RIVERSIDE
County

Pictorial Research by Harry W. Lawton
"Partners in Progress" by Patricia Mastick Young

Foreword by Stephen A. Becker
Editorial Consultant, Thomas W. Patterson

Produced in Cooperation with the
Riverside County Historical Commission and the
Riverside County Board of Supervisors

Windsor Publications, Inc.
Northridge, California

Harvest of the Sun
An Illustrated History of
RIVERSIDE
County

James T. Brown

Windsor Publications, Inc.—History Book Division

Publisher: John M. Phillips
Editorial Director: Teri Davis Greenberg
Design Director: Alexander D'Anca

Staff for *Harvest of the Sun*
Senior Editor: Pamela Schroeder
Picture Editor: Susan Wells
Text Editor: Lissa Sanders
Director, Corporate Biographies: Karen Story
Assistant Director, Corporate Biographies: Phyllis
   Gray
Editor, Corporate Biographies: Judith Hunter
Editorial Assistants: Tricia Cobb, Patricia Pittman,
   Lonnie Pham, Kathy M. Brown
Designer: Alexander D'Anca
Layout Artist: J.R. Vasquez

Library of Congress Cataloging in Publication Data
Brown, James T., 1954—
   Harvest of the sun.

   Bibliography: p. 244
   Includes index.
   1. Riverside County (Calif.)—History. 2. Riverside
County (Calif.)—Description and travel. 3. Riverside
County (Calif.)—Industries. I. Young, Patricia Mastick.
Partners in progress. 1985. II. Riverside County
Historical Commission. III. Riverside County. Board of
Supervisors. IV. Title.
F868.R6B85   1985   979.4'97   85-6417

Honorary Advisors
The publisher wishes to acknowledge the following individuals, who lent valuable assistance in
the preparation of this volume:

Stephen A. Becker
History Division Director,
Riverside County Parks Department

Fred Reinhardt
General Manager,
Riverside County Department of Development

Thomas W. Patterson
Editorial Consultant

Riverside County
Board of Supervisors
Patricia A. Larson
Walter P. Abraham
Melba Dunlap
Kay Ceniceros
A. Norton Younglove

Riverside County
Historical Commission
B.J. Mylne
Erin Port
Mary Haggland
Kitty Kieley Hayes
Van Perkins
Joseph Byrne
Esther Trunnell
Katherine Siva Saubel
Esther Klotz
Vincent Bautista
Bill Jennings

Overleaf: *This photograph was taken from a
hill overlooking Central and Victoria avenues.*
Photo by Michael J. Elderman

Contents

Preface

A popular tale among the Palm Springs Cahuilla Indians was that of "The People
Who Went to See the Sun." Long ago, an Indian
people lived near a spring called *To ba*. They
studied the heavens carefully. They recorded the
tracks of the planets and stars and the risings and
settings of the moon and sun. Some felt the sun's
course to be very close, others reasoned that it
was actually very far away. Finally, many of the
villagers, including the youngest and strongest, set
out with their families to find the home of the
sun.

The journey stretched out into years. The weak
and the irreverent died away, until only one
young man, *Suwet tawa*, "the Star Found Him,"
was left. At a great river he grew despairing, and
with the cry *"Hi ca,"* that asks for help further on,
he threw himself in. There he was discovered by
the sun and the morning star, and the sun took
him in.

The young man saw in the home of the sun
many surprising things—a willow tree that burned
at sunrise and then grew green again—a tree that
supplied corn in endless quantities. But the young
man grew lonely and asked to be taken back to
his people. The sun agreed, and advised *Suwet
tawa* to tell nothing to his people for a little
while; in return the young man would learn all
the secrets of the sun.

Suwet tawa returned home. The villagers had
long since despaired of seeing him again. They
overwhelmed him with questions about his ad-
ventures. By nightfall he could resist no longer.

He told his people to build a great fire and began
the tale of his journey. The following morning, as
the sun rose, *Suwet tawa* fell dead.

The pages that follow tell the story of a county
reclaimed in large part from the sun. It is made of
many little stories, some, in their own way, a reit-
eration of the young Indian's odyssey. As the
years pass, the sunbelt grows more and more irre-
sistible. For those who have obeyed its advice, the
sun has nurtured a bountiful harvest.

Writers of history, too, can fall victim to such
bedazzlement, tempted to say too much, too soon.
Errors in fact or omission are, of course, entirely my own, but the following people helped to
cushion my oft-times Icarian journey. Pamela
Schroeder of Windsor Publications proffered
timely support and sage advice. Stephen Becker,
through his own example and the facilities of the
County Historical Commission, constituted a valuable resource. Harry Lawton's contributions—as
historian, critic, and friend—brought him perilous-
ly close to co-authorship. Throughout my journey,
Tom Patterson preceded me. His work speaks
loudly from many places in the text. May he not
be too critical of its uses.

I extend my thanks to Monica O'Keefe and
Karen Huffman for their remarkable transcrip-
tions. Finally, there wait Janet and Rebecca, my
sisters, and, of course, Bob and Shirley Hine.

This book is dedicated to the memory of
Suwet tawa.

*The ancient Santa Ana River on the western
edge of Riverside County glimmers beneath a
setting sun. Photo by John Kleinman*

Mount Cucagmona in the San Gabriel Range towers over an older orange grove at the University of California's Citrus Research Center and Agricultural Experiment Station in Riverside. Matthew Gage's pioneering canal first brought water to these lands, at that time undeveloped, on the east side of the city. Photo by Robert Platt

Foreword

It is one of those magical late winter days in Riverside, a day of warm breezes, brilliant sunlight, bright blue skies, and clear, wide vistas. The snow-capped peaks of Mt. San Jacinto and Mt. San Gorgonio beckon me toward the oases of the Coachella Valley and the high desert beyond. James Brown's final manuscript is ready to join Harry Lawton's expertly selected historic photographs to become *Harvest of the Sun,* a new history of our county. Today, Jim's words and Harry's photos bring alive the stories of the people of these valleys, mountains, and deserts. It is their histories which reach out to me and implore me to travel and explore. On a day like today, it is easy to see how this place has lured so many.

The past is prologue—a proverbial reminder from Shakespeare—and indeed so it is with this book. At least four other county histories have preceded this one, each peculiar and particular to the era in which it was written: Elliot's 1883 *History of San Bernardino and San Diego Counties* (from which Riverside County was later carved), Holmes' 1912 *History of Riverside County,* Brown and Boyd's 1922 *History of San Bernardino and Riverside Counties,* and Arthur Paul's 1954 *Riverside Community Book.* It is over thirty years since an attempt has been made to recount the history of Riverside County. Through Windsor Publications and the tremendous support of our corporate and business sponsors, the Riverside County Historical Commission and the Board of Supervisors are pleased to present this volume, a new, fresh look at our history and heritage.

A number of people served as prologue to this volume as well, providing, through their endeavors in the recent past, a context for the publication of this book. We owe much to the county's first Historical Committee members, out of which our county history program has grown. Among those who led the way in the 1960s were Donna Bouer Babcock, the committee's first chairman

and later the first secretary of the County Historical Commission, Harry Creasey, Robert T. Anderson, Norman Davis, John Gabbert, Leonard Grindstaff, Edward Walker, and Robert Hine. It is interesting to note, and a reassuring pleasure to remember, that two people with a direct hand in this volume, Harry Lawton and Tom Patterson, were also members of this first organization, founded by the Board of Supervisors to enable the county to seek ways to preserve its history.

We are indebted to all who have seen fit to preserve our county's heritage; it is through their actions, words and writings we remind ourselves that every place has its own important niche in time, its own victories, its own failures. And every place and every era has its great pioneering spirits. *Harvest of the Sun* brings that picture back to life for Riverside County. In his landmark book, *Southern California, an Island on the Land,* historian Carey McWilliams writes, "It is difficult to appreciate that, not so many years ago, this was a semi-desert, rimmed by great mountains, described in early chronicles as barren and bereft." Author James Brown reminds us in this book that with water and great will the people of Riverside County have reaped a plentiful harvest, blessed by the sun. We harvest oranges; they are our golden nuggets. We harvest dates; and they are our delicate mystery. But it is our story, our narrative heritage, and a knowledge of those who have shaped our homes and our communities which is truly our greatest treasure.

—Stephen A. Becker
History Division Director,
Riverside County Parks Department and
Historical Commission

Left: *The San Jacinto Valley—where Mission cattle once roamed—still remains a lovely pastoral setting dotted with farms despite the onrush of urbanization in some areas. Photo by John Kleinman*

Below left: *Clouds loom over Soboba Road near the San Jacinto River. Photo by John Kleinman*

Below: *Cattle graze on the lush green hills near Soboba Indian Reservation in the San Jacinto Valley. Photo by John Kleinman*

Left: *This photograph shows some of the San Jacinto Valley's wild vegetation. Photo by John Kleinman*

Below left: *These trees near Idyllwild carry touches of a Southern California snow. Photo by John Kleinman*

Below: *A field of alfalfa waves softly in the breeze near La Sierra. Photo by John Kleinman*

I When the Earth Stopped Shaking

This Temperamental Land

In the beginning there was nothing but darkness. Sounds, humming or thunder, were heard at times. Red, white, blue, and brown colors came all twisting to one point in the darkness. These were acting all together—twisting. These came together in one point to produce. This ball shook and whirled all together into one substance, which became two embryos wrapped in this placenta ... formed in space and darkness. These were born prematurely; everything stopped for they were stillborn. ...

Then again all the lights whirled together, joined, and produced. This time the embryos grew fully—the children inside talked to one another. While they were in this sack they rolled back and forth; they stretched their arms and knees to make a hole so they could get out. Then they named themselves Mukat and Temayawit.

—Alejo Potencio, a Pass Cahuilla Indian relating, in February 1925, the birth of the twin gods, Mukat and Temayawit.

With the halting efforts of those primal colors—red, white, blue, and brown—to create, to

The Whitewater River, photographed when it was almost dry, sweeps out of the San Bernardino Mountains onto the floor of the San Gorgonio Pass, continuing into the Colorado Desert below. Early Palm Springs pioneers tapped the river to provide water for their community. Photo by John Kleinman

The Yuman or Quechan Indians of the Colorado River were friendly to the first Spanish explorers crossing their territory, but throughout the early nineteenth century they encountered thousands of immigrants traveling to Southern California. Incursions on their crops and other unpleasant meetings resulted in their often fierce resistance to the white man and their warlike reputation. By the 1850s they had partially adopted European dress as shown in this sketch made by a member of Lieutenant Joseph C. Ive's expedition, which explored the Colorado River for the United States Army Corps of Topographical Engineers in 1857-1858. Courtesy, Special Collections Department, Library of the University of California, Riverside

Among the Indian groups along the Colorado River were the Mojave Indians, known for their elaborate tattooing and as being fierce warriors. This 1856 lithograph was made from a drawing by the noted artist H.B. Mollhausen and depicts three Mojaves as seen during the U.S. Government railroad expedition of 1853-1854 when government engineers were surveying a railroad route from the Mississippi River to the Pacific Ocean.

merge and spawn, the great epic of the world's birth had begun. Potencio's clan, the *Kauisiktum* ("from the rock"), lived in a village in the looming shadow of Mount San Jacinto, near present-day Palm Springs. Serving as *net*, or ceremonial leader, Potencio had just finished supervising the Mourning Ceremony of his clan. Near the ceremonial big house ("the center of everything"), the wood and grass images of relatives who had died in the last year were put to the fire. Their spirits were mourned and released in a manner that mourned, as well, the death of Mukat long, long ago. Now, tired and still transported by the long ceremony, he chose to relate the tale again for a visiting ethnographer, William Duncan Strong. For a county called Riverside, the ancient stories of Mukat and his twin even today retain a unique validity.

The young twins set about to make the earth, the sky, the oceans, and fill the world with animals. All the things of the earth were their creatures. But as they worked, they argued, as boys do—over who was older, wiser, more creative. Temayawit, who lost every dispute, grew very angry:

I will go to the bottom of the earth, whence I

came, and take all my creatures with me—the earth, sky, and all my other creations.' Mukat answered, 'You can take yours, but all mine will stay.' Then Temayawit blew and his breath opened the earth. His creatures went down with him; all save the moon, the palm tree, the coyote, the wood duck, and a few others. He tried to take the earth and sky with him; a fierce wind blew and the earth shook all over, while the sky bent and swayed.

But Mukat put one knee on the ground, held one hand on all his creatures, and with the other held up the sky. He cried, 'Hi! Hi! Hi! Hi!' (which is the way all people do now when an earthquake comes). In the struggle all the mountains and canyons appeared on the earth's surface, stream beds were formed, and water came out and filled them. At last Temayawit disappeared below, all became

Although earthquakes are a recurrent phenomenon in Southern California, only one quake has resulted in a loss of life in Riverside County. The San Jacinto Valley earthquake of December 25, 1899, caused the deaths of several Indian women, who died in the collapse of this old adobe home on the Soboba Indian Reservation. Photo by Frederick H. Rogers, courtesy, Clarence Swift Collection

quiet, and the earth stopped shaking, but its rough uneven surface remains until today.

Within the creative structure of myth, the Cahuilla Indians preserved the memory of the processes by which their homeland took shape. While Mukat and his brother fought, great geological forces were struggling to mold the tremendous landforms we recognize as Riverside County. See in Temayawit's exodus the loss of many potential flora and fauna, leaving much of Mukat's homeland sparsely occupied. See too, if you choose, in Temayawit's wind, so fierce that "the sky bent and swayed," the angry resonance of the seasonal Santa Ana winds as they sweep down from the north through the passes in spring and fall, to dry the earth and cleanse the sky for the sun.

Riverside County stretches nearly 200 miles, east to west, across the multiform surface of South-

The Cahuilla Indians of the Colorado Desert were one of the few tribes on the North American continent that dug wells. Their desert wells were terraced with steps sometimes descending twenty feet. An artist for the 1853 Lieutenant R.S. Williamson expedition of the U.S. Army Corps of Topographical Engineers attempted to render the scene at Deep Well between today's Palm Springs and Indio. The well was located in the grove of mesquite trees. Courtesy, Special Collections Department, Library of the University of California, Riverside

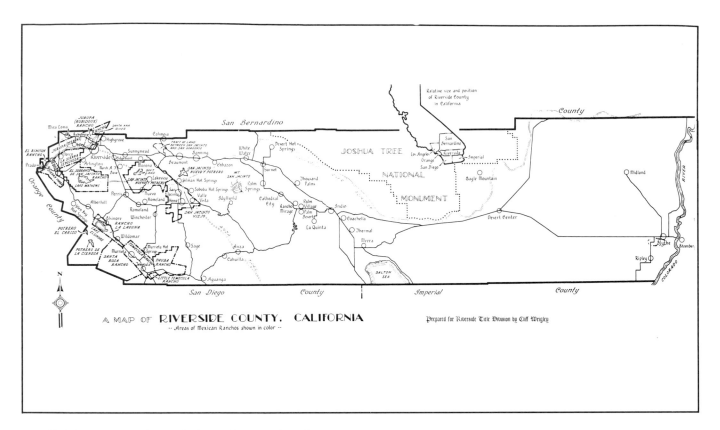

A MAP OF **RIVERSIDE COUNTY, CALIFORNIA**
·· Areas of Mexican Ranchos shown in color ··

Prepared for Riverside Title Division by Cliff Wrigley

This map of Riverside County was made by Riverside Title in about 1974, and illustrates the size and shape of this vast county.

ern California. It is bounded on the east by the Colorado River, on the west by the Santa Ana Mountains and the river of the same name. North, the great San Bernardino range as well as the Pinto, Granite, and Big Maria mountains straddle the boundary; while, to the south, the boundary cuts across the Santa Rosa Mountains, the Salton Sea, and the desolate Chocolate Mountains. The county's 4.5 million acres straddle parts of four natural provinces: the Peninsular and Transverse ranges, the Colorado Desert, and the Salton Trough. They embrace one of the sheerest vertical thrusts in the West—rivaling the Sierras and Tetons—where Mount San Jacinto soars more than 10,000 feet from the desert floor. They share nearby in the Salton Basin, the largest area below sea level within the United States. Temayawit's heritage is secure.

The Transverse ranges consist of the San Gabriel, the San Bernardino, and the Little San Bernardino Mountains. Against the grain of most California ranges, they strike due east from the Pacific near Santa Barbara and divide the Mojave

Desert from the Colorado Desert. In Mount San Gorgonio Southern California knows its highest peak. South of "Old Grayback" the Peninsular ranges swing as though on a hinge. The San Jacinto, Santa Rosa, Agua Tibia, Vallecito, and Laguna mountains reach to the international line, where the system becomes the spine of the Baja Peninsula.

The hinge point of these two great geological entities is San Gorgonio Pass. There Mount San Gorgonio stares miles across the floor of the pass toward its eternal rival, 10,831-foot San Jacinto. The term "hinge" is more than simply descriptive. Here, on its journey toward San Francisco, the San Andreas Fault is ever so slowly, but inevitably, sheering the two Californias away from the rest of

North America, and opening the Colorado Desert to the Sea of Cortes. Like monuments to the twin gods, San Jacinto and San Gorgonio seem to strain toward each other, in love or in anger, and only the greater tectonic muscle of the fault has kept them apart.

The dazzling surface variation of Riverside's western region is the work of this fault along with her younger sisters, the San Jacinto and Elsinore faults. Where the San Jacinto and San Andreas faults come nearest together, a barren, jumbled wall plays havoc with sun and shadow. This is the Badlands, a section of wrinkled earth that divides San Jacinto Valley from San Timoteo Canyon. Parallel and further west are the Temescal Valley and the broad, shallow Lake Elsinore, for which the third fault is named. Between these three canyons stretch fertile valleys, mesas, (remnants of the floor of an ancient sea), and countless rivers and streams. Most of these drain northward into the Santa Ana River Valley, which cuts, in turn, through the Coast ranges to the sea.

Western Riverside County is a land of sagebrush, chaparral, and riverine canyons. It breathes the sea-spray of the Pacific and basks in a Mediterranean climate. Temperatures rarely dip below freezing, even in the coldest winters, and the 100-plus temperatures of summer are tamed by a regular afternoon coastal breeze. The phenomenon of the "false spring," as Carey McWilliams has called it, is at home here. The land, parched to a brown and golden stillness, receives its first gentle fall rains. Suddenly the hillsides blossom with an alpine florescence. The meadows pass from gold to green in a few short weeks. Through the storm and glory of winter the soil becomes swollen with moisture. This rainy period is a matter, almost exclusively, of the fall and spring seasons. When the cycle of rain fades in May or June, a second desert spring unfolds briefly—until the fierce Santa Anas and rising temperatures turn the hillsides once again to bronze.

Here one learns to know the scrub oak, whose dark green leaves ease the weary eye in any sheltered canyon or streamside. The chamise, or grease-wood, blankets higher elevations. On the drier slopes the gray brittlebush and several varieties of sage predominate. Throughout the region, wherever there is sufficient water, the canyons and washes wear the pale green and bright yellow of several species of the willow family. Arching prominently above them is the elegant sycamore, or plane tree, with its false maple leaf and dangling buttonball seed clusters.

Before man the foothills and canyons teemed with fauna—from the ubiquitous black-tailed jackrabbit to the stately mule deer. Bobcat and bighorn sheep roamed widely in this region. Now the coyote, the jackrabbit, and the kangaroo rat prevail. Above, the red-tailed hawk still dominates the sky, while, if you're lucky, you'll spot a roadrunner doing battle with a diamondback. Its sad cry, so out of character, might later give you pause. Above all one remembers two very common birds, each with its striking and strikingly different songs. The mourning dove, whose long, white-tipped tail feathers paint brush strokes in the sky, repeats a persistent melancholy cooing which, if it catches you alone on a dark day, may send you stumbling back toward civilization— "Never send to know for whom the bell tolls." For an antidote there is the Western meadowlark, whose delightful song, an accomplished rendition of bright, cheerful notes, never fails to lift the heart. On the western end of the county, the Santa Ana River shelters a wide variety of migratory ducks and geese.

Between the brush country of the west and the desert to the east stand the greatest of the Transverse ranges: the San Jacinto Mountains. Here arctic storms, spiraling inland from the Pacific, give up the last of their moisture in rain and snow. The brows of the San Jacinto and Tahquitz peaks frame mountain meadows fringed with lodgepole and sugar pine. In the distance, seen at its best as the sun sets against its cheek, is Cahuilla Mountain—smaller in stature than Tahquitz, but possessed of a profile worthy of any prophet's contemplation. Between them are the highlands— Anza and Garner Valley—where chaparral shades into yellow pine. Plummeting eastward toward the bone-white bed of the Whitewater River, these mountains divide the Western Chaparral from the Sonoran environments. Between the two worlds San Gorgonio Pass hosts an ongoing battle of tremendous ferocity as ocean and desert air masses butt together like bighorn sheep—like Mukat and Temayawit.

The county touches the upper Mohave and the lower Colorado Deserts. Northern basins are the home of the Joshua tree. Below, the Chuckwalla and Chocolate Mountains stand guard over a desert floor that shares the aesthetic of the moon. For at least four consecutive months the temperature exceeds, sometimes far exceeds, 100 degrees. Three inches of rain per annum is "reasonable." But look more closely; Mukat's creatures flourish here, too. Consider their names: brittlebush, smoke tree, ironwood, creosote, the rattlesnake, and iguana. Here one finds the hardiest breeds of survivors. Beware the colonies of cholla cactus, each with its clinging white barbs. But return, if you can, in the spring, when wildflowers and cactus blossoms turn a season's spare ration of moisture into a cacophony of color. There, ahead on the roadside: the ocotillo, resembling nothing so much as the bones of an old umbrella stuck in the sand, until with spring each stem bursts with scarlet.

The heart of the desert lies at or below sea level: the Coachella Valley, the Salton Sink. Along its fringes, where the last trickle of mountain streams sink into sand, are the stately Washingtonias: the native palm first described by Emory in 1848 as "cabbage trees." Here, too, sprawl colonies of the forbidding agave. In the sink itself: salt bush and alkali desolation.

The Salton Trough has been partially filled by the Salton Sea since 1906. Ringing its perimeter is evidence of much older and greater volumes of water. Imagine, instead of the bleak, arid basin that surrounds you, a freshwater lake over 100 miles long, thirty-four miles at its widest, and 300 feet in depth, fringed with tule and bullrushes, a haven for waterfowl, clams, and fish! Imagine, too, that this ancient sea, Lake Cahuilla, had not one

lifetime but many, the latest thought to extend from approximately A.D. 900 to 1500.

Freshwater . . . indeed, the Gulf of California once extended almost as far as San Gorgonio Pass, but even in geological terms that was ancient history. In a sense the county has been touched on *two* sides by the Colorado River, for Lake Cahuilla flowed with the river from the deep snowpack of the Rocky Mountains. Even as the San Andreas Fault seeks to divide California from the continent with an ever wider sea, the Colorado has always succeeded in bridging that sea with sand. After tapping the Green, the San Juan, and the Virgin rivers, it turns abruptly south, bearing the suspended silt of the Grand Canyon over the Colorado Desert. Over the centuries it had created a huge delta, divided the Salton Trough from the gulf, and alternately filled it to capacity or allowed it to dry entirely.

A thousand years ago Lake Cahuilla shimmered under the sun. The sun looked down, too, on a busy and prosperous people settled in villages along the shore. They harvested clams from the rocks, fished in the marshes, and circled the foothills for the game that descended gingerly to the cool shore. Then the lake was bountiful, villages prospered, and the middens (refuse heaps) ringing each settlement swelled with the cracked shells, little bones, and broken tools discarded after long use.

As these ancient people watched, the lake rose and fell seasonally, some years more dramatically than others, and the Colorado continued to flow in its direction. Then the inevitable occurred. Sometime near 1500 the accumulated deposits of delta silt blocked its path once more. The Colorado turned back toward the gulf. It need not have taken long—possibly the lifetime of one man—but the waters disappeared. First to suffer were the aquatic plants, the cattail and bullrush; next, the shellfish Anodanta. Today researchers can outline evidence of the human disruption. Abandoned fish traps, horseshoe rings of stone, line the lakebed in concentric rings. As the water fell, the desperate fishermen built again further

Top left: *Generations of Indian students attended church services in the St. Boniface Chapel at St. Boniface Indian School in Banning. The school was self-supporting and eventually was closed down when it could no longer compete with public schools. Courtesy, Leonard McCulloh*

Top right: *St. Boniface Indian School was established in 1889 on an eighty-acre site north of Banning by the Bureau of Catholic Indian Missions. Even as late as the 1930s there was an attendance of about 150 Indian reservation students, who were also given manual arts training. Courtesy, Leonard McCulloh*

Above: *Indian children from Riverside County reservations also received education at Sherman Institute, which the United States government built in Riverside in 1902 because of lobbying by Frank Miller of the Mission Inn. Since the 1960s Sherman Indian High School has offered a comprehensive vocational and college preparation program to Indian youngsters mostly from Arizona, Nevada, and New Mexico. Courtesy, Lorne Allmon*

down. Archaeologist Philip Wilke has mapped seven generations of these traps tirelessly rebuilt, again and again, until the last two species of fish, the bonytail and the humpbacked sucker, could no longer survive the brackish water.

The first Europeans in the Coachella Valley saw the old beachlines high on the hillsides and heard the Cahuillan legend of great water and its subsidence "poco, poco." Years later, the Cahuilla would speak as well of white-winged birds that bore little men across the water. This cryptic tale has sent treasure-seekers across the dunes, searching in vain for what may be the hulk of a Spanish galleon buried in the sand. Did one of explorer Francisco Ulloa's shallow-draft vessels in 1539 break through a thicket on a channel of the delta and sail into the broad lake? No treasure, so far, has been unearthed, but the legend persists.

The drying of Lake Cahuilla devastated the Cahuillas' ancestors. Their food system disappeared quickly and that of the desert was slow to replace it. One by one, villages and clans split away, fanning out in search of new food sources. The environment became even more forbidding, but they proved adaptable. Juan Bautista de Anza, the first Spaniard to record their presence, found them as they have continued to be—a proud and self-reliant people.

The Cahuillas continued to occupy the floor of the Salton Trough, utilizing natural springs and deep spiral wells for water, but they settled, as well, in the San Gorgonio Pass and seasonally occupied the Perris Plain at its eastern edge. They ascended the San Jacinto and Santa Rosa mountains, and could soon claim a wide territory of varied ecology and resources.

Holding off Spanish subjugation, the Cahuillas have been able to retain much of their way of life. They provide us with one of the few clear pictures of native culture in Southern California. At the time of European contact, each Cahuilla was a member of a clan, based on a common lineage. Generally these clans occupied permanent villages grouped near the ceremonial big house and the residence of the clan leader, or *net*. The *net*, a po-

sition most often passed down from father to son, served many roles. He adjudicated disputes and organized hunting and gathering activities. Most importantly, he was responsible for the care of the *mayswit*, the ceremonial bundle that contained the sacred symbols of authority, lineage, and ritual.

The Cahuillas constructed sturdy permanent homes of brush and pole and moved to temporary camps elsewhere only when food gathering or trade required. They hunted and trapped the

Constructed of poles, brush, and mud, the temescal or sweathouse was common in most California Indian villages, including those of the Cahuilla Indians. After their bodies were perspiring fiercely, the Indians would plunge into a cold stream, spring, or lake. From Wallace W. Elliott, History of San Bernardino and San Diego Counties, *1882*

small game of the desert and the great ecological diversity of their environment gave them access to a wide variety of plants and food products. Ethnobotanists in cooperation with Cahuillan informants have documented over 250 plants and their utilization. For food, the acorn, mesquite, screwbean, piñon, and cactus bulbs were utilized. Large raised granaries were built to hold the surplus through lean seasons.

The great majority of plants were used medicinally, to cure disease, infection, and heal wounds. The *puvulam* (shaman) and the *tingavish* (doctor) were specialists, classifying, experimenting, and treating with remarkable precision. Many plants had several uses—for example *Baccharis viminea*, the seep willow, was a favorite wood for house construction, and its leaves, when steeped, were used as an eyewash to prevent blindness, a shampoo for baldness, and leaves and stems together as a hygienic agent. The saltbush seed served for flour, the leaves for soup, and flowers and stems as an inhalant for congestion.

Though long considered solely hunters and gatherers, new research suggests that the Cahuillas were skilled in agriculture as well. Anthropologists note that their creation myth incorporates Mukat's gift of domesticated plants. Mukat's rough treatment of his creatures, his penchant for playing tricks, caused some of them to plan and carry out his murder. But when Mukat was cremated, an unexpected thing happened:

Then in the place where Mukat was burned there began to grow all kinds of strange plants, but no one knew what they were...

Palmitcawut, a great shaman, journeyed to the home of Mukat's spirit to find out what the plants signified: 'We, your creatures, do not know what the strange things are that grow where your body was burned.' Mukat's spirit answered him: 'You need not be afraid of those things. They are from my body.'

Mukat's final gifts to his people included tobacco from his heart, squash from his stomach, corn from his teeth, as well as watermelons, wheat, and beans. These plants have been cultivated as far back as the Cahuillas remember in isolated canyons and rain basins in the Coachella Valley.

For the Cahuillas, competitive games were the principal organized recreation. These ranged from arduous footraces to what the Spanish called *peon,* a gambling game requiring both a poker face and remarkable sleight of hand. Songs were the principal musical expression. They memorialized everything from romance to tribal history and religion. The Cahuillan belief system emphasized tradition, the wisdom of the aged, industry, cooperation and sharing, order and moderation. Ritual permeated every aspect of community life. It celebrated existence, helped solve conflict and equalize wealth, educated, and propitiated the spirits of plants, animals, and the gods, on which that existence depended. Clans participated in many ceremonies, including those for boys' and girls' adolescence, marriage, and death. Some songs recall the activities of different humanized birds. The Eagle Ceremony celebrated the phoenix-like immortality of the eagle. As part of a ritual dance, an eagle was killed and buried to the accompaniment of great mourning. Ritual costumes were refurbished with its feathers and guests solemnly exchanged gifts. Even today, bird dances continue to be a social event where many gather to relax, share food, and dance.

Most important in the ritual life of the Cahuillas was *nukil,* a week-long ceremony held once or twice a year to honor the souls of those recently deceased. Preparations were carefully made by the sponsoring clan over a period of months. Foodstuffs were stockpiled for the many expected guests. For several nights, as visitors continued to arrive outside the ceremonial enclosure, the shaman led in the recitation of complex song cycles such as the creation myth. While the relatives of the deceased sat quietly at the rear of the enclosure, singers painstakingly reconstructed the complex Cahuillan cosmology, the balanced pattern of life and death. Long into the nights old men continued to chant. By the sixth night, the sacred

mayswit had been introduced, gifts exchanged, and the images of the dead, dressed in animal skins, and eagle feathers, made ready.

At the dawn of the seventh day all gathered to witness the final ritual acts. The *net* and his assistant carried the images around the enclosure. Behind them followed women sweeping with pieces of cloth to erase the tracks of the dead. The procession arrived at the cemetery where the images were burned. Their spirits at peace, the dead must be forgotten.

The foothills and valleys of western Riverside County appear to have been shared by several tribal groups: the Serranos, the Luiseños, the Cupeños, as well as the Cahuillas. These first three groups were purely hunters and gatherers. Archaeological evidence from Lake Perris suggests the Cahuillas established intensive settlements in this area late in "prehistoric" times before the arrival of the Spanish, possibly around 1500, and were the final native presence there. Western Riverside, however, contains many reminders of earlier occupations: hundreds of pictographs and petroglyphs painted or etched on boulders throughout the region. The origin and purposes of rock art are a fascinating study, but answers are elusive. Early on, anthropologists like Julian Steward and William Strong suggested a connection between the predominating style of these pictographs and the ceremonial practices of the Luiseños who inhabited the Temescal Valley and the ranges west. Such work established one of the few firm links between pictographs, their creators, and their purposes.

As recorded by Strong, *We-enic,* the Luiseños girls' adolescent ceremony, was celebrated whenever several females reached womanhood. In a sacred brush enclosure called *wankic,* a large pit was dug and lined with reeds. With great ceremony the girls, who had been hidden away, were brought out and placed in the pit which had been warmed with heated rocks. Attended by their mothers and lectured constantly on proper behavior, they would remain in the pit for at least three days, leaving only as it was reheated or to eat a small bit of food.

The ceremony closed with a race to a chosen rock where each girl painted a long vertical design in red, often composed of linked diamond shapes. These patterns, said to represent rattlesnakes, appear almost everywhere throughout western Riverside County. Like the tender memories they recall, the images fade slowly, peacefully, in the sunlight—unless they are senselessly destroyed by modern vandals.

Another style of petroglyph found in western Riverside County is the so-called "maze stone." These isolated etchings take the form of complex, carefully elaborated labyrinths. The best known of

One of the most famous Indian rock carvings in Riverside County is the Hemet maze stone, an intricate petroglyph seen on this boulder in the San Jacinto Valley. The maze was probably carved centuries ago by Luiseño or Cahuilla Indian inhabitants of the region. A legend has arisen, however, that it was carved by Buddhist monks shipwrecked long ago on the shores of California. Courtesy, Horace Parker Collection

these is the Hemet Maze Stone in Reinhardt Canyon. Research into the calendrical and astronomical uses of such rock art may yet unlock their purpose.

For the Cahuillas the land of the dead lay to the east. Indeed, the eastern desert beyond the Salton Sink is a land of nearly intolerable aridity. No one lived in the fiery basins between the Orocopia, Chuckwalla, and Chocolate mountains. Prehistoric Indian traders braved the desert to capitalize on the lucrative shell trade between coastal tribes and those of the deep interior, their trails leading from shelter to waterhole to oasis, but little else of man's presence in this region is visible even today.

Once the desert crossing is made, however, there is a moment of respite from the fiery landscape. East of the Salton Sea, the Colorado Valley widens for nearly thirty miles, north to south. There one finds fertile alluvial soil, dark green

In 1853 a group of U.S. Army topographical engineers commanded by Lieutenant R.S. Williamson crossed the San Gorgonio Pass and descended into the Colorado Desert, seeking the best route for a railroad from the Mississippi River to the Pacific Ocean. These explorers were the first to note the waterline of the ancient Lake Cahuilla, which centuries before had covered much of the Coachella Valley. Courtesy, Harry W. Lawton

thickets, and sloughs. The Spaniards called the valley Palo Verde, probably because of the green-barked palo verde trees. But *palo* also means "stick" or "club." This too has significance, for conflict and turmoil, like the Colorado itself, have swept the valley again and again, leaving it, each time, transfigured.

The lower Colorado was the center of the Yuman Culture Complex, a multi-tribal civilization unique in the Southwest. It included, from north to south, the Mohave, Halchidoma, Kamia, and Quechan cultures. Far more than other tribal or linguistic groups in this region, they had cemented themselves into cohesive national units.

The Halchidomas occupied the area centered on the Palo Verde Valley. They relied on the river for most of their diet. As often as twice a year the men would pierce the moist alluvial soil with digging sticks to plant corn, beans, pumpkins, and watermelons. In turn, the women would tenderly harvest them. Clustered together in villages, each family group worked the fields husbands had inherited from fathers and passed on to sons. The Halchidomas supplemented the agricultural staples

Centuries before the first steamboats chugged up the Colorado, the Indians of the Colorado River plied this waterway on reed rafts. Courtesy, Special Collections, Library of the University of California, Riverside

through hunting with their mesquite bows and spring traps. Trading widely—with the Cahuillas, whom they considered allies, and as far east into Arizona as the hilltop towns of the Hopis—they wore fine blankets and adorned themselves with shells. This earned them the reputation (and envy) as the best-dressed people on the Colorado.

The Halchidomas flirted with a truly national consciousness. Apparently the chief of the most populous village served as tribal spokesman. They recognized no leader similar to the *Kwoxot* (strong man) of the Quechans. Spiritually, they shared many of the traditions of other Yuman peoples, and the Cahuillas as well. For the Halchidomas, reality existed on two levels, a tangible one and one of dreams. Only those who dreamed singular and powerful dreams, hearing their personal songs first in the spirit world, could aspire to the duties of leader or shaman.

With the Cahuillas, the Halchidomas shared a tradition of dual creators, Cipas and Blind Old

ROBERTS Sc.

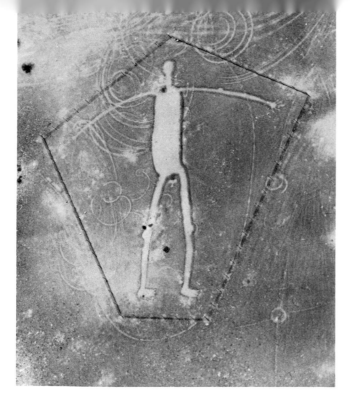

One of the great mysteries of Riverside County are the strange anthropomorphic geoglyph rock alignments known as the "Blythe Giants" in the Palo Verde Valley. These humanoid and animal figures, which reveal themselves fully only from the air, were constructed by early Indians of the region removing rocks from the desert pavement. A fence has been built around the Blythe giant shown above to protect it from motorcyclists and off-road vehicle users, who created the circles that were threatening to destroy the geoglyph. Courtesy, Harry Casey and Imperial Valley Barker College Museum

Man. Like Mukat and Temayawit, they argued, and the loser, Blind Old Man, stormed away. Cipas, too, was killed by his own creatures. His son, Kwistamxo, returned with powers just as remarkable and taught the Halchidomas how to plant and to reason. Like the Cahuillas, and unlike their neighbors north and south, the Halchidomas mourned the dead by burning them in effigy. A mock battle always preceded the burning, with some men representing Halchidomas and others, the enemy. In the end, the fighters broke their weapons and tossed them into the flames. For the unfortunate Halchidomas, real wars were not so easily resolved.

War, above all other nonessential pursuits, occupied the minds of the Yuman nations. The Mohaves and Quechans constituted one powerful alliance. Pinched between them, the Halchidomas, with their allies, the Maricopas, were hard-pressed. Yuman tribes had evolved a style of warfare that rivaled in formality that of Napoleonic Europe. Ranging in divisions as large as 200 soldiers, each side faced the other in long lines. Led by a general and several captains, each of whom proudly wielded his feathered lance—a symbol of fearlessness—the armies would advance. Soldiers would hammer their opponents with short, vicious war clubs until senseless or dead. In this grand style, the great, prosperous nations of the Colorado conspired to reduce each other to ruin.

Some researchers have seen the growing Spanish slave trade as a motive for these wars. Others saw a limited and overstrained environment forcing each group to seek expansion of its territory. Whatever the reason, from the first European contact the record is one of constant warfare. Father Francisco Garcés, the remarkable explorer-priest, passed through the Palo Verde Valley in 1776, recording his valuable impressions of their vanished lifeways. He brought with him two Halchidoman girls purchased from the Quechans. Returning them to their people, he sought to extract the promise that no tribe would war again with another. Garcés' "truce" lasted only as long as it took a Mohave war party of eighty men to march southward past him toward the Halchidomas.

By 1825 the Halchidomas had been thoroughly mauled by their enemies. Reduced to a few desperate villages, the once proud people concluded that escape alone would prevent annihilation. Some fifty years ago, Kotux, one of the last Halchidomas to remember the stories of his people, described their preparations to Leslie Spier:

Next day they dug holes under their houses; stored their beans, corn, black-eyed peas, and everything they had in pots; and buried them deep in the ground. Long after, the Mohave told how they had discovered this hoard.

Victoriano, the last hereditary chief of the Soboba Indians of the San Jacinto Valley, posed with his third wife in the 1880s in Professor H.J. May's photographic studio in San Jacinto. Victoriano was said to have been 136 years old when he died in 1888, but it seems likely his age was exaggerated. Courtesy, Clarence Swift Collection

Exodus took the few remaining Halchidomas to Sonora, where they found welcome among the Yaquis. After an epidemic, the last Halchidoma families drifted north to the Gila River and their old allies, the Maricopas. There they were absorbed and the nation lost forever.

On a bench of the Big Maria Mountains, northwest of Blythe, are the best-known examples of prehistoric rock art in Riverside County: the giant Desert Intaglios. Sometimes as long as 160 feet, huge figures were painstakingly patterned out of the desert gravel. Here, a giant hunter lies transfixed by the sun; there, a giant animal similarly frozen in time—perhaps this was his prey. Discovered by air in 1930 when a pilot, George Palmer, noticed "giant horsetracks" leading from the Colorado to the mountains, the huge creations remain a mystery.

Perhaps the explanation disappeared with the nation called Halchidoma. Exodus and absorption might have been enough to destroy the link. But one fascinating coincidence remains: the tale, told by Kotux to Leslie Spier, and published in 1932. It concerned two brothers who lived with the "old people." One was a giant, Man Who Wiggles Because He Is Tall. While crossing the Colorado River the brothers argued and fought. To this day, those footprints lie pressed into the mountains.

The truth about the Halchidomas concerning their lifeways, as well as the intaglios, will probably never be known. That which no one remembers is never restored. Kotux, himself an old man, ended his tale in the traditional fashion of his people: "Nyupai." It is gone.

II Of Captains, Cattle, and Conquest

The Frontier of a Castillian King

One can easily imagine the scene set in the last decades of the eighteenth century. His Majesty Carlos III, King of Spain, stares down upon a map of his empire. He follows with his finger the rough line that represented the northern Pacific shore. In the shafts of soft light that fell from a palace window, in the air of quiet order, the royal policy had made sense. A small strip of seacoast, so easily navigated on the map! He pressed firmly the name of each mission outpost, added so recently that the ink seemed still damp. San Diego de Alcala, San Gabriel Arcangel, San Antonio de Padua, San Carlos Borromeo ... the whispered sounds rolled from his tongue. Now his finger fell on the great bay named for Saint Francis, where only fog and seacliff had been before. Only a precious few outposts in Alta California stood against the Czar, moving south from the Arctic Sea, and from the English. In all of Alta California only five missions, two presidios, seventy soldiers! And in nearly four years it was becoming obvious that no ship could set sail from La Paz and beat for Alta California with assurance of arriving there on schedule, or even intact. The

In about 1890 a group of leaders from the Mission Indian reservations of Riverside and San Bernardino counties posed for San Bernardino photographer H.B. Wesner. Left to right in the front row are: Captain Habiel, Captain Will Pablo, Chief Hervasio Cabezon, Captain Manuel, and Captain José Maria. Left to right in the back row are: Captain Ramon, Captain Jim, and Captain Lastro. Courtesy, Malki Museum, Inc.

Russians, the Apache—and now, of all things, the currents of the Pacific Ocean—were against him. A route overland from New Spain, from Sonora, even Santa Fe, must be established. The sea, he waved his hand, was useless.

The king lifted one corner of a stack of colonial correspondence. Now, consider, this man Anza. A mere borderland captain, doubtless a crude Indian fighter, yet he offers just such a service. He appears to be sincere; his plan has its friends, even the difficult Padre Serra. Could it be, at last, I have a captain? One who will succeed at this simple task—not lose himself foolishly in the desert or, like Diaz, fall on his own lance? Surely, this one can make a road, crowd it with settlers, secure California . . .

Juan Bautista de Anza was a born frontiersman. His grandfather and his father held the Sonoran border against the Apaches, the Pimas, and the Seris for sixty years. It had been his father's secret desire, plotted over and over by the fire on rare peaceful evenings, to put through a trail to Alta California. Only a well-aimed Apache arrow could have prevented his going. And when this happened, Juan Bautista de Anza not only inherited his father's isolated garrison at Tubac in Arizona, but his great plan as well.

A day's ride to the north, at Mission San Xavier del Bac, Father Francisco Garcés also felt the weight of an inheritance. It was from San Xavier that his predecessor, Father Eusebio Kino, took to wandering, alone and without arms, a true missionary. As a consequence Kino had opened up vast realms of territory in the Southwest peopled by natives wholly innocent of God. Already Garcés had followed the Gila River from one receptive tribe to the next, crossed El Camino del Diablo (the Devil's Highway) on the desert to the west, and turned back in 1771 at the foot of the Santa Rosa Mountains. Together, Garcés and Anza planned to complete the journey and descend on the San Gabriel Mission from the east.

The region today called Riverside County had until 1772 played no part in the brief settlement of Alta California. The Spaniards clung to the

seacoast, their missions and presidios as near to good harborage as practicable. But a prominent feature of the county did receive a name early on. Leaving Serra and most of his soldiers at San Diego, Captain Gaspar de Portolá and Father Juan Crespi had continued in search of the "good" harbor at Monterey. In late July 1769 they camped near the mouth of a river flowing west from a steep canyon. Experiencing here California's first documented earthquakes, they christened the river Santa Ana, Rio de Los Temblores.

The county's first European guest would enter and leave quickly, in pursuit of very practical goals. In 1772, a year after Garcés turned back, Lieutenant Pedro Fages, the military governor at San Diego, set out with a small party of soldiers in search of deserters. Eastward he skirted the Santa Rosas, and ascending Carrizo Creek, crossed back over the mountains at a difficult pass. He descended toward Mission San Gabriel across the San Jacinto Valley. He never found the deserters, but he had crossed Riverside County. Unknown to each other, Fages and Garcés had surveyed Anza's entire route.

Soon after, a reluctantly Christianized Indian made the entire crossing to Sonora. Late in 1775, Sebastián Tarabal, his wife, and a relative ran away from Mission San Gabriel. Losing the other two in the sand dunes east of the river, Tarabal wandered, parched and delirious, into the Quechan villages. His trek would have gone unnoticed had he not been turned over to Anza. When the first expedition left Tubac on January 8, 1774, it consisted of the captain, fathers Garcés, Díaz, a scout and courier, twenty soldiers, a few mule teams, and Sebastián Tarabal as guide.

Anza's route was toward the north, into Papagueria, the land of the nomadic Papagos. He reached the Colorado at Yuma by February 7, and with pomp and a small display of force made an ally in Quechan *kwaxot* (leader), Salvador Palma. The powerful Quechans held the vital river crossing; there could be no road without their approval. They were friendly, and provided ferry service across the river. Confronting the dunes on the other side, Anza altered his route, moving south into the thickets and bayous of the overflow channels that fed sometimes into the Salton

Sink. Even there, in early spring, adequate water was hard to find. After getting lost several times, the desperate Anza divided the company, sending the debilitated pack animals and most of the supplies back to Yuma. On the 14th of March he entered Coyote Canyon at the foot of the Santa Rosa Mountains. His weary horses lifted their heads to the unmistakable scent of good water. At a spring they named for Saint Catherine in a lovely area called Lower Willows, the travelers pitched a relieved camp.

By the evening of the next day, Anza had crest-

33

ed the brow of a gap between the peaks. Calling it the Royal Pass of San Carlos, he took time to describe in his journal the land that lay before him as "beautiful green and flower-strewn prairies, and snow-covered mountains with pines, oaks, and other trees that grow in cold countries." At its western edge rose the handsome face of Cahuilla Mountain etched by the setting sun.

Anza entered the San Jacinto River Valley. He named a lake (now San Jacinto, or Shadow Lake) for his viceroy, Antonio de Bucareli, describing it being as "full of white geese as of water." Nearing the Santa Ana River, probably through Riverside's Sycamore Canyon and Tequesquite Arroyo, Anza camped near what is now Pedley Narrows. The river was high and his men felled trees to improvise a bridge. At sunset on March 21, the pathbreaker entered the mission compound at San Gabriel to considerable celebration. Carlos III had chosen correctly.

Anza returned to Tubac on May 26, four-and-a-half months after he left it. Viceroy Antonio Bucareli awaited him in Mexico City, holding documents of promotion heartily approved by Carlos III. Together they planned a second expedition, to establish a pueblo at San Francisco Bay. Preparations were complicated, but by September 28, 1775, the new lieutenant colonel had assembled all the elements of his expedition. The list was long: three officers, three priests, thirty-eight soldiers, twenty-nine soldiers' wives, and 136 "miscellaneous" (mostly children). Two families took nine children, and most averaged four apiece. They were to be the nucleus of San Francisco. There were as well twenty muleteers, three vaqueros, seven servants, and a commissary. Over and above 240 people, there were 695 mules and horses, and 355 head of cattle!

On October 22, 1775, the colonists began their journey from Tubac. Together they formed all the elements of a civilization uprooted, an entire town afoot. At Sahuarita on October 23, a woman died in childbirth. By Tucson, however, Father Font had already married three couples. All Souls Day called for nine masses under the brilliant sky, at-

tended by a horde of Indians who impressed Font with their "quiet and silence." Then, as Anza reached the Gila River, the weather turned bitter cold.

At Yuma, the natives remained hospitable. Fathers Garcés and Eixarch stayed behind, settling near Salvador Palma to build their two beloved missions. With Palma's help, it took only three hours for the entire entourage to ford the Colorado. Once across, Anza again resorted to division to conquer El Camino del Diablo. Soldiers had dubbed Signal Mountain "Cerro de Impossible," for no matter how hard they traveled, the mountain never seemed any closer. Though a cold December, the dunes of the desert floor still offered little water. Three staggered groups permitted the sluggish waterholes to refill. To make matters worse, a violent snowstorm pummeled the expedition, falling on sand too deep for easy travel. What a curious form of hell—snow on the desert, no firewood. Anza himself, coatless in the cold wind, dug at the pitifully small wells of Santa Rosa. Women, children, and horses all suffered in the four-day crossing.

The mountains to the west lay deep in forbidding snow. On December 23 Anza camped once again at Lower Willows on Coyote Creek. The following day the cumbersome expedition began the rough ascent toward San Carlos Pass. There are singular times when events, distilled from circumstance, seem to hang in the air for a moment. The Old hesitates for a while at a high divide. The Old prepares, self-consciously, to become New. That morning, at his command, "Everybody mount," Anza bequeathed that future one special moment. The lumbering caravan ascended Coyote Canyon on a cold, clear Christmas Eve, entering future Riverside County. At the crest they celebrated not only the birth of Christ, but that of an unknown new era. December 24, 1775: 3,000 miles away, citizens of the British colonies were surging together, soon to declare a bold new independence from King George. Even farther, across the Atlantic, the monarch Carlos III struggled to extend the waning moments of his vast empire.

Outside his tent, under the stars, Padre Font listened to the soldiers celebrating the Holy Night of the Nativity with their holiday rations of *aguardiente*. He had protested to the commandante about the drinking but to no avail. Straining toward where the families huddled together, he caught, faintly, the anguish of another expectant mother.

In the afternoon they called me to confess the wife of a soldier who since yesterday had been suffering childbirth pains. ... She was very fearful of dying, but having consoled her and encouraged her as best I could ... at half past eleven at night she very happily and quickly gave birth to a boy.

Here, no manger, no stable walls—only the wet canvas of a tent. But for the founding members of a new civilization huddled together in the still solemnity of the night, their warmth and strength alone had to suffice. Two days later, the pass surmounted, Temayawit, deep below, marked the moment with what Anza thought at first to be "a heavy distant thunder." It was an earthquake, lasting fully four minutes.

The expedition continued with little incident, though some women wept at the continued presence of so much snow. Soon, however, descending to the San Jacinto Valley, they marveled at the bright green fertility of the valley floor. Anza noted many sites for future ranchos and villages. At the River of the Señora Santa Ana, they found their bridge of logs intact. They traveled on, hampered only by lack of firewood. The expedition reached Mission San Gabriel Arcangel on January 4.

The colonists went on to found the Presidio of San Francisco on September 17, 1776. Little did they know that the English colonists were already thick in a fight which would eventually affect the entire province. Anza returned to Sonora. He would live out his days as governor of New Mexico. Father Garcés, his great-hearted co-conspirator, would suffer martyrdom. In 1781 Palma and his tribe turned suddenly on the missions, clubbing Garcés and Eixarch to death, closing the road to the west Garcés had done so much to open.

During its five years of use, the Anza Trail guided an estimated thirty-five to fifty percent of California's colonists to their new home. The newcomers owed their livelihood to the road—the first private stock entered California by way of San Carlos Pass. Closure by the Quechans left the distant province wholly dependent again on insecure sea traffic and an occasional trading caravan from Santa Fe.

For decades the great Pass of San Gorgonio, the only true pass south of the Transverse ranges, had gone unused. Under the general direction of the Mexican Captain José Romero of Tucson, several expeditions were organized to open a direct route from the pueblo at Los Angeles to the land of the Cocomaricopas in Arizona. Romero's party traversed the mighty pass late in 1823, but lack of water turned them back before they reached the Colorado. Romero would try again and succeed in crossing in 1825, but events would prevent Mexico from utilizing the new route.

Likewise, settlement in Riverside County was slow to start and fitful at best. Even the western region, sixty miles from the coast and occupied by unmissionized tribes, held little attraction. Leandro Serrano is credited as the county's first permanent European. The son of a soldier from the Portolá-Serra expedition, he obtained permission from the priests at San Luis Rey to take up five leagues of land in the Temescal Valley in 1818. Serrano had served as mayordomo at the mission and proven his ability to deal judiciously with the "neophytes" (Christianized Indians). He was allowed to settle in the valley in return for securing the padres' northern flank against the unchristianized Luiseños and Cupeños.

The Temescal Valley lies between two arms of the coast ranges. As the outlet for the San Jacinto River, the canyon wears a bright necklace of cottonwood and sycamore set at the center with shimmering Lake Elsinore. Serrano chose a spring near the middle of the valley for his homesite, and with Indian help drove out the bears and

In the 1840s Trujillo ditch brought water from the Santa Ana River to the community of La Placita (later known as Spanishtown). Between 1875 and 1876, after the first canal was engineered for the Riverside Colony, this older ditch was enlarged and extended. This photograph of what became known as the Lower Canal, which took over the intake site of the Trujillo Ditch, was taken sometime in the 1890s. Courtesy, Tom Patterson

mountain lions. From the coast, he brought his family and a herd of cattle and sheep and began construction of his home. Serrano planted an orchard and a vineyard, and would father thirteen children. In turn their homes, too, would spring up around him.

Serrano's growing settlement stood alone in Riverside County during the era of Spanish control. It wasn't until 1821 that the fathers of San Gabriel Mission established a rancho run by Indian neophytes at the far end of the San Bernardino Valley. There they dug a *zanja*, an impressive canal headed at Mill Creek. Soon after, in 1824, another neophyte rancho, San Gorgonio, was established near where Banning and Beaumont stand today.

The pace of settlement exploded with Mexican independence and the passage of the Secularization Act of 1833. Through this act, the missions were immediately downgraded to parish churches and their vast land holdings broken up. Neophytes were to be released from the mission way of life to which they'd become accustomed and resettled as citizens on those lands. *Comisionados*, appointed by the governor, would supervise the transition.

The process proved disastrous, both for the missionaries and their charges. The neophytes were unprepared for their expulsion, and the missionaries, in bitterness, resorted to desperate measures. One of these was the wholesale slaughter of thousands of head of cattle for the sale of their hides. They left in their wake thousands of carcasses rotting on the sun-drenched hillsides.

Some neophytes, when banded together, did, by protest and petition, protect their rights. Under the leadership of Pablo Apis, for example, a group of Luiseños from San Luis Rey regained some of the mission land given Governor Pío Pico as Rancho Temecula. But most, abandoned and bewildered, never received their allotments. Some wandered back to their tribal grounds, only to find them deserted. Many took up migratory work as field hands or *vaqueros*. All too many drifted aimlessly into pueblos and succumbed to

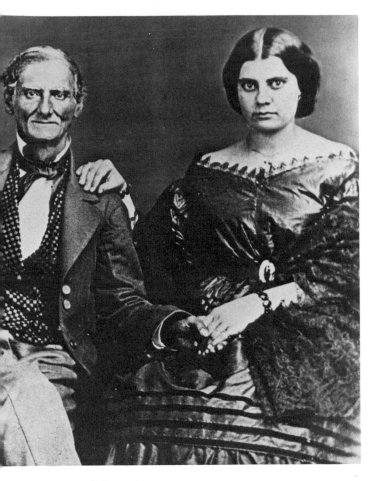

32,000 acres. A year later he requested and was granted El Rincón (which he called "the pocket"), the fertile Prado Basin near today's Corona. Bandini's first home, an adobe, stood on a high bluff overlooking the river. Nearby was a *rancheria* where Indians tended his cattle and tilled his crops. At El Rincón he built a larger adobe, hauling lumber from the San Bernardino Mountains to help steady its two stories. In 1841 he sold El Rincón to Bernardo Yorba, who gave it to Maria, one of his daughters, and Leonardo Cota, her husband. Bandini then turned his attention to San Juan Capistrano, where he had received an additional grant.

In terms of acreage, however, even Bandini was outdone by the Estudillo family—José Antonio received the 35,000-acre Rancho San Jacinto Viejo in 1842. His daughter, Maria del Rosario, and her

Left: *In 1838 Don Juan Bandini, shown here with his daughter, Ysidora, acquired the Jurupa Rancho in what is now Riverside County. Courtesy, Riverside Municipal Museum*

Below: *In 1839 Don Juan Bandini acquired the Rancho Rincon, extending the Rancho Jurupa grant along the choice pasture lands of the Santa Ana River's Prado Basin. This adobe home slightly northwest of Corona eventually became the property of Leonardo Cota and was often referred to as the "Cota home." Courtesy, Press-Enterprise Company*

vice and despair.

Comisionados were, of course, in a perfect position to take advantage of secularization. Under governors Alvarado, Micheltorena, and Pico, the number of privately held ranchos leapt from twenty, during the Spanish regime, to around 500 during the Mexican. The legal limit for such grants was to be eleven leagues (seventy-six square miles) but this was often exceeded. By 1845, out of a statewide European population of around 7,000, a handful of men had become a powerful class called *ranchero*.

Sixteen ranchos were granted within Riverside County, all at its western end. First of the great rancheros was Juan Bandini. Born in Lima, Peru, in 1800 and an accomplished politician, Bandini, as comisionado of San Gabriel, received vast acreage. In 1838 he was granted Rancho Jurupa, stretching for nearly seventeen miles across the Santa Ana River Valley, and consisting of over

husband, José Antonio Aguirre, were granted the 48,000-acre Sobrante de San Jacinto, centered around present-day Lake Mathews. Another relation, Miguel Pedrorena, received the 48,000-acre San Jacinto Nuevo y Potrero, adjoining Estudillo's original grant and taking in most of the Moreno Valley and Perris Plain.

For a brief period the rancheros established a way of life as colorful as their domains were vast. The principal livelihood was cattle, but the principal occupation was leisure. The existence of cheap Indian labor and the willingness of cattle to multiply uncoaxed made it possible. The ranchero filled his season with an unstudied nobility and an unending hospitality. Bandini, for instance, was touted as the best dancer in Southern California. Weddings, rodeos, and holy days occasioned three-day fiestas, in which everyone performed the *jota*, the *borrego*, the *jarabe*, the *fandango*, the *bamba*, and the stately *contradanza* to exhaustion. Education (apart from intricate dance steps and incredible horsemanship) scarcely existed at all. Historians estimate that in 1845 in the entire state no more than one hundred souls could read.

Life for the ranchero couldn't always be one of gaiety. Distances were immense and articles of trade were rare. Most of all, the depredations of marauding Indian bands, especially Ute and other northern tribes, were incessant. In 1839 the Bandini family witnessed a raid, probably spearheaded by the notorious Ute chieftain Walkara, and assisted by famed mountain men Pegleg Smith and Jim Beckwourth. Gathering 5,000 horses by swooping down on the western ranchos, the thieves raised a giant column of dust during their retreat and disappeared over Cajon Pass like a tornado.

Rancho life was rendered even more colorful by the infiltration of some singular Americans. Hide and tallow brought American ships to the coast and publicized the charms of the countryside. Wanderlust and the search for beaver pelts impelled fur trappers over the deserts and Sierras. Jedediah Smith crossed the Mojave and stopped at

the *asistencia* at San Bernardino, reaching San Gabriel Mission in 1826. Though officially unwelcome, he traversed the state and made the first known crossing of the Sierras in 1827. David Jackson, Smith's lieutenant, retraced the Anza route in 1831. Joining Ewing Young, who had been exploring the Pacific Coast as far as Oregon, Jackson left the province by the same route the following year.

From Santa Fe, along what became known as "the Old Spanish Trail," trading parties set out for California by way of Cajon Pass. Benjamin Wilson, arriving with the Rowland-Workman party of 1841, soon began negotiating for the purchase of Rancho Jurupa from Bandini. By 1847 he had married one of Bernardo Yorba's daughters, Ramona, and settled on Rancho Jurupa as *alcalde,* or local judge. Louis Rubidoux, of the well-known St. Louis fur-trading family—one that, according to Bernard De Voto, "practically dug the Missouri" —was already a Mexican citizen in Santa Fe, but he, too, succumbed to the lure of California. In 1847 he purchased 6,700 acres in the center of Rancho Jurupa.

Another fur trapper, Isaac Williams, married into the Lugo family and took possession of nearby Chino Rancho. With his crony Pauline Weaver, an old mountain man, he petitioned Governor Pico for the mission neophyte rancho at San Gorgonio. While awaiting official title, "Paulino" Weaver took up residence there in the old adobe headquarters.

Abel Stearns, of a distinguished Massachusetts family, took early to wandering. Naturalized in Mexico City, he arrived in California in 1829, looking for a land grant. Settling in Los Angeles, he proved himself adept at both politics and economics. Dubbed "Cara de Caballo" ("Horseface") by the natives, he nevertheless managed a marriage to one of Bandini's daughters, the beautiful Doña María Francisca Paula Arcadia Bandini. By the end of Mexican rule, Don Abel Stearns

Top: *In 1842 Benjamin Wilson bought a portion of the Jurupa Rancho and built an adobe home for himself and his bride, Ramona Yorba. Wilson sold his Jurupa property to Louis Rubidoux in 1847 and moved to Los Angeles where he became that city's first mayor. Rubidoux expanded the adobe homestead greatly and was known as a genial host to travelers. The homestead began deteriorating in the 1890s, when this photograph was taken, and the main building (at left) was gone early in this century. Courtesy, Riverside County Parks Department*

Above: *This photograph shows the Louis Rubidoux homestead in 1906. Today a California state historical marker commemorates the site of the old Rubidoux adobe. Courtesy, Tom Patterson*

would be the largest of the rancheros, and the wealthiest. Included in his estate were the 13,000-acre La Laguna (encompassing Lake Elsinore) and the original Wilson portion of the Jurupa grant.

Accompanying "Benito" Wilson in the Rowland-Workman party was a remarkable frontiersman, Lorenzo Trujillo. Trujillo had been settled near Abiquiu, New Mexico, an outfitting center for the Santa Fe trade. He was a *genízaro*, a Christianized Indian reared to Spanish culture. Wilson referred to him as "my faithful Comanche"—others said he was Pueblo. What is certain is that genízaros, by dint of their skill in Indian fighting and their hardy pioneering ways, were granted territory throughout the frontiers of Spanish New Mexico. They established small irrigated farms and grouped their homes into central protected villages.

The Lugos of Rancho San Bernardino offered Trujillo and his neighbors land on the Santa Ana River near Colton in return for defense against raids. Trujillo and twenty other families settled at La Politana. But genízaros were primarily farmers, and friction soon developed between the village and the Lugos, whose stock trampled their fields. Consequently through Wilson, Bandini offered them roughly 2,000 acres nearby—the "Bandini Donation"—and most of the families quickly relocated. By 1844 Wilson had helped them lay out farms of 550-foot frontage along the southern bank of the Santa Ana River, at the base of the La Loma Hills. Trujillo and his neighbors dug an extensive irrigation system. They built their homes around a small plaza and the village became known as La Placita de Los Trujillos. Across the river, under a high bluff, more New Mexicans established Agua Mansa, the name sometimes used for both settlements. They marked their fields with willow stakes which would eventually sprout into rows of bright green trees. Between them, in the rich bottomland soil, they planted fruit trees, grapes, grain, and vegetables. On the high mesa southeast, where the city of Riverside now sprawls, they pastured their horses, sheep, and cattle.

It was a community unique to California in many ways, a pastoral village amidst sprawling ranchos and grafted from Spanish and Indian stock. Joining them in 1854 was Danish sea captain Cornelius Jensen, abandoned by his gold-hungry crew in San Francisco. Jensen came south and opened a much-needed store in Agua Mansa. Marrying Mercedes Alvarado, Jensen fathered twelve children and, by 1870, had purchased from the Rubidoux holdings enough property to build a home and a winery out of sturdy red brick. They stand today; preserved as a county park, the ranch will soon again produce grapes, apricots, and oranges as a living museum. The house re-

mains, an anomaly in the Danish Vernacular style.

The Agua Mansans were a strong community, closely knit and devoutly Catholic. At Agua Mansa they built a small adobe church, named for San Salvador, and began a cemetery. Their church bell hung from a tree nearby but was never rung, for it was cracked and useless. In 1863, at the urging of Father Peter Verdaguer, neighbors began to contribute scraps of metal, even jewelry. Three years later, with hundreds of people in attendance, a new bell, cast at the church, was broken from its mold. The crude inscription was legible, but two small holes flawed its tone. It didn't make a difference. The bell hung proudly on a frame near the church for many years.

All the while, Agua Mansans paid dearly for the "Bandini Donation." Encounters with marauding Indians were frequent, and over the course of time several of Trujillo's sons were injured in Indian battles. Even so, the abandonment of the earlier townsite of La Politana by the genízaros left the Lugos feeling defenseless. Filling the gap was another native leader, Cahuilla Captain Juan Antonio, with the features of a lion and skilled in horsemanship and weaponry. The most dramatic example of a new class of Indian leader, Antonio ruled by force. Encouraged by the Spanish, strongmen such as Antonio took on the role of chief within their tribes and began to maintain at least titular control over all clans, superseding the traditional lineage *net*. Antonio's desert counterpart, Cabazon, at one point delivered the heads of two thieves to Alcalde Benito Wilson in return for noninterference with his desert people.

American conquest of the area—the "California theater" of the Mexican War, shattered the balance worked out by the region's diverse occupants. Wartime alliances between the three antagonists —the Californios, the Anglos, and the Indians —shifted confusingly. Here, in the south, it became a war of suspicion, neighbor against neighbor, and would leave bitterness and antagonism in its wake.

The first phase was relatively bloodless. Commodores Sloat and Stockton of the Pacific Squadron

One of the oldest structures in the Riverside area is the Cornelius Jensen home, built by a Danish sea captain who established a store at Agua Mansa in 1854. Construction of the house began in 1870, based on the design of Jensen's boyhood home on the island of Sylt, Denmark. Jensen acquired large holdings of land in Riverside County and his sheep grazed on the Riverside plain. Courtesy, Riverside County Parks Department

"captured" the capital at Monterey and formally took possession of California on July 7, 1846. But after occupying Los Angeles, imposing an unneeded martial law, and managing to insult nearly everyone, Stockton precipitated a counter-rebellion. At stake was Californio pride and the rancheros proved on several occasions that damaged pride could make an enemy even more formidable.

On September 24, 1846, the American garrison at Los Angeles, under Sergeant Archibald Gillespie, was surrounded and forced to surrender. Three days later, rebels surrounded the home of Isaac Williams at Chino. Within was a mixed group of recent American arrivals and old American rancheros. Among them: Joe Rowland, Benito Wilson, and Louis Rubidoux. Outside, among the native cavalry, were the Lugos.

Wilson felt the newer American arrivals "had a very contemptible opinion of the Californians' courage and fighting qualities. . . . I hoped they had not underrated the natives." With the roof ablaze, the Americans surrendered and were taken prisoner. Wilson mourned the loss of Carlos Ballesteros, who died charging the walls: "A very

good man and one who had ever been amongst my best friends."

Farther south the Army of the West under General Stephen W. Kearny was nearing the end of an exhausting 2,000-mile march from Fort Leavenworth to join the embattled Americans in California. Descending Warner's Pass, his bedraggled force camped at San Pascual. Kit Carson, who accompanied him, also underestimated the Californios' fighting qualities. Carson promised

Kearny an easy fight. At dawn on December 6, the Californio cavalry under Andres Pico pitted lance against saber. Kearny's force suffered defeat. One of Louis Rubidoux's brothers, Antoine, was among the wounded.

After the battle a few Californios hid at Serrano's rancho in the Temescal Valley. Taking advantage of the chaos of rebellion, Luiseños and Cupeños nearby attacked the ranch, killed the fugitives, and raided the stock. In return, under José Lugo, Juan Antonio and his Cahuilla warriors captured and slaughtered as many as one hundred Luiseños and Cupeños in the so-called "Temecula Massacre," truly the bloodiest "battle" of the Conquest. Three weeks later, late in January 1847, Captain Antonio Garra, literate and ambitious chief of the Cupeños, guided the Mormon Battalion, bringing reinforcements to Kearny, as far as Temecula. In return, the battalion protected the mourning Indians while they buried their dead.

After Mexico was defeated and the Treaty of Guadalupe Hidalgo ceded most of today's Southwest to the United States in 1848, Garra realized these new conquerors were more dangerous than his old enemies. Already American bureaucrats in San Diego were demanding taxes from his impoverished people. Unpaid taxes were being collected by seizing Cupeño cattle. In 1851 Garra launched an uprising that terrorized American settlers and, in defeat, marked the end of Indian organized resistance. Garra struck first at a party of sheepmen crossing the Colorado into California. Killing five Americans and one Sonoran, Garra then assaulted an army post and raided Warner's Ranch. Unsure of his next move he tried to draw his old rival Juan Antonio into the rebellion. His letter to the Cahuilla leader is a testament to a proud people's desperation: "If we lose this war, all will be lost—the world."

While Garra hesitated, time was running out. A survivor of the sheepmen's attack had managed to crawl across the desert to Paulino Weaver's rancho at San Gorgonio. Paulino reached Juan Antonio

Above: *A former fur trapper and mountain man, Louis Rubidoux bought 6,700 acres of the Jurupa Rancho in 1844 and established the Rubidoux Ranch. Rubidoux served as justice of the peace, raised cattle and grain, and fought with the American forces at Chino in the Mexican War. Between 1852 and 1854 a military detachment was stationed at the Jurupa Outpost on his ranch. After his death in 1868 a portion of his ranch became part of the Riverside Colony. From Brown and Boyd,* History of Riverside and San Bernardino Counties

Left: *In 1876 the United States established Indian reservations in California, but for many years there were still white complaints of isolated Indian groups squatting on ancestral lands now owned by white settlers. One of these groups, the Cupeño, occupied Warner's Valley and extended into parts of southern Riverside County. In 1902 the Cupeño people were rounded up, evicted from their scattered homes, and taken in wagons to a new reservation established for them in the Pala Valley of San Diego County. Photo by Charles F. Lummis*

first. And when the two great native leaders agreed to meet that December in the desert near Coyote Canyon, Antonio (probably accompanied by Weaver) chose loyalty to the Americans over ethnic bonds, and took Garra prisoner. Antonio turned Garra and his son over to American military authorities.

Garra was executed on January 10, 1851, by firing squad. The Conquest over, and all rebellions quashed, Americans and Californios settled down to becoming "Californians." Urged on by land-hungry Anglos who were appalled to discover so much unoccupied land in California claimed as private property, the Land Commission of 1851 began to pass judgment on the "validity" of Mexican land grants. Some of their decisions now seem unjustified. The heirs of Leandro Serrano, though entitled, never gained their patents. Furthermore, rancheros whose titles remained secure often later succumbed to drought, fiscal ineptitude, and voracious legal fees. The day of the ranchero was over.

In years following, Juan Bandini and Abel Stearns, both falling on hard times, would attempt to retrieve in court the Bandini Donation from Agua Mansa. Both would fail. In the end, the terrible flood of January 22, 1862, would begin the settlement's decline. A wall of water high enough to snarl at the steps of the little church swept away most of the homes on both sides of the river. No lives were lost—perhaps this was the night when San Salvador's first bell cracked in urgent tolling. Though the community rebuilt, precious land-title documents and much fertile topsoil were lost forever.

In contrast, Paulino Weaver, whose land grant claim had no legitimacy, was able to sell his rancho, unchallenged by the commission after eighteen years. But Weaver, like many other mountain men, couldn't stay put. Perhaps it was the shadow of Mount San Jacinto sweeping past his doorstep every day, or the howl of the fall Santa Anas down the shoulder of Old Grayback ... He would go on to lead gold rushes at La Paz and Prescott, skirmish with Apaches, and die in Arizona in 1867.

The year of the great flood, 1862, another legend was wiped away. At Sahatapa, in San Timoteo Canyon, Juan Antonio and his people were experiencing the first discomforting symptoms of smallpox. It never took long for this, the most virulent of the white man's diseases, to wipe away a culture. All his villagers dead or deserted, an old man lingered in helpless agony. Dragging himself from his shelter, as befits a warrior, Juan Antonio crawled into the sun to die.

III A Fruit Appropriate to Paradise

The Land Finds Its Value

California entered the Union in 1850 as a free state—part of one more uneasy compromise in the nation's gradual fragmentation into civil war. The whole country agreed a railroad from sea to sea was desperately needed, but Congress, split North and South, could not settle on a route. In 1853 the legislators authorized study of five possible routes. One of the teams of the Pacific Railroad Survey traversed the region of future Riverside County, entered the San Gorgonio Pass, retraced the Old Emigrant Road through Warner's Pass, and crossed to Yuma. Their geologist, William Blake, noted the high shoreline marks of prehistoric Lake Cahuilla, and recorded the Indians' tales. For a time, in his honor, it was known as Blake's Sea. But, despite the surveys, Congress failed again to endorse any of the routes suggested.

Instead, they compromised. In 1857 Congress passed an appropriation for overland mail service. A company headed by John Butterfield of New York was awarded the lucrative contract. A fleet of sturdy Concord coaches, drawn by at least four

The first true packinghouse in Riverside was
Griffin & Skelley, which opened in 1884 in a
new building on Eighth Street near Ninth. Its
main product at first was muscat raisins, but as
the orange industry grew and prospered it
concentrated on citrus. Courtesy, Riverside
Municipal Museum

horses or mules, traveled a circuitous 2,800-mile route from St. Louis, passing through Arkansas, Texas, New Mexico, Arizona, Los Angeles, and then through the Central Valley to San Francisco. Over 800 employees at stations eight to twenty-five miles apart swapped teams and fed the parched and often addled passengers. The route entered California at Fort Yuma, with local stations at Warner's Ranch, Oak Grove, Aguanga, Temecula, Laguna Grande (Elsinore), Temescal, and Chino Ranch. The Butterfield Overland ran this southern route without a break in service until 1861 and the Civil War.

On Sunday, January 20, of that year, botanist William H. Brewer crouched in his cold tent and, fighting the onset of rheumatism, made a long entry in his journal. As part of the Josiah Whitney Geological Survey, it was his responsibility to collect and classify the flora of California. But, only a month in the field, and following the route of the Butterfield Overland Mail, Brewer's advance party had met its first obstacle—the floodwaters of the Santa Ana River near present-day Corona. Unknowingly, he would memorialize the waning moments of a passing era.

The Overland passes here—that miracle of undertakings—over plains and deserts, over mountains, through gorges, into rivers, yet always inside of scheduled time. . . . The river here is quite a stream—several rods wide and up to the sides of our mules as we ford it. I have not seen a bridge in Southern California, nor is there timber enough here to make them.

The Whitney Survey followed the Butterfield Route as far as Temescal Station, where a tin strike nearby had been drawing considerable attention. Camped near hot springs at Glen Ivy, Brewer warmed his aching joints at the bathhouse and recorded the excitement:

People are 'crazy' about tin ore, every man has from one to fifty claims, while poor devils with ragged clothes and short pipes talk as they smoke

of being the wealthy owners of one hundred or two hundred tin claims, each in time to rival Cornwall or Banca.

The next day, Brewer's party ascended the steep side of the canyon to examine the diggings.

We rode to the principal mine, four miles distant—found it a splendid humbug. Many black streaks are found in the rocks; some of which contain some tin. Many claims are made and entered. One man has invested $14,500, and has commenced mining operations—that is, has sunk a shaft in the granite to look for richer ore. All thus far is mere speculation, and will end in that, I think.

But while the Whitney Survey continued northward, a gold strike would shake the sleepy region and open a new stage route through San Gorgonio Pass. In 1862 Paulino Weaver brought Los Angeles news that gold had been sifted from a gulch near La Paz, Arizona, across the Colorado from the Palo Verde Valley. The rush was on immediately, heightening the demand for a supply route from Los Angeles directly east to the Colorado. W.D. Bradshaw, smitten with "the fever" and guided by a Maricopa Indian who knew the old Halchidoma trade route, successfully made his way across the Colorado Desert from the pass. The Alexander Company, a newly formed subsidiary of Wells Fargo, wasted no time. That September the surprised miners at La Paz looked up from their work long enough to watch a dusty coach and six foaming horses arrive from Los Angeles.

Agents Warren Hall and Henry Wilkinson were experienced stagemen, and their desert route had been carefully planned. Incredibly, the farthest distance between water holes was only fourteen miles. Unfortunately, only a month after their coaches had begun to roll, Hall and Wilkinson came to believe an employee at Isaac Smith's San Gorgonio Ranch was stealing bullion from the stage. During their investigation at the ranch both men were stabbed to death. (The employee was

released by authorities at San Bernardino after claiming self-defense!)

Though the rush at La Paz dwindled quickly, the Bradshaw Road had proven more efficient than the indirect climb through Warner's Pass. Several operators—including Phineas Banning, developer of Wilmington as well as the first railroad in Southern California—ran stages through the pass to Yuma. Banning left his name behind for one of the towns that later grew up around Weaver's old ranch.

Despite mining rushes and galloping stages, despite the distant bloody war that would soon devastate the South, the two decades following California's statehood were relatively peaceful ones for the "cow counties" of Southern California. Louis Rubidoux successfully weathered the transition brought on by Americanization. His ranch, situated on the rich bottomland soil of the Santa Ana River channel, produced abundant wheat, grapes, and peaches. At its most prosperous, in 1861, he milled a record harvest of grain and produced nearly 2,000 gallons of wine, as well

as 500 gallons of peach brandy. A thousand head of beef and 2,000 sheep grew fat on the green pasturage along the river. Rubidoux's small canal system protected him from the severe droughts that periodically swept the higher plains. The Santa Ana River Valley was a long, narrow oasis of dependability in a land where rain patterns were notoriously inconsistent.

East of the river the region remained unpopulated and isolated. It would take a gigantic effort to bring water from its source on the river to the mesas above. And without a valuable cash crop, one whose sale could reward investors for their gigantic outlay, that effort would not be made. Great areas would remain empty, dry, a land only of stages and strikes.

The first successful effort to bring water to the highlands straddling the Santa Ana River had its roots in an aging Easterner's utopian vision.

John Wesley North was born near his father's sawmill at Sand Lake, New York, in 1815. Raised in the rough-and-tumble Methodism of the frontier, the young man "experienced religion" at a camp meeting and at thirteen felt the call to the Methodist ministry. In 1838, as a licensed preacher, he entered Wesleyan University at Middletown, Connecticut.

Here he fell in with a group of earnest young students who debated the latest and most volatile issue dividing the country: slavery. "Going to and fro as a flaming brand," North crisscrossed Connecticut, raising support for what was yet the dangerously unpopular abolitionist cause. Thin,

ORANGE GROVE & HOME OF A.J. TWOGOOD, RIVERSIDE, SAN BERNARDINO CO. CAL.

energetic, with prominent cheekbones and large, earnest eyes, North was an arresting figure on the speaker's platform and soon became well known.

With his young bride, Ann Loomis from Syracuse, New York, North soon moved to the brisk air and unspoiled frontier that was Minnesota in the 1850s. North, hoping to create a new free state, soon allied himself with the pioneer capitalists and developers of Minneapolis/St. Paul. By 1855, at forty, North had organized the new abolitionist Republican Party, as well as two cities, Faribault and Northfield, and assumed the presidency of the new state's first railroad company.

But North's decline in Minnesota was as rapid as his rise. A severe economic depression found him overextended and, as railroad president, his close ties with politicians left him open to accusations of graft and scandal. Nearly nominated for

This 1882 crayon lithograph depicted the home and orange grove of A.J. Twogood. Twogood, one of Riverside's first settlers, came west from Iowa in 1870 with the James P. Greves excursion party to California. He built this home in the Pachappa area, served in a number of civic capacities, and helped organize the town's first library. From Warren W. Elliott, History of San Bernardino and San Diego Counties, *1882*

governor at one time, North now found himself penniless.

But North's service to the Republican Party would not go unrewarded. He had done much to see Lincoln elected in 1860. After several meetings with Lincoln, North received the promise of a job. But the new President, hoping to stave off civil war, now sought to diffuse the inflammatory potential of his more radical associates. When

North's appointment reached him, its duties and location were both somewhat obscure. The Railsplitter was sending his radical safely to the Far West. North would be surveyor general of the new, silver-rich Nevada Territory.

Between 1861 and the end of the war in 1865, North served as surveyor general, judge of the territorial court, and president of Nevada's constitutional convention. But perhaps his greatest chance for immortality came in the field of literature. A brash young newspaperman found in the ministerial North a hilarious target for his columns in the *Territorial Enterprise*. The judge, however, soon got his revenge. When the young man publicly accepted a challenge to a duel, North gave Samuel Clemens two options—a guaranteed jail sentence, or a permanent vacation from the territory. Thus "Mark Twain" was impelled to the next stage of his legendary writing career—in the goldfields of California.

With the end of the war, North, at fifty, made

plans to go where he could do the most good—to take part in the radical reconstruction of the defeated South. He wrote his wife from Nevada: "I long to go down there, after the war is over,

Among the more elegant early Riverside homes was that of Thomas W. Cover at the southwest corner of Jurupa and Brockton avenues. Cover, who made his fortune in the historic strike at Alder Gulch, Montana, helped found Riverside and supervised the digging of its first canal, a major enterprise for the period. A restless man, he set out with a friend in 1884 to hunt for the lost Peg Leg Smith goldmine on the Colorado Desert. When their wagon overturned, spilling the water supply, the friend walked on alone to Indio for help. The rescuers could not find Cover, and his strange disappearance became one of Riverside County's legends. From the Special Collections Department, Library of the University of California, Riverside

to help build up good society. . . . To heal the wounds the war has inflicted."

With the profits from his mining investments, he bought and reopened a foundry in Knoxville, Tennessee. But his New England manner and Northern attitudes made him few friends in Knoxville, and his championship of free blacks brought him white hatred. North shamed a mob of Fourth of July revelers from their intention to lynch a freedman, only to find his foundry boycotted and his presence extremely unwanted. No longer a young man, North's failure to reform the South devastated him. His investments dwindling away, North felt poor and alone: "My friends do not reproach me as much as Job's did him, neither do they visit me as his did. They simply content themselves with staying away."

But North's despair was not entirely his own. He shared in a great disillusionment brought on by the failure of Reconstruction to significantly alter the shape of the South. A whole generation of dedicated reformers—in religion, temperance, abolition, pacifism—found themselves aged and falling behind in the growth of a giant industrial nation. Post-Civil War America was tired of reforms—it was to be, in the sardonic phrase of North's old friend Twain, a "Gilded Age."

North cast about in his mind for a solution. Nearly broken, an old man reached back to the villages of his New England youth and a vision of the perfect society. On April 17, 1869, he wrote:

I have often thought how pleasant it would be to live in a society wholly made up of educated, enterprising, progressive people; where every neighbor is a companion and a friend; where each will vie with the other in building the schoolhouse, the church, the lyceum, the library, and the reading-room; and where the views of all would harmonize in an onward march toward all that is pure, and beautiful, and good.

North's dark times in Knoxville were brightened somewhat by his renewed friendship with Dr. James P. Greves, whose burly, bearded, and somewhat sad demeanor stood in sharp contrast to North's wiry energy. Born in 1810 in upstate New York, Greves had crossed paths with North several times. He practiced medicine in Michigan, Milwaukee, St. Louis, and the South. Like North, Greves was an ardent abolitionist, and took his needed services to the freedmen of the Sea Islands, off the coasts of Georgia and the Carolinas, where resettlement under the Union Army promised a new era to former slaves, as yeoman farmers. But Greves' health had failed in South Carolina and he left the Sea Islands experiment before new Reconstruction policies turned the freedmen off the land once more.

Greves joined North in Nevada Territory. At the end of the war they met again in Knoxville. Together the old friends began plans for a colony in California. Circulating letters and pamphlets among friends and acquaintances, they drew encouraging replies from groups in New York, Michigan, Iowa, and Massachusetts. In May 1870, nearly one hundred prospective colonists boarded the transcontinental railroad for a trip to "see the elephant"—California. Together with Greves and Ebenezer Brown, a merchant and temperance advocate from Belle Plaine, Iowa, North traveled up and down the state searching for potential sites. At San Pascual, the site of the future Pasadena, in April of 1870, North found 1,700 acres that seemed suitable. While North, nearly convinced, returned to San Francisco, Greves and Brown lingered in Los Angeles. Brown worried that San Pascual was still too close to the temptations and vices of the rowdy cowtown, Los Angeles.

Nearby, what had begun as a promising business venture on the Rubidoux Rancho was fast failing. The first plan to develop the highlands along the Santa Ana River came from an exotic source—the silkworm. Disease in the French silk industry and a statewide bounty for the planting of mulberry trees and the production of silk cocoons promoted a profitable export industry for Californians in the mid-1860s. In 1869 the California Silk Center Association purchased the entire eastern section of the Rubidoux Rancho, a plain

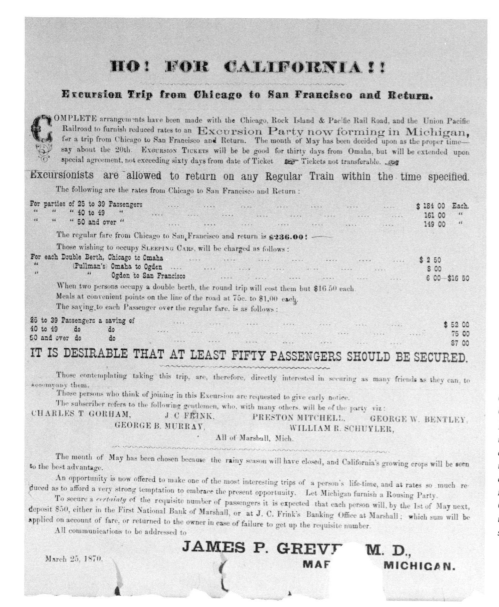

HO! FOR CALIFORNIA!!

Excursion Trip from Chicago to San Francisco and Return.

COMPLETE arrangements have been made with the Chicago, Rock Island & Pacific Rail Road, and the Union Pacific Railroad to furnish reduced rates to an **Excursion Party now forming in Michigan,** for a trip from Chicago to San Francisco and Return. The month of May has been decided upon as the proper time—say about the 20th. EXCURSION TICKETS will be be good for thirty days from Omaha, but will be extended upon special agreement, not exceeding sixty days from date of Ticket ☞ Tickets not transferable. ☜

Excursionists are allowed to return on any Regular Train within the time specified.

The following are the rates from Chicago to San Francisco and Return :

For parties of 25 to 39 Passengers	$ 184 00	Each.
" " " 40 to 49 "	161 00	"
" " " 50 and over "	149 00	"

The regular fare from Chicago to San Francisco and return is **$236.00!**

Those wishing to occupy SLEEPING CARS, will be charged as follows :

For each Double Berth, Chicago to Omaha	$ 2 50	
" (Pullman's) Omaha to Ogden	8 00	
" Ogden to San Francisco	6 00—$16 50	

When two persons occupy a double berth, the round trip will cost them but $16 50 each.
Meals at convenient points on the line of the road at 75c. to $1.00 each.
The saving to each Passenger over the regular fare, is as follows :

25 to 39 Passengers a saving of	$ 52 00	
40 to 49 do do	75 00	
50 and over do do	87 00	

IT IS DESIRABLE THAT AT LEAST FIFTY PASSENGERS SHOULD BE SECURED.

Those contemplating taking this trip, are, therefore, directly interested in securing as many friends as they can, to accompany them.
Those persons who think of joining in this Excursion are requested to give early notice.
The subscriber refers to the following gentlemen, who, with many others, will be of the party viz :

CHARLES T GORHAM,   J C FRINK,   PRESTON MITCHELL,   GEORGE W. BENTLEY,
GEORGE B. MURRAY,   WILLIAM R. SCHUYLER,
All of Marshall, Mich.

The month of May has been chosen because the rainy season will have closed, and California's growing crops will be seen to the best advantage.
An opportunity is now offered to make one of the most interesting trips of a person's life-time, and at rates so much reduced as to afford a very strong temptation to embrace the present opportunity. Let Michigan furnish a Rousing Party.
To secure a *certainty* of the requisite number of passengers it is expected that each person will, by the 1st of May next, deposit $50, either in the First National Bank of Marshall, or at J. C. Frink's Banking Office at Marshall ; which sum will be applied on account of fare, or returned to the owner in case of failure to get up the requisite number.
All communications to be addressed to

JAMES P. GREVE, M. D.,
MAR   MICHIGAN.

March 25, 1870.

Once they had decided to organize a colony in California, James P. Greves and Judge John W. North distributed broadside announcements to friends and acquaintances throughout the east who might be interested in looking over the state. Greve's announcement featured an excursion trip. In September of 1870 the two men and other backers formed the Southern California Colony Association and purchased the future site of Riverside. Courtesy, Riverside Public Library

sloping toward what surveyors had labeled a "high detached hill," Mount Rubidoux. They intended to plant mulberry trees—culturing, with Indian labor, valuable silk thread. French-born Louis Prévost, a silk-culture expert, headed the group. Another investor, Thomas W. Cover, recently of Virginia City, Montana, intended to supervise the construction of the necessary canals. But the cancellation of state bounties, combined with Prévost's untimely death in San Jose, permanently stalled the Silk Center. The disgruntled directors returned the 8,600 acres to the market.

Tom Cover hung on, still hoping to dig his canals. Years earlier, as a young man, he had left Ohio, another victim of gold fever. Unsuccessful in California, in 1863 he struck gold in Alder Gulch, Montana, and by 1868 had arrived in Los Angeles, handsome and self-assured, with a wife and an estimated $75,000 fortune. He brought with him as well an intimate knowledge of flume construction and hydraulic mining techniques. In the arid West such knowledge would prove invaluable in the development of an agricultural technique unfamiliar to the Eastern yeoman: irrigation. But, in a depressed market, Cover's land went unsold. He could find no investors equal to his vision. Had it not been for the Civil War, waged hundreds of miles away from the placid counties of Southern California, the land in the shadow of the "high, detached hill" would have remained pasturage.

Cover, following a lead, caught up with Greves and Brown at their hotel. According to Greves:

Mr. Cover called on Mr. Brown and myself, and urged us to examine the tract before a final purchase. To us at the time, it seemed too far inland for our use, when we declined. Mr. Cover then offered to take us to the tract free of expense. As we were temporarily at leisure, and wishing to see more of Southern California, we accepted his offer.

Dashing Tom Cover doubtless made the most of his skills at salesmanship. Crossing the Santa Ana River in a dusty buggy, the little party climbed to the brow of a bluff and stared out across the vast plain that would be Riverside. Cover swept his hand across the broad panorama, then pointed out the little rill of earth one of his employees had made at the river's edge to hold the water claim. The canal he would build, its impressive length, a sinuous band of blue, and the village it watered, rose into view like a mirage. Greves wired North in San Francisco to make no purchase until he'd seen this land.

Soon the aging judge would stand with a few like-minded companions—old abolitionists, temperance advocates, reformers—on the edge of a broad, barren plain in the shadow of a steep, isolated mountain. The air was warm, the sky crystalline, the region empty and new. An unlikely place for a New England village, but possibly worth another effort. The high hopes of the Civil War and its disillusioning aftermath brought a few dispossessed New Englanders to this barren place, where they might once again move "toward all that is pure, and beautiful and good." Few cities are born with such an earnest endowment.

Accompanying North when he inspected the site was Congregationalist minister J.W. Atherton. Twenty-seven years later he recalled:

What a place and scene met our crew! Above, dry, sun-kissed and wind-swept mesa stretched for miles toward the south—and having not a tree or a shrub in sight, and only the scantiest possible remains of what we assumed to have been, at one time, a growth of grass.

"I think we have found the place," North wrote Anna.

Charles N. Felton was another native New Yorker drawn to California in '49. He had been so toughened by his life of prospecting that he could serve as sheriff of Yuba County during its brawling days. His sharp stare spoke of intelligence and warned of a single-minded sense of purpose: profit. Felton had placed some of his fortune into partnership with a relative in Nevada who, as territorial judge, was well-placed to supervise developments. Later allied with William Ralston's notorious "ring" in San Francisco, Felton would shake off accusations of graft and corruption to become a United States Senator. Now, in 1870, Felton was convinced of the advantage of depressed land prices in Southern California, and decided to invest. The colonists could not meet the combined purchase price and costs for canal construction, totaling in the end around $70,000. North turned to Felton, from whom family ties and success in Nevada promised a friendly ear. Without ever wanting to see the land, Felton invested nearly $50,000 in the colony, becoming its principal owner. It was a necessity North would soon rue.

On September 19, 1870, a fifty-five-year-old judge and a sixty-year-old doctor crossed the shallow Santa Ana River and pitched a tent against the unobstructed wind that swept across the site of their new town. On the evening of his first day on the site North wrote his Anna: "I am at last located on the site of our future city. . . . This is a great undertaking that I am engaged in, but it

The upper canal was begun in the fall of 1870 and brought water from the Santa Ana River from a point on a hill a few hundred yards below the present Colton Bridge to the lands of the Southern California Colony Association. This photograph, taken in 1899, shows the Riverside Water Company canal south of Russell Street. Courtesy, Tom Patterson

promises well, and I firmly believe it will prosper." The following morning Captain John Broadhurst, as well as Los Angeles surveyors Goldsworthy and Higbie, arrived with Tom Cover. While the surveyors began setting out stakes, the principals gathered within the crowded tent. Together they organized the Southern California Colony Association, with North as president, Broadhurst vice president, Greves secretary, and John Stewart, another colonist, treasurer. Tom Cover became superintendent of canal construction.

In the center of the SCCA tract, the surveyors laid out a mile-square grid, the nucleus of a yet nameless village. They divided the square north to south by streets numbered first through fourteenth, and east to west by streets named for shade trees (excluding Market and Main). The center block was reserved for a plaza. Within, there were 169 blocks of two acres each. Outside, they staked out 257 small ten-acre farm plots.

An engineering necessity revitalized the long-lost New England tradition of small farms. The cost of distribution works kept the farms close to-

gether. One irrigated acre could produce an income equal to much larger dry-farmed acreage, but, more important to North, the small farms would promote community. Farmers would now be able, he wrote, "to enjoy the society of near neighbors." In addition, Goldsworthy and Higbie fixed the grade for Cover's ditch, and unofficially surveyed a chunk of government land south of the colony, though it was still unopened to homesteading.

The first pioneers were arriving almost daily. A partial list of early settlers, many of whom came with their families, included: North and Greves, Tom Cover, Captain Broadhurst, Dr. Sanford Eastman, D.C. and A.J. Twogood, Lyman Waite,

53

T.J. Wood, J.W. Linville, S.O. Lovell, and Luther C. Tibbets.

While the canal wound slowly southward from its intake at the La Loma Hills, butcher A.R. Smith hauled domestic water from Spring Brook for twenty-five cents a barrel. The first building, the SCCA's office, was finished in September 1870. The few hardy settlers scattered over the dusty colony site or "squatted" on the Government Tract to the south. On December 14, 1870, stockholders held their first meeting. There was a lively discussion concerning the town's name, including such suggestions as "Jurupa," after the Indian-Spanish name for the area, as well as "Joppa," for the Mediterranean city, and even, simply, "New Colony." The idyllic "Riverside" was chosen by majority vote. Looking back, pioneer James Roe found the name "prosaic"—but he added, philosophically, "it has answered very well up to date."

Work on the canal proceeded more slowly than expected. Winding circuitously around arroyos, in some places blasted from bedrock, it required, as well, several wooden trestles—flumes—across the deepest chasms. The longest flume, 528 feet, lay to the east of La Placita de los Trujillos and was dubbed the Spanishtown Flume. Its plankwork leaked so badly that while nearly 800 miner's

Soon after the Riverside Colony was founded in 1870, a band of Cahuilla Indians assembled in a village on the slopes of Little Rubidoux hill northwest of the town. Their frame-and-brush homes were rectangular, unlike the domed dwellings of their native culture. The Indians formed the earliest work force for the community, helping dig the first irrigation canal and working as laborers in the fields and servants to the colonists. Courtesy, Avery Field Collection, Riverside Municipal Museum

inches of water entered it, only 600 left it. Designed to be twelve feet wide, sloping to eight feet at the bottom, and three feet deep, the canal rarely achieved its goal. Of the water diverted by a brush-and-sand wing dam from the Santa Ana, most never reached the colony, lost to seepage, gopher holes, and cracks in the 1,100 feet of flume. The first trickle of water entered the colony in mid-1871. Though recollections disagree, Anne L. Shepard, writing in 1929, placed it in May:

What an excitement there was that night .. when the water finally came! Men on horseback kept us informed of its slow progress toward our home, I think it was about half past nine when it finally came....We had a bonfire—not a large one, for all our firewood had to be hauled from the river bottom. I can still see the little group standing about in the flickering light ... When the trickle of precious moisture reached a point opposite our house, my father led us in three cheers and my brother John fired the family shotgun.

Despite its early weaknesses, Tom Cover's ditch remained a remarkable achievement, for it proved that irrigation need no longer be confined to the narrow, riverine bottomlands. The Riverside Canal signaled a new, explosive era in California agriculture.

North liberally distributed rights to the precious trickle. As the canal crossed the deep Tequesquite Arroyo via a graceful flume, he extended those rights to Government Tract settlers. Many helped dig the canal, though none had officially purchased shares in the colony. In addition, North announced that irrigating water would be free to all for the rest of the year.

Even before the canal began service, North had thumbed through his Bible for what biographer Merlin Stonehouse called "a fruit appropriate to paradise." The colonists, most of whom had been businessmen or professionals and unfamiliar with

agriculture, threw themselves into experimentation with refreshing energy and imagination. They planted all manner of citrus and deciduous fruit, as well as wine and raisin grapes, almonds, walnuts, and even the esoteric cash crop, the opium poppy. Only the hardier plantings survived the withering blasts of the seasonal Santa Anas.

In the end, two of the colony's most unique citizens, Luther and Eliza Tibbets, discovered the land's real value. Luther Tibbets, among the first pioneers, took up squatter's rights on the Government Tract in December 1870. By all accounts he was an irrascible and argumentative character, a man of high principles but a rather loose grasp on reality. Tibbets was constantly embroiled in controversy, and had an insatiable appetite for lawsuits. For a time he manned a small stockade,

The raisin grape industry was launched by Riverside's earliest pioneers, and encouraged by Judge John W. North. It failed to succeed in Riverside, and North left his community in 1880 to found another town, Oleander, in the San Joaquin Valley and begin the raisin grape industry of California. Two Chinese men are shown harvesting grapes and placing them on trays to produce raisins. Courtesy, Riverside Municipal Museum

Above: *This rare photograph of the two original parent navel orange trees in the yard of the home of Luther and Eliza Tibbets was taken around the turn of the century by John Henry Reed. Reed was the first city tree warden for Riverside, and started a campaign in 1898 that led to the establishment of the Citrus Experiment Station. One of the parent navel orange trees still survives, transplanted to a small park at the corner of Arlington and Magnolia avenues in Riverside. Courtesy, University of California Citrus Research Center and Agricultural Experiment Station, Riverside*

Right: *Chinese formed much of the labor force in all phases of the early citrus industry in Riverside. In 1885 they were driven from their first Chinatown in the Mile Square of downtown when a ban was passed against commercial laundries. The new Chinatown in the Brockton Arroyo during its heyday in the 1890s was an endless source of fascination to Riversiders, with its exotic shops and gambling and opium dens. Courtesy, Riverside Municipal Museum*

complete with gunports, to protect his corrals from marauders, and was once seriously injured by a shotgun blast during an argument with a neighbor over a grain crop. Eliza, a spiritualist, cultivated the appearance of Queen Victoria, whom she admired, and indulged in seances and other exotica. She had remained behind in Washington, D.C., while her husband prepared the homestead, and she arrived with Riverside's first known black resident, the mysterious little girl known only as Nicey. Possibly the product of a Civil War dalliance on the part of Eliza's son, James, Nicey's background always remained discreetly shrouded in Victorian silence.

It was Eliza Tibbets who, before leaving Washington, contacted William Saunders, a horticulturist at the Department of Agriculture, hoping to take with her new varieties of fruit for Luther to plant. Saunders had received a shipment of exotic orange trees from Bahia, Brazil, and was seeking people to plant them. They were "navels," their seeds clustered at one end of the fruit. He sent two of the young trees to Riverside, where Luther and Eliza planted them sometime in 1873. During water shortages, local legend has it, Eliza nursed the little trees with her dishwater. Upon maturing, the fruit was found to be superior in every way. Bud sales were brisk, and the two trees, ringed with barbed wire, became famous. Although officially called the Bahia, the fruit was soon dubbed the Riverside Navel, and its popularity eventually made Riverside a citrus center and prosperous showplace. But that was yet to come—it takes several seasons for an orchard to mature. Meanwhile, the colonists planted conventional crops in the rows between their trees, and hunted game in the riverbottom or the plains to the east.

The first child born near the colony was Mary Broadhurst, late in 1870, to the sea captain John Broadhurst and his wife. But because they settled on the government land, and because the captain soon returned to the sea, Jessie Riverside Smith, born in 1871, of A.R. Smith, more often bears the honor. Three years later the little community contained upwards of 300 citizens. The telegraph had reached Riverside and John G. North, the founder's son, worked as telegrapher. A stage made daily trips to Colton, San Bernardino, and Los Angeles. A small public library functioned out of the new schoolhouse on Sixth Street, only recent-

Above: *Riverside's reputation as the orange-growing center of Southern California was assured in 1885 when the city captured the top gold and silver medals at the New Orleans World's Industrial and Cotton Centennial Exposition. The Riverside Board of Trade immediately launched strong promotion programs that were later emulated by other citrus belt cities. Shown above is the cover of a tiny brochure of the period, measuring three by six inches, with two pages of text describing the city's orange industry. Courtesy, Lorne Allmon*

Top: *Eliza Tibbets has been credited with persuading the U.S. Department of Agriculture to ship two navel orange trees that originated in Bahia Province, Brazil, to her home in Riverside, where they flourished and provided the bud grafts that started the Washington Navel orange industry. Legend says that Eliza kept the trees alive with her dishwater. Courtesy, Special Collections Department, Library of the University of California, Riverside*

Left: *The Citrus Fair Pavilion was erected by Riversiders in 1882 to stage their popular annual citrus fairs and other public entertainments. Novelist Helen Hunt Jackson, author of Ramona, visited the 1882 fair and described displays of citrus fruit so colorful that "the whole place was fairly ablaze, and made one think of Arabian Nights' Tales." Courtesy, Riverside Municipal Museum*

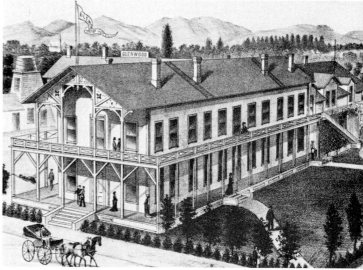

Above: *The jumping-off place for settlers bound for the Riverside Colony until the coming of the Southern Pacific Railroad to Colton in 1875 was the small town of Spadra, located in the Pomona Valley, and then the farthest eastward extension of the railroad. From here future settlers took a stage across a desolate desert waste to the townsite of Riverside. Courtesy, Pomona Public Library*

Above right: *Rivaling Riverside's Mission Inn in the 1890s was the Arlington Hotel at Eighth and Lime streets, constructed in 1888 by H.B. Everest, who made a fortune refining gasoline from crude oil. The building later became the city's first courthouse, and later became the Tetley and then the Riverside Hotel. Courtesy, Riverside Municipal Museum*

Right: *Riverside's Mission Inn started in 1876 as a two-storied gabled adobe building known as the Glenwood Cottage. In 1882 owner Frank Miller remodeled the building with this two-story addition and it became the Glenwood Hotel. Miller ransacked Europe for statuary and other artifacts that led to its final rebuilding stage as the Mission Inn early in the twentieth century. Several presidents and hundreds of famous guests have signed its ledgers throughout the years. Courtesy, Special Collections Department, Library of the University of California, Riverside*

ly plastered. Here also, the community "Lyceum" met regularly and, under Judge North's guidance, debated such remarkably perennial topics as, "Should the Bible be discontinued in the public schools?" A.R. Smith had erected a restaurant, meat market, and rooming house. E.G. Brown had finished the first structure on the site of his famous "Anchorage" estate on Colton Avenue. A two-story hotel and several proprietors of general merchandise occupied the fledgling business district.

Several informal church groups were organized, including members of the Methodist, Baptist, and Episcopalian faiths. There were, as well, free-thinkers and spiritualists. There was only one church, however, and it served the whole community. Situated on the corner of Sixth and Vine streets, it was a small, charming, New England-style shrine, complete with spire. All members of the colony had contributed funds and labor for its construction. Although affiliated with the Congregationalist organization and pastored by the Reverend Atherton, it was called appropriately the First Church of Christ in Riverside, for everyone attended services there. Long after they had formed separate organizations, the little church remained their meeting place.

Christmas Day of 1874 witnessed a true community Christmas party, held in the schoolyard around a stove where tables had been improvised from planks and sawhorses. Lyon and Rosenthal's General Store contributed candy, nuts, and eating utensils. There were candles from Clift's Drugstore, as well as mittens and stockings from the bright material Anna North purchased in Los Angeles. Youngsters strung popcorn to decorate the Christmas tree, cut from the distant forest in the San Bernardinos. While the colonists feasted on roast pig, chicken, biscuits, mince pie, and apple sauce, Lettie Brown played her father's melodion. Afterwards everyone sang "Praise God From Whom All Blessings Flow." James Roe, remembering such early "hard times," memorialized an era that passed all too quickly:

Above: *Riverside's second schoolhouse was an adobe building in La Placita (then called Spanishtown) located a few miles north of the colony. James Roe, grouped between the girls near the doorway, was the first school teacher and later one of the city's first historians. The Spanishtown flume is in the background at the left near the base of La Loma Hills. Courtesy, Riverside Municipal Museum*

Below: *This 1876 photograph is the earliest known street scene of downtown Riverside. The view looks south along Main Street with Pachappa Hill on the right. In the right foreground, the brick building is the Lyon and Rosenthal general merchandise store, situated at the corner of Main and Eighth streets. Courtesy, Riverside Public Library*

Newcomers were introduced and made welcome, and all the citizens fraternized together, without regard to possible religious, political or social differences. There were not enough people to form cliques, coteries or parties; and the old residents have often told me that these were their happiest days.

During the mid-1870s land sales for North's little colony were slow. Charles Felton, in his San Francisco office, grew more unhappy with his returns. But the promise of Riverside's future had already reached distant ears. In 1874 Samuel Cary Evans, Sr., a banker from Indiana, in combination with William T. Sayward, a speculator from San Francisco, purchased 8,000 acres south of the colony's Government Tract. They planned to dig another canal and develop the southern half of the Riverside plain. Laying out the "New England Colony," and the "Santa Ana Colony," they began work on an extremely long canal commencing just south of the Riverside Canal and cutting through the middle of the Riverside Colony, terminating near present-day Corona. The canal was poorly conceived and it was soon found that costs would far exceed original estimates. Furthermore, under Judge North, the SCCA refused to grant the necessary right-of-way. Samuel Evans found himself blocked.

In late 1874 Evans, seeking a compromise, contacted Charles Felton in San Francisco. Felton and Evans agreed to merge, Felton combining his majority of shares in the Southern California Colony Association with Evans, subsuming the original colony in Evans' larger enterprise. By April 1875, Evans, Sayward, and Felton had formed the Riverside Land and Irrigating Company.

The era of the association, with its high-minded and intimate little group of settlers, was ended. Judge John North, whose restless energy and vision of a New England village had brought Riverside into existence, was removed from control. At sixty, the old abolitionist gave up control of the colony, and opened a law office in San Bernardino. He would several times in the future represent colonists in the struggles against Evans and his company, but after 1879, would live there no more.

In 1874 Samuel Cary Evans and a group of associates purchased a large block of land lying south of the original Riverside Colony and gradually began consolidating nearly all the territory of the valley under control of a corporation known as the Riverside Land and Irrigation Company. Evans' venture squeezed out Judge John W. North, ended the colony period of Riverside, and gave him a major role in shaping the city's history. Courtesy, Tom Patterson

With Sayward supervising, the RL&I Co. subdivided the entire southern plain. They linked their townsites of Alvord and Sayward (Arlington) with a wide thoroughfare called Magnolia Avenue. At a width of 132 feet, with a center divider, and planted in eucalyptus, grevilla, pepper, and

The most elegant and distinguished home of its period in Riverside was the Casa Grande, built in 1878 by James Benedict, a wealthy former judge from New York. Ramona High School now occupies the site of the house, which was located on Magnolia Avenue near Madison. Courtesy, Riverside Municipal Museum

magnolia trees, it became the postcard showplace of early Riverside.

Under the RL&I Co. sales improved. Evans and Sayward promoted the healthful climate and genteel lifestyle, the country homes and tidy orchards. The enterprise appealed no longer to disgruntled reformers seeking to escape the Gilded Age, but to the "gilded" themselves, people of independent wealth. One of these, New Yorker James Benedict, built Casa Grande, an imposing adobe mansion facing Magnolia Avenue while nearby his sister built Casa Blanca, complete with tennis courts. Here a growing Riverside elite gathered on balmy afternoons. Friends and relatives followed Dr. Joseph Jarvis from Kingston,

Ontario, and began to settle along the "Canadian Tract" on California between Adams and Jackson streets. Among them was George Chaffey, Sr., whose son, George, Jr., would go on to develop Etiwanda, Ontario, and the Imperial Valley. Another friend of Jarvis was Matthew Gage, a jeweler, who opened a little shop downtown. No one

knew yet his importance to the future growth of Riverside.

Downtown experienced a building boom. At Eighth and Main, B.D. Burt and Brother, General Merchandising, completed Riverside's first brick building in 1875. Soon after, Lyon and Rosenthal, Hamilton's Drugstore, John Boyd's Saloon, and a Public Hall all rose in brick. Otis Dyer opened the town's first bank near Main and Ninth streets.

But the proprietorship of the Riverside Land and Irrigating Company led more and more to social conflict. Colonists suffered Sayward's obnoxious personality. One pioneer, looking back, described him as "conceited, ignorant, and lecherous." Evans' stern devotion to profit alienated other segments of the new town. Most trouble-

Above: *Bicycling was as big a passion as jogging in the Victorian age in Southern California. The Riverside Wheelman's Club (shown here) staged nine annual Admission Day bicycle meets for cyclists throughout the southland beginning on September 9, 1892. Courtesy, Riverside Municipal Museum*

Right: *Organized in 1876, the Riverside Cornet Band provided plenty of weekend "oomp-pa-pah" in the bandstand at White Park. Its director, John McCrary, is seen in the upper left corner. Courtesy, Riverside Municipal Museum*

some was the Government Tract, now a mile-wide wedge between the northern and southern sections of company development. Initially the company attempted to float old rancho boundaries in an effort to claim much of the government land as their own. Judge North, representing the squatters (he had claimed eighty acres himself), took the fight as far as Washington, D.C., where his appeal to the General Land Office would eventually succeed. Meanwhile, the company placed the Mile

Square's plaza block on the market for business sites, donating in retribution a swampy tract to the southwest for a future park site (now, after filling, the lovely White Park).

But the greatest cause of conflict lay in the most important commodity: water. Under North's beneficence, Government Tract settlers had received water rights as needed. Sayward, under Evans' direction, announced that settlers on non-company lands must pay $20 per acre for that water right (a phenomenal sum in those early days) or relinquish half their property in return for water on the other half.

At the behest of the Government Tract settlers, John W. Satterwait successfully introduced in 1876 a state act preventing water companies from cutting off water to lands they had already begun serving. In effect, the Satterwaite Act wedded the right of water to land. (This is the water law doctrine now known as "appurtenancy.") Under the act a settler named William Price, with Judge North again as counsel, successfully sued the RL&I in 1877. An appeal by the RL&I that went as far as the state supreme court delayed Price's victory until after 1880. By this time Price had given up and gone back to Iowa. In his place a wealthy newcomer, O.T. Johnson, constructed a large home with a mansard roof and tower.

William Price and James Roe were relatives. Each had settled near the other on the Government Tract. Roe, a druggist, grew to be one of the most active critics of Evans and the company and, as a by-product, became Riverside's greatest pioneer newspaperman. As a member of the news department of the community's first paper, *The Riverside News,* founded on November 27, 1875, he published the battle over water rights. The newspaper passed through several hands until folding completely in 1877. Roe then took control of *The Riverside Press* soon after its founding on June 28, 1878, by George Weeks of Crafton. Roe and subsequent owner L.M. Holt established a tradition of aggressive community service, one which maintains *The Riverside Press-Enterprise* to this day.

In 1878 the RL&I Co. split off the less profitable canal into a wholly owned subsidiary, the Riverside Canal Company. The following year Evans raised the rates from three cents per miner's inch to four, and six cents for non-company lands. The outcry was great, and several public protests were organized. The colonists won a temporary victory in 1880 when the county board of supervisors reduced the rates under provisions of the new state constitution. Evans countered by

cutting back canal maintenance. Settlers now feared water shortages as each new buyer received his own water rights from Evans.

In November of 1882, a year when rainfall was at the lowest recorded level, conflict reached its highest pitch yet. Water rates had risen to 7.5 cents per miner's inch. Irate landowners formed the Citizens Water Company, a political action group bent on breaking Evans' water monopoly. Within a year, the revolt was almost total. Out of 4,500 irrigated acres, 4,200 acres were represented by the Citizens Water Company.

The Riverside area now contained close to 3,000 people. It sprawled from the northern limits of the Mile Square thirteen miles southward to Arlington, an area of nearly sixty square miles. Within, the community was experiencing all the growing pains of a frontier community. Liquor traffic, crime, drinking water, and a public school system were hotly debated.

Leaders of the Citizens Water Company began to agitate for incorporation as a city, hoping to gain local control of water rates. On September 25, 1883, 228 white male adults voted in favor of incorporation, while 147 voted against. To historian Tom Patterson:

Riverside became a city like no other. For an estimated 3,000 or fewer persons (including women, children, Chinese and other persons without votes) there were fifty-six miles of incorporated area ... San Francisco, then the state's most populous city and until then the largest in area, had only forty-six square miles for 300,000 persons.

Evans began to weaken. Faced with growing competition, he offered to sell the canal company to the citizens, but at a price the irrigators felt outrageous. Negotiations seemed interminable, until a compromise designed by newspaper editor Luther Holt was accepted by both sides. In 1884, after nearly ten years of combat, the Citizens Water Company and Riverside Canal Company merged to become The Riverside Water Company, a mutually owned utility operated for the

Left: *In 1884 Matthew Gage began the first large-scale artesian water project in Southern California. Tapping the underground San Bernardino Valley basin, he engineered a twenty-mile canal that brought water to the undeveloped upper plain of Riverside. The Gage Canal paved the way for other large irrigation projects in arid Southern California. From* Rural Californian, *1885*

Above: *Riverside's frontier days had ended by 1885, and its Main Street was beginning to acquire a Victorian veneer. The Riverside Banking Company occupied the building with the tower at the corner of Ninth Street. Across the street from the bank was the Public Hall. Courtesy, Riverside Municipal Museum*

had sent him as a young man to the goldfields of Montana—the perennial itch of the perennial prospector—never left him. Cover became convinced he could find the legendary lost gold mine of Peg Leg Smith, thought to be somewhere northwest of Yuma. That year, 1884, Cover disappeared in the desert east of Borrego Valley. His remains have never been found.

That year, as well, the elderly Judge North was far to the north, in the Central Valley, promoting another development called Oleander. His children grown, his wife in almost permanent residence in Washington, North lived alone in a small frame house where, nearly penniless, he wrote letters and read Robert Ingersoll. The defeat of Felton, Evans, and the RL&I Co. must have pleased but not greatly surprised him. His optimism had always been unshakable. On occasion, he thought proudly of his son, John G. North, who had stayed in Riverside, led the battle against the RL&I Co. and was now serving ably as superintendent of the new Riverside Water Company.

Judge North died in 1890 at his sister's home in Fresno. It was Washington's Birthday. Behind were remarkable achievements, born of a lifetime filled with remarkable energy. He had fathered railroads, universities, constitutions, and cities. Once, during some of their darkest days, he had written Anna: "If we had given our minds to money we could have been rich and as mean as people that we know .. {but} we have children great men might be proud of."

Indeed.

John Wesley North was buried in Riverside.

benefit of its users. Riverside was safely on its way toward remarkable prosperity.

Tom Cover's contribution to the colony had brought him new wealth, a commodious home near Jurupa and Brockton, and a respectable role as community pioneer. But the restlessness that

IV Cities on Rails

Building a New County

More than six years of back-breaking labor, mostly Chinese, separated the Central Pacific Railroad from completion. At Promontory Point, Utah, on May 10, 1869, California was united with the rest of the country by a great transcontinental railroad. In an age of automobiles it may be hard to conceive of the power of a nineteenth-century railroad. But to the farmer, the rancher, and the potential city maker, those twin, cold iron rails four feet, eight and a-half-inches wide, were the arteries of life. As water meant a harvest, so railroads promised a market. And without a railroad, as without water, land in Southern California seemed useless, crops went unshipped and unsold, towns dwindled and died.

Early California railroad capitalists like the "Big Four"—Leland Stanford, Charles Crocker, Collis P. Huntington, and Mark Hopkins, of the Central Pacific—soon wielded great economic power. The Big Four—or "the Associates," as they called themselves, began their consolidation of a transportation empire soon dubbed "The Octopus." It would dominate the development of California until the twentieth-century. Testing their great power, the Big Four gained control of Oakland and San Francisco's waterfronts and the "Shasta Route" of the California and Oregon Railroad. To the south, the fledgling Southern Pacific Railroad

The Southern Pacific Railroad line was completed across the San Gorgonio Pass in 1876,
eventually uniting Los Angeles with Arizona.
It wasn't until March 1881 that a thorough
eastern connection was made when the Atchison, Topeka, and Santa Fe hooked up with
the Southern Pacific at Deming, New Mexico.
This turn-of-the-century photograph of a
Southern Pacific train was taken at the Banning depot. Courtesy, Leonard McCulloh

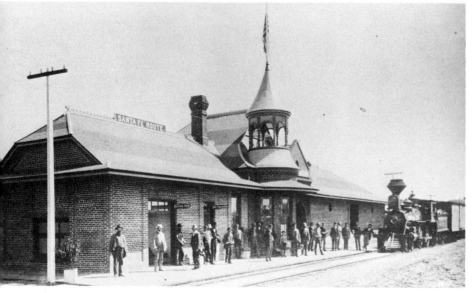

Top: *In 1853 Dr. Isaac Smith of Maine purchased mountain man Paulino Weaver's claim to a one-third portion of the old San Gorgonio Rancho and built his home midway between Banning and Beaumont. The home became a stage station on the Bradshaw Road running from the west to the Colorado River. This photo was taken in about 1915 of what is now known as the Highland Springs Resort, the oldest resort establishment in Riverside County. Courtesy, Lorne Allmon*

Center: *Southern Pacific held the railroad monopoly in Southern California from the 1870s into the land boom of the early 1880s, charging whatever it felt the traffic would bear. In 1882 construction crews of the California Southern Railroad drove a line from National City through the eastern outskirts of Riverside to Colton, linking it up three years later with the Santa Fe line through Cajon Pass. The arrival of the first California Southern train at the Perris depot on July 10, 1882, marked the end of a hated monopoly and the start of the railroad rate wars that resulted in cheaper transportation and shipping. Courtesy, Evaline Morrison Collection, Sherman Library, Corona Del Mar*

Bottom: *The Southern Pacific Railroad line from Los Angeles first reached Colton, several miles north of Riverside, on July 30, 1875. The railroad threw its influence into building up the town with a large hotel and other improvements. With the building of the Santa Fe and Union Pacific, Colton became a major junction for Southern California's three great lines. This photograph of the railroad yards at Colton was taken in about 1900. Courtesy, Leonard McCulloh*

Although mountain man Paulino Weaver was the first white man to occupy the San Gorgonio Pass, he soon moved on to found Prescott, Arizona. The development of the Pass begins with the arrival of Dr. Isaac William Smith, who bought Weaver's portion of the old San Gorgonio rancho in 1853. The Smith ranch, located where the Highland Springs resort is today, served as a station for stages on the Bradshaw Road and other lines between California and Arizona. Although Dr. Smith planted fruit trees and grapes, he made no attempt at commercial growing, and concentrated primarily on raising cattle. Courtesy, Leonard McCulloh

Company proposed laying track to Los Angeles and San Diego, and east from there to complete a southern transcontinental route. In 1870 the Southern Pacific, now under the Big Four's control, began reaching southward through the San Joaquin Valley.

Towns curried a railroad's favor with donations of rights-of-way and with outright cash grants. In Los Angeles Crocker demanded gifts of the Los Angeles and San Pedro Railroad and a cash subsidy of $600,000. Failure to satisfy the railroad meant bypass, as happened at San Bernardino in 1873 when the Southern Pacific, heading eastward from Los Angeles, established the "spite town" of Colton as a division point.

The arrival of the railroad was cause for rejoicing in the struggling little colony at Riverside. Though still miles away and across the Santa Ana River, Riverside was promised access by the Southern Pacific to a national market for the first fruits maturing in the colony. But the Big Four manipulated freight rates with equal imperiousness. For a while Riverside growers found it less expensive to cooperate in freight-wagon shipments to Newport, from there chartering steamer service to San Francisco. By 1880, however, the Southern Pacific, assuming the control of the Pacific Mail Steamship Company, had sealed off even this complicated form of relief.

In 1876 the rails from Sacramento finally pierced the San Gabriel Mountains at Newhall and met those reaching out from Los Angeles. The rail crews of the Southern Pacific now labored eastward toward a meeting with the Colorado. Rising through Juan Antonio's old haunts in San Timoteo Canyon the roadbed crested San Gorgonio Pass southwest of Pauline Weaver's "Roost." There work crews installed a small turntable at Summit (elevation 2,480) and a station at San Gorgonio. Nearby was the home of Dr. Isaac Smith, who had purchased Weaver's interest in Rancho San Gorgonio in 1863. Smith raised stock and deciduous fruit in the cool highland climate. Called variously Smith Ranch or Smith's Station, it served as a stage stop on the Bradshaw Trail and later, as Highland Home and Highland Springs, as a resort.

The Southern Pacific struck out across the high benchland toward the neck of the pass. Eight miles east of Smith's Ranch lay another pioneer stage stop, the Gilman Ranch. Here José Pope, Weaver's overseer, had taken up another segment of Rancho San Gorgonio, building a small adobe home in 1854. The ranch passed from Pope to a sheepman named Chapin and thence to Newton

Above: *James Marshall Gilman helped bring civilization to the San Gorgonio Pass, purchasing his Banning ranch in 1869. Gilman ran cattle, planted fruit orchards, developed a sawmill in Water Canyon, and operated a general store. He was active in political and civic affairs in the San Gorgonio Pass throughout most of his life and played a major role in the development of the local school system. Courtesy, Leonard McCulloh*

Below: *James M. Gilman pioneered fruit growing in the San Gorgonio Pass, setting out some of the first orchards in the 1870s. The region has long been known for its almonds, pears, peaches, apricots, cherries, and other horticultural products. Gilman's wife, Martha (right), and two of her daughters are shown here picking fruit in one of the Gilman orchards. Courtesy, Leonard McCulloh*

Noble who, in 1868, established a stage station and post office.

In 1869 James Marshall Gilman, a native of New Hampshire, purchased Pope's original 160 acres, and later another 360 acres. Gilman's Ranch was the nucleus for early pioneering activity in the area. Marrying Martha Smith, daughter of Isaac Smith, Gilman established the first general store and stocked the ranch with cattle and horses. Soon after the completion of the railroad, he built his landmark home and began the cultivation of almonds, apricots, and prunes. The ranch property is now a county historic park.

By New Year's Day, 1876, the SP rail crews reached Whitewater, where they tapped nearby gravel beds for ballast and Snow Creek for water. As the road veered southeasterly across the desert floor, the company piped this water to new stations at Cabazon and Palm Springs. The route skirted the eastern shore of the dry Salton Sink where well-drilling crews began searching for water. That year an observer, Lieutenant Eric Bergland, coolly described railroad working conditions as "not one which a sane person would select in which to spend the summer." The wells flowed, however poorly, with stops at Indio, Woodspur (Coachella), Thermal, Walters (Mecca), Salton, Pope, Wister, and "Flowing Wells" (near Niland). The rails reached the Colorado at Yuma in May 1877.

To provide the railroad with ties and cordwood, in 1875 Colonel William Saunders Hall, the Southern Pacific grading contractor, laboriously constructed a steep road from the floor of the pass near Cabazon to an area near Lake Fulmor in the San Jacinto Mountains. Twenty-percent grades and razor-sharp turns on one of the steepest mountain faces of the continent spilled lumber wagons, killed drivers and teams, eventually bankrupting Hall's company.

A more successful lumbering operation was established on the opposite side of the pass, in San Gorgonio Canyon. In partnership with Phineas Banning, whose stages and freight wagons had made him familiar with the area, a Baptist minis-

Top left: *Banning's first hostelry, the Bryant House, opened in 1884 at Livingston Street and Ramsey Avenue. It was renamed The Banning in 1890, and some years later became the San Gorgonio Inn. Today the San Gorgonio Inn is still in business as the San Gorgonio Pass's favorite restaurant. The register of the old hotel may be seen under glass in the lobby and contains such illustrious names as those of Ulysses S. Grant and Grover Cleveland. Courtesy, Leonard McCulloh*

Bottom left: *Banning's first permanent land-*

mark was an adobe structure built in 1854 by José Pope, mayordomo for Colonel Isaac Williams, claimant of a half interest in the San Gorgonio Rancho. The adobe was used for years as a station for stages on the Bradshaw Road between California and Arizona. It was later used as a blacksmith shop by James M. Gilman, who in 1869 bought 160 acres of land that included the adobe. Courtesy, Leonard McCulloh*

Top right: *In the 1890s the center of Banning clustered along San Gorgonio Avenue. This*

scene was taken looking north from the Southern Pacific railroad tracks. Courtesy, Leonard McCulloh*

Bottom right: *The second oldest business structure in Banning was the Charles A. Reid building, located on the northeast corner of Livingston Street and San Gorgonio Avenue. The building was erected in 1884 to house both a general store and the Banning post office. It was taken over by Reid soon after his arrival in the San Gorgonio Pass in 1890. Courtesy, Leonard McCulloh*

ter named Scott felled timber at an upper elevation and, utilizing a long flume, floated cut wood
down the canyon to the railroad. Scott's manager,
Dr. Welwood Murray, began to consolidate water
rights and land claims in the area. A settlement
named for Banning grew up around the water
source at the terminus of the flume, and in 1878
the SP sanctified the development with a new
siding and station.

Arthur Paul described early Banning as "a
town of one house and several saloons ... glamor-
ized by brawls, street killings and at least one
lynching." But the lumberjacks, miners, gandy
dancers, and teamsters of the early days soon gave
way to more sedate citizenry. By 1883 lots and
acreage were selling at anywhere from $50 to $200
an acre. Soon small farms were producing almonds, grapes, peaches, and other deciduous
fruits.

Beaumont's inception nearby was marked by
an even greater agricultural diversity. Laid out
as a townsite called San Gorgonio, early settlers
"sky farmed." Here the railroad shunted the extra
locomotives needed for the steep grade. The Beaumont, a Victorian-style hotel of gigantic propor-
tions, served as the new city's showplace. Beaumont "blossomed" rather than "boomed"—the
first cherry orchard was set out in 1888 and to
the north, at Oak Glen, apple orchards began
commercial production.

A decade after the Southern Pacific placed its
brand on the future Riverside County, its domi-
nance in the region was challenged by another
railroad with transcontinental aspirations, the
Santa Fe (then called the Atlantic and Pacific). In
1886 Congress authorized subsidies for a new
southern rail route. The Santa Fe, with its eastern
terminus at Chicago, laid track to the Colorado
River at Needles, where they constructed an impressive cantilever bridge. There the Santa Fe met
the ubiquitous Southern Pacific, whose tracks had
crossed the desert from their mainline at Mojave.
But the young corporation wasn't satisfied with
shared track: finding its transcontinental inten-
tions blocked at Los Angeles, the Santa Fe looked

southward toward San Diego. The company assisted a group of investors in National City in funding the California Southern Railroad.

Under engineer Fred T. Perris of San Bernardino, the California Southern began construction
near San Diego Bay. In 1881 it had reached Temecula Canyon, where the northerly route turned
east to climb through the Coast ranges. There,
along the Santa Margarita River, crews of indomitable Chinese laborers chipped and blasted a
winding grade through the granite canyon walls.

The California Southern soon began "negotiating" for subsidies from communities nearby. The
railroad demanded $6,000 from Riverside, 500
acres of land from the Riverside Land and Irrigat-

Far left: *Originally known as San Gorgonio and later as Summit, Beaumont came into existence in November of 1887 when the Southern California Investment Company, headed by H.C. Sigler of Beaumont, Texas, purchased holdings at the summit of the San Gorgonio Pass and platted a townsite. The Luxurious Edinburgh Hotel, also called the Beaumonter, was erected during the boom days under Sigler. Courtesy, Leonard McCulloh*

Left: *Every up-and-coming community in Riverside County had to have its opera house, and most of them were built in the 1890s. It wasn't until 1913, however, that Banning boasted the opening of an opera house, which opened to a capacity crowd for a Schubert symphony troupe from Chicago. Courtesy, Lenoard McCulloh*

Bottom: *Early settlers in the San Jacinto Valley depended on stages to the Southern Pacific station in San Gorgonio (Beaumont) or to the California Southern station in Perris for travel to and from the valley. The boom years of 1886-1887 finally saw construction of many feeder lines to isolated communities. On April 30, 1888, a Santa Fe Special train from Los Angeles became the first train into San Jacinto making possible full agricultural development of the region. Courtesy, Clarence Swift Collection*

ing Company, a depot site, and complete right-of-way. The New England settlers at Riverside bridled at such extortion, and the California Southern shrugged its corporate shoulders. Emerging from Temecula Canyon, the railroad ascended Murrietta Creek to the Laguna Grande (Elsinore) at the head of Temescal Canyon. There, instead of continuing down the canyon and proceeding north through future Corona and Riverside, as the colonists hoped, the railroad turned abruptly northeast, ascended Railroad Canyon, and emerged on the Perris Plain. Proceeding by way of Box Springs Grade, the railroad did provide Riverside with a station—three long miles away, near Point of Rocks at Sugarloaf Mountain. The lesson

was learned. Riversiders would be less proud in the future.

As California Southern construction neared Southern Pacific tracks south of San Bernardino, SP officials ordered a special train to the intended point of crossing—where it stayed for over a year. The California Southern could advance no farther. Inside the train armed guards led by Virgil Earp kept a tense vigil until the San Bernardino sheriff, wielding a court order and backed by a mob of citizens armed with pickaxes, convinced the Southern Pacific to make way. The first train from San Diego to San Bernardino passed through Riverside on September 13, 1883, and by 1885 the cocky California Southern had linked

MURRIETA COLONY!

The New Land of Promise!

On Line of the California Southern Railroad, San Diego County, California,

Which for Richness of Soil, Salubrity of Climate, Excellence of WATER and HEALTHFULNESS cannot be Excelled.

To get there, you should, if East, take the cars at Kansas City for San Diego, via the Atchison, Topeka and Santa Fe Route, through Colton and past Riverside, Stopping off at the Station at Murrieta, where you will find parties ready to show you the Land.

THE AGENTS:

CHAS. CHARNOCK and ASA ADAMS, can be consulted at No. 12 Court Street, Los Angeles, about these or other lands, as they have a good list of city and country property for sale.

Above: Southern California's flourishing boom of the 1880s led to the extravagant promotion of dozens of new townsites—many short-lived and resulting in the ruin of their backers and colonists. The Murrieta Colony was one of several townsites that sprang up in Riverside County along the route of the California Southern Railroad between San Bernardino and San Diego. *Courtesy, Horace Parker Collection*

Facing page, top: This ceremonial photograph is believed to depict the arrival of the first train of the California Southern Railroad (Santa Fe) in Riverside in 1882. The first station was at the foot of Sugarloaf Mountain, and the railroad line linked San Bernardino with San Diego. *Courtesy, the Bordwell Collection, Riverside Municipal Museum*

Facing page, bottom: Once a stock ranch for Mission San Luis Rey and the oldest community in Riverside County, Temecula began its development as a stage stop in the 1840s on the old southern route to the east. This photograph looking northeast from the Temecula River was taken in about 1899. The old Welty Hotel, better known in later years as the Hotel Temecula, is the two-story building near the bridge. The hotel is today a private residence which has been restored with historic furnishings. *Courtesy, Horace Parker Collection*

Above: In 1884 a syndicate purchased the townsite of Murrieta along the new California Southern Railroad to San Diego. The following year the Fountain House Hotel (above) was erected. During the boom of the 1880s, the town flourished briefly and by 1887 had three newspapers. After the collapse of the boom, the community became known as a resort with its famous Guenther's Murrieta Hot Springs. *Courtesy, Horace Parker Collection*

with the Santa Fe. A second transcontinental line had been established.

Temecula's history extends back to prehistoric times, when it was a prosperous Indian village. During the Mexican era it served as a crossroads and the center of ranching activities in the area. There in 1852 the Treaty of Temecula, a generous land settlement with the United States, was signed by Juan Antonio at Pablo Apis' adobe headquarters. By 1873 Alsatian Louis Wolf had built an adobe store and John Magee built another nearby to serve the stage route. Around them were other adobe homes, gardens, and corrals. With the construction of the railroad through the canyon in

1882, a new townsite was established near the tracks on Murrieta Creek and three miles northwest of "Old" Temecula. A railroad station and post office, Temecula's third, was established there on January 24, 1883. Ironically, "New" Temecula was made a Historic Preservation District by the Riverside County supervisors in 1980, thereby given protection, while the remains of older Temecula are threatened by the more recent real estate developments surrounding Rancho California.

Farther north on the California Southern route lay the equally old settlement at Murrieta. Here Juan Murrieta raised sheep during the Mexican era. With the Conquest and subdivision, Murrieta

became a shipping point and center of commerce for local ranchers and farmers. At the hot springs a hotel and sanatorium were constructed, drawing health seekers from each arriving passenger train.

The railroad established a station where it followed the San Jacinto River through Railroad Canyon. Called Laguna after the lake nearby, it was soon renamed Elsinore, after a new town founded in 1883. Partners Franklin Heald, Donald Graham, and William Collier had purchased over 12,000 acres there and begun subdivision. Margaret Graham, wife of one of the partners, drew on her schooling in Shakespeare for the name, citing its "pleasant sound" of immortality. Over nearby hot springs proprietors built a small A-frame building with a wooden tub. Its popularity grew, and in 1887 the Crescent Bathhouse was constructed, a multi-storied structure in the Victorian Moorish style, including within "modern conveniences for furnishing hot mud baths."

Nearby at Wildomar, Collier and Graham laid out another townsite. Here a hotel was constructed in 1887, and a large Presbyterian church. Elsinore became a center of olive culture in the area when a Missourian named Albers set out the first 135 acres of trees. By the turn of the century, Elsinore (now Lake Elsinore) had become a popular and prosperous resort community nestled in a dramatic setting.

The railroad met the Perris Plain at Pinacate, where a mining district was building toward a boom. The largest mine, the Good Hope, operated a stamp mill. The railroad placed a boxcar on a siding and the post office was moved to the site. By 1885, however, settlers two miles north of the boxcar lured the station away and a new town was laid out. It was named Perris, after California Southern's chief engineer. Soon a well was sunk, and a hotel and post office built. Citizens erected an impressive station of brick. Hook Brothers and Oak established a general store and a newspaper, *The Perris Valley Leader,* commenced publication.

Early development of Perris and other communities nearby relied on an impressive engineering achievement that brought the promise of abun-

Above: *In the late 1890s the small community of Elsinore boasted both a pier and a bathhouse and was well on the way to becoming Riverside County's first resort community. The name Elsinore was chosen from Shakespeare's Hamlet. Courtesy, Riverside Press-Enterprise Company*

Left: *One of Southern California's most fashionable spas beginning in the early part of the twentieth century was the Lakeview Hotel in Elsinore, a community that has thrived as a health resort. The hot sulphur water from natural springs has made the city a popular resort since its founding in 1888. Photo by E.N. Fairchild, courtesy, Riverside Municipal Museum*

Below left: *James H. Schanck, an immigrant from Illinois, established a jewelry store in Elsinore in 1887. One of the resort community's leading civic figures, he ran the post office, shown here, and the Wells Fargo franchise from his store. Courtesy, Riverside Press-Enterprise Company, from the Evaline Morrison Collection*

Bottom: *The city of Elsinore, incorporated in 1893, was a thriving health resort adjoining the largest natural lake in Riverside County when this photograph of its high school class was taken in the same year. Courtesy, Riverside Press-Enterprise Company*

dant water to the dusty plain. In the early 1880s, E.G. Judson, a New York stockbroker, and Frank E. Brown, a New England engineer, were casting about for a more secure water supply for their new real estate development called Redlands. They determined that snowmelt runoff from Bear Valley in the San Bernardino Mountains represented an enormous potential for water storage. In 1884 Frank Brown built a single-arch masonry

dam at Bear Valley. When the dam was completed it drew worldwide attention and praise—a heady experience for a twenty-eight-year-old engineer. Called Big Bear Lake, the reservoir was the centerpiece of an engineering marvel. The stored waters were released for collection at the base of the mountain and delivered by five miles of canal and pipeline to Redlands. Redlands boomed.

The success of the Bear Valley water system spurred Brown on. Further south, across the San Timoteo Canyon and the Badlands, lay Moreno Valley and the Perris Plain, just waiting for Bear Valley water to turn them green. Under Brown's supervision investors in the valley organized irrigation districts and bought shares in the Bear Valley Water Company. Brown began construction of a lengthy aqueduct over the steep slopes south of Redlands and through the Badlands via a long masonry tunnel. Two new towns, Moreno and Alessandro, as well as Perris, boomed. By 1892 several impressive brick buildings had been completed at Moreno, and the block-long Moreno Hotel was under way. Citizens enjoyed a meat market, fruit stand, blacksmith shop, drugstore, and nursery. Twenty-five thousand acres were dotted with commodious homes.

West of Moreno, along the California Southern route, Alessandro flourished. Laid out by William H. Hall, state engineer, assisted by the firm of Frederick Law Olmsted, designer of New York's Central Park, Alessandro soon sported a hotel, store, railroad depot, and school. F.H. Austin began publication of the weekly *Alessandro Indicator*. In August 1894 the valley's first carload of citrus fruit left the depot.

The first water, a trickle, arrived by temporary pipeline in 1891. But something was wrong— terribly wrong. Late in 1894 the Bear Valley Water Company began behaving suspiciously. First it asked quietly if it could reduce the amount of water it was obligated to provide. It soon became apparent that Frank Brown had miscalculated. There simply wasn't enough water to go around. Citizens formed the Alessandro Defense Organization, seeking in court to assure their rightful share of water. Years of litigation, bankruptcy, and thirsty hardship followed. Redlands' claim to priority was eventually upheld and nearly all water, even domestic, was cut off from the Perris Plain.

Frank Brown began extensive well drilling to save what face he could, but the wells were not enough. More and more settlers began the sad journey away. The homes surrounding Moreno and Alessandro were dubbed the "City on Wheels" as giant steam tractors dragged the huge Victorians to Riverside or Perris. Many settlers returned from an absence to find their houses already gone—stolen by impatient contractors. The new towns disappeared, a sorry end to the short-lived blossoming of the Perris Plain.

Brown would not give up. It may have been that his judgment, so rudely challenged by the Moreno disaster, had been permanently impaired. Incredibly, in 1909, Brown convinced other developers of the prospect of settlement near Anza's beautiful Lake San Antonio de Bucareli. A lake as unpredictable as the seasonal river flow that sometimes fills it, it has known many names: Lake San Jacinto, Shadow, and Mystic Lake. Brown's development, which he named "Brownlands," consisted of fifty-acre tracts ringing the lake. By 1913 a curving street paralleled the shore, intended for a future street railway. Settlers came, built homes, established businesses.

Poor Frank Brown. His lots had been laid out during a very dry cycle of seasons. In 1916 the cycle shifted and floodwaters poured down the San Jacinto River. Charles Van Fleet, a local pioneer, recalled that, when he visited Brownlands, all he could see were a few rooftops above the muddy waves. There is no trace of "Brownlands" today.

Meanwhile, the Santa Fe was busy preparing for its final assault on the Southern Pacific—its own terminus at Los Angeles. Surveyors established the grade for the Los Angeles and San Gabriel Valley Railroad, from San Bernardino to Los Angeles, as well as the Riverside, Santa Ana and Los Angeles Railroad, from the California Southern at Highgrove to Los Angeles via the Santa Ana Canyon.

Riverside had learned a lesson when it failed to secure a route through the settlement from Fred T. Perris' California Southern. Now, three years later, the city offered the Riverside, Santa Ana and Los Angeles complete right of way along Olive Street as well as a station site. The Riverside Land and Irrigating Company provided even more land. Construction reached Riverside's Tequesquite Arroyo from Highgrove by December 10, 1885. The old station at Point of Rocks was relocated to the tracks between Seventh and Eighth streets and, in 1886, a new station house was dedicated. Declared "the prettiest one on the road" by the *Riverside Press,* it sported corner bay windows and a broad Gothic roof. During railroad construction regular passenger trains arriving on the California Southern from San Diego backed the several miles from Highgrove to Riverside before continuing to San Bernardino. By 1900 twin eastward passenger trains originated at Los Angeles and (with one through Pasadena, the other through Santa Ana Canyon to Riverside), joined at San Bernardino for the remainder of the trip.

Delay in completing the RSA&LA postponed the abandonment of a troublesome section of track in Temescal Canyon. Rails were washed out by flood in 1884, remaining out through the winter. By 1891 Santa Fe's "surf line" to San Diego had been completed and when floods again washed out the rails they remained abandoned, splitting permanently California Southern's historic trans-continental link and making Temecula the terminus of a long spur line from Highgrove.

That spur was enlarged in 1888 by yet another Santa Fe subsidiary, the California Central. From Perris the line described an arc through Winchester to the heart of the San Jacinto Valley, terminating at San Jacinto. Old San Jacinto dates back to the days of the Estudillo Rancho. A rancheria had continued on at Soboba. The fertile countryside was well watered by the river and artesian springs. The climate was mild due to the region's higher altitude. A small community grew up around Procco Akimo's store, built near Hewitt Street. By 1870, twenty-three families, mostly

Top: *One of the earliest hotels in the San Jacinto Valley was the luxurious old Magnolia Hotel in Valle Vista, furnished with ornate trappings that came around Cape Horn. Marshall Stone (shown here) and his wife, Eliza, opened the establishment in 1888. Courtesy, Clarence Swift Collection*

Center: *Automobiles were becoming as familiar a sight as buggies on San Jacinto's Main Street when this photograph was taken in 1914. The fourth man from the left is John Shaver, who was a Riverside county supervisor for the Fifth District. Courtesy, Clarence Swift Collection*

Below: *One of San Jacinto's earliest brick buildings was the Palma Hotel, which after a stormy feud between Riverside and San Jacinto became Riverside County Hospital in 1897. After a strong earthquake on Christmas morning of 1899, its brick walls collapsed. Fortunately, there was no loss of life. Courtesy, Horace Parker Collection*

farmers, had settled. A school on South Central Avenue and a post office had been established. Promoters located New San Jacinto on their own lands west of the original settlement. Here the California Central established its terminus in 1888.

San Jacinto grew quickly. The wood-frame Lockwood Hotel was finished before the railroad and advertised "a table supplied with the very best the market affords." Victuals were prepared by Chinese cooks from vegetables sold at the Chinese Vegetable Garden on South San Jacinto Street. Nearby, the Domenigoni Block was occupied, in part, by a bathhouse. The Hotel Vosburg soon became the most prominent hotel and social center. Originally the San Jacinto, then the Farmer Hotel, it was purchased by William and Annie Vosburg, and in 1913 they renamed it the Hotel Vosburg. William Vosburg soon expanded the charming building, with its shade trees and elegant Southern-style porticos, to include the entire block on the corner of Ramona and San Jacinto. The Citizens Water Company was developing the

Above: *With the coming of the railroads to Riverside County, lumbering activity became intense in the San Jacinto Mountains to supply railroad ties. This photograph of oxen hauling logs was taken on the 8,000-acre Hancock-Johnson Ranch in the San Jacinto Mountains about 1900. Courtesy, Clarence Swift Collection*

Facing page, top: *Dry grain farming has always been a significant part of the agricultural picture in Riverside County. Reaping the harvest was made easier in the late nineteenth century by the invention of large combines. This thirty-two-mule combine reaper was used by the Billy Newport Ranch in Menifee Valley. Courtesy, Riverside Municipal Museum*

Left: *Lumbering was a major activity in the San Jacinto Mountains, beginning with the construction of the Southern Pacific Railroad through San Gorgonio Pass in the 1870s and extending up to World War II. Anton Scherman, Jr.'s, Dry Creek Mill at Mountain Center, shown here in 1902, was one of the major mills in the mountains, providing lumber for much of the San Jacinto Valley. Courtesy, Clarence Swift Collection*

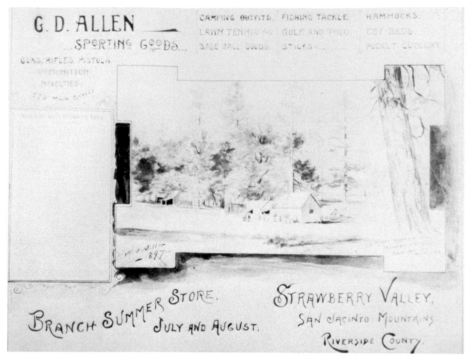

Left: *Beginning in the 1870s, the San Jacinto Mountains saw heavy lumbering activity, particularly during the building of the Southern Pacific Railroad through San Gorgonio Pass in 1876. By the 1870s it became fashionable to visit Strawberry Valley as a mountain resort. Artist W.J. Miller depicted the resort in this watercolor for advertising purposes in 1897. Courtesy, Riverside Public Library*

Below: Eggs were only fifteen cents a dozen and butter thirty cents a pound when local photographer H.J. May took this 1898 picture of San Jacinto's thriving corner grocery at Five Points. Courtesy, Clarence Swift Collection

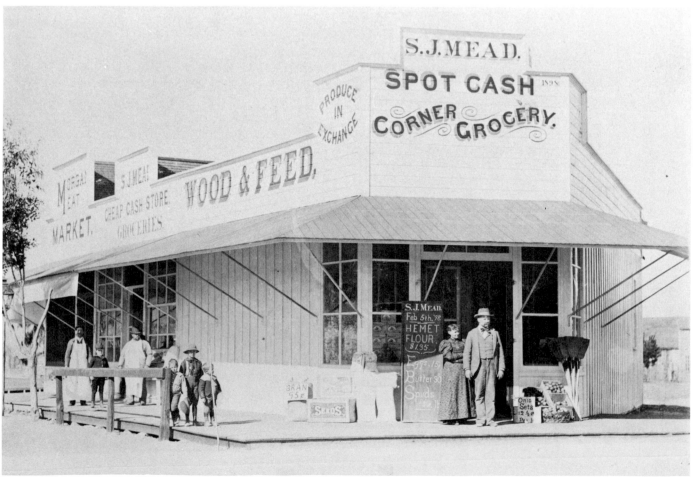

Left: *The oldest newspaper in the San Jacinto Valley was the* San Jacinto Register, *founded in 1884. It was located on the north side of Main Street between San Jacinto and Sheriff streets when this photograph was taken about 1898. The two-story structure at the right was the William Vawter Building. Courtesy, Clarence Swift Collection*

Below: *San Jacinto Valley settlers found relief from the summer heat by camping for weeks at a time in the San Jacinto Mountains. This photograph taken in 1896 by Thomas Millhollin captured some of the ancestors of the late valley historian Clarence Swift. Left to right are Jacob Swift, grandfather of Clarence Swift, his father, Rufus Swift, Mrs. W.A. Ballou, his father's sister, Mrs. Frances Swift, his grandmother, Claire Ballou, and W.A. Ballou, an uncle. The camp was set up at Keen's Mountain Resort in Strawberry Valley. Courtesy, Clarence Swift Collection*

water-storage potential of the Ciénega on the river, and guests at the Vosburg were often entertained there at the hastily decorated artesian sites. Apricots, peaches, walnuts, and citrus fruit, as well as grain crops, brought steady prosperity to the valley.

To serve the growing settlements, pioneer lumbermen expanded their operations in the San Jacinto Mountains nearby. William Hall's old road up the sheer north face of San Jacinto had early on proven unusable. In 1877 Joseph Crawford began the construction of another access road from the canyon of the San Jacinto River eastward. Equally steep, Crawford's road had the advantage of shorter length. By 1878 a water-powered sawmill and a small hotel had been established at

Strawberry Creek. Pioneers in the high, pine-scented valleys included Charles Thomas and his family, who in 1861 settled what is now called Garner Valley. Samuel Tripp is remembered through Tripp Flats, while a lumber teamster, Sam Temple, was preparing to take his villainous place in Western lore. In 1880 Amasa Saunders purchased the mill at Strawberry Creek and built a home on the site of present-day Idyllwild School. Saunders converted his mill to steam power and began cutting incense cedar. In 1884, under Anton Scherman, timbering expanded to mills at Fern Valley and Dutch Flat. The recreational value of the high country competed from the beginning with its value as a timber source. Mary Keen and her husband John operated Keen Camp for many years. Their resort was the most popular of the early rustic recreation camps.

A hunting trip in the San Jacintos first brought C.L. Mayberry and W.F. Whittier, a San Francisco paint manufacturer, to Charles Thomas' valley in 1886. With the recent success of Frank Brown's Bear Valley Reservoir fresh in their minds, they conceived the idea of a dam and reservoir of their own. Stored and released into the south fork of the San Jacinto River, this water could assure a constant supply for the dry lands west and below in the San Jacinto Valley. That year Whittier, Mayberry, and others purchased 1,000 acres from Charles Thomas as a dam and reservoir site. Below, as the Hemet Land Company, they purchased 6,000 acres, half from H.T. Hewitt, a San Jacinto pioneer, and half from Francisco Estudillo, for $20 an acre. In 1887 they embarked on the construction of a dam and the development of the town of Hemet along the California Central.

Mayberry supervised the clearing of a new road. Its legendary switchbacks eased the grade that had made Crawford's old road so dangerous. Huge granite blocks, quarried at the site, were mortared with Belgian cement to form a spectacular single-arch masonry dam 110 feet in height. Designed by James D. Schuyler and finished in 1893, the dam was later expanded several times until, by 1923, it was 135 feet tall—in its time the tallest masonry

Above: *The original San Jacinto, later known as "Old Town" and Bowers, sprang up in the 1870s and boasted this large brick building on Hewitt Street, which housed the Palma Hotel below the cupola on the right, H.T. Hewitt's store, and a saloon. Time passed this district by, until the San Jacinto Land Association bought a large tract of land in the valley and launched the town of New San Jacinto in the summer and fall of 1883. Courtesy, Clarence Swift Collection*

Above, far right: *Nestled beneath the sweep of the snow-covered San Jacinto Mountains, the small town of San Jacinto still resembled a western frontier town in the early 1890s. This photograph was taken looking east on Main Street from Five Points, which is in the foreground. Courtesy, Clarence Swift Collection*

Right: *At the turn of the century ostrich farms flourished throughout much of Southern California to provide plumes for hat and dress decorations. The Cawston Ostrich Farm started a breeding ranch near Seventh and Sanderson streets in the San Jacinto Valley and flourished for many years until fashions changed and there was no demand for ostrich plumes. Courtesy, Lorne Allmon*

dam in the West. Lake Hemet was capable of storing nearly 11,000 acre-feet of water.

At the mouth of the South Fork a small diversion dam channeled the flow into a three and-a-half-mile flume. In turn, a steel pipe two miles long crossed the river and discharged into a five-mile canal. A terminal reservoir at the townsite supplied over thirty miles of distribution ditches and flumes.

With an assured water supply, the five- to twenty-acre parcels in the Hemet Tract soon sported groves of apricots, peaches, pears, nectarines, prunes, and figs. The town of Hemet grew quickly. The first edition of the *Hemet News* was issued on December 9, 1893. It announced that the Hotel Mayberry and a grammar school were nearing completion, that Heffelfinger and Company's general merchandise and the A.E. Boalich Lumber Yard were experiencing brisk sales, and that the new town still needed a bank, a restaurant, a shoe shop, a barber shop, a drug store, and a dentist.

By 1906 Hemet had all these, and more: cement sidewalks, an opera house, telephones, and electric lights! Violet Tapper, an early resident, described the town's "growing pains":

Harvard was the 'main street' in 1905. None of the streets were paved at that time but were deep with dust in the summer and a sea of mud in the winter. . . . Hitching posts lined Harvard Street with a water trough for the horses on Front Street at Harvard. [Once] dogs sighted a jackrabbit just outside the business district. The rabbit ran north on Harvard and under the horses at the hitching posts. . . . The startled horses began to rear and kick, resulting in much damage to the fronts of the buggies and wagons.

This photograph of the Great Hemet Dam was taken by S.I. White shortly after water started rushing over it for the first time on April 2, 1906. The dam, built under the supervision of E.L. Mayberry, was the most important event in the history of the San Jacinto Valley, opening vast new lands to cultivation. Courtesy, Clarence Swift Collection

By 1910, with a population of 992, mayor T.S. Brown could preside over the first meeting of a city council. Hemet was truly a boom town.

The growth of the San Jacinto Valley was periodically interrupted by earthquakes, the worst of which occurred on April 21, 1918. That pleasant Sunday afternoon the first in a series of violent shocks swept the valley. One-hundred-foot geysers leapt into the air along the artesian basins near the San Jacinto River. Headstones toppled in the cemetery. The business districts of Hemet and San Jacinto were devastated as brick buildings like the Hotel Mayberry toppled to the ground. Of first concern, however, was the great dam high in the mountains—a break would have meant hundreds being swept to their deaths. The dam stood, a testament to its sturdy construction.

The Bank of Hemet, however, was so badly damaged it was soon razed. For a year the bank shared quarters with Roulston and Spaulding's undertaking parlor. The vault, which had survived the quake, stood alone on the bank lot while money and bookkeeping materials were carried back and forth by hand. Funerals continued unabated in the room behind the teller's window.

South and west, the RSA&LA was transforming Bernardo Yorba's old "pocket" rancho in the Prado Basin. A company headed by R.B. Taylor, Adolph Rimpau, and Samuel Merrill, former governor of Iowa, purchased 12,000 acres from Yorba's heirs. The South Riverside Land and Water Company hoped to capitalize on the popular success of the Riverside Colony by laying out a city and subdividing the remaining acreage to small citrus ranches. H.C. Kellogg, a civil engineer from Anaheim, surveyed a unique circular boulevard three miles in circumference called Grand Avenue. By spring of 1887, a $45,000 pipeline had been completed, drawing water from side streams in the Temescal Canyon.

The year 1887 saw the arrival of the first settlers from Iowa, as well as a scattering from other states and Canada. A. S. Garretson, another proprietor of South Riverside, built the lavish Hotel Temescal on the block between Main and Washburn

and Sixth and Seventh streets. A Congregational church rose at Eighth and Ramona, followed by the Citizens Bank, completed in August of the same year. But water problems lingered, and each morning long lines formed at the new settlement's single domestic well.

THE FIRST NATIONAL BANK OF HEMET

Building continued. Soon the pioneers boasted of a railroad station, a post office, and a newspaper, the *Bee.* Acre upon acre of citrus orchards were planted. Such rapid expansion proved the original water plan to be far too small for adequate supply. Under the Temescal Water Compa-

San Jacinto Valley's second great earthquake (the first was in 1899) struck on April 21, 1918, causing extensive damage to homes and businesses in both Hemet and San Jacinto. The quake demolished the First National Bank of Hemet. Photo by S.I. White, courtesy, Clarence Swift Collection

ny, sources farther and farther up the canyon were tapped to meet the increasing demand. From the springs and artesian wells at Glen Ivy, near Coldwater Canyon, the company constructed a steel pipe capable of 220 miner's inches of flow. By 1892, however, over 2,500 acres of oranges and lemons had been planted. Two years later officials were looking for another source of supply. At Lake Elsinore they constructed a large pumping plant at the end of a long pier. The company began to drain the lovely lake dry.

In 1896 a general election approved incorporation, and the new city had a new name: Corona. In 1898 citrus growers discovered that the high alkaline content of Elsinore water was poisoning their trees. The pumping plant at Lake Elsinore was abandoned. In 1901 the Temescal Company emerged from the canyon, buying up water-bearing lands and drilling wells at Ethanac, near present-day Romoland. A redwood pipeline and an eighteen-mile ditch delivered water to the canyon and a power plant at Ethanac generated the electricity to drive the pumps.

In 1903 citizens in Corona began construction of a gas and electric plant. Soon Main Street sported new gutters and grading. In 1914, 100,000 spectators jammed Grand Avenue to cheer Eddie Pullen while he succeeded in breaking the 300-mile speed record in a pioneering new sport—auto racing. Barney Oldfield, though not the winner, drove his Maxwell nonstop for the entire 300 miles at an astonishing average of 85.5 miles per hour!

Corona grew with equal rapidity. Over-pumping lowered the water table at Ethanac and turned it saline. The Temescal Water Company abandoned its wells there and, in 1929, built a dam in Railroad Canyon with the hopes of storing the annual flood of the San Jacinto River. Removing its tracks in Railroad Canyon, the Santa Fe constructed a spur to Alberhill from Corona via Temescal Canyon. Track laying began on August 30, 1926, and utilized some of the old grade from the defunct 1888 Pomona and Elsinore Railway. The spur served the large coal and clay mining

operations at Alberhill. But Railroad Canyon Dam proved almost valueless for irrigation, filling only for short durations at flood. The Temescal Water Company continued its search in a region where local sources were dwindling, buying into water companies as distant as Agua Mansa and Colton. Even part ownership in the Riverside Water Company, including the extension of the Gage and Riverside canals to Corona, did not satisfy. Not until the completion of the Colorado River Aqueduct would the Corona area know water security.

While farmers and city builders through the region set out their network of survey stakes, Indians, already devastated by war, disease, and social disruption, found themselves squeezed into the dwindling interstices between settlements. Ethnologists and philanthropists had only recently turned their attention to the remnants of California's "mission" tribes. During the early 1880s Abbott Kinney and Helen Hunt Jackson, special agents for the Bureau of Indian Affairs, crisscrossed Southern California—interviewing, observing, taking testimony. On an uncomfortable buckboard along dusty roads and broken trails, Jackson and Kinney visited countless reservations and rancherias. In 1883 Jackson submitted her report "On the Condition and Needs of the Mission Indians of California." According to Jackson, the Indians of the region occupied an increasingly

The notorious Sam Temple (seated), who shot Cahuilla Indian Juan Diego in 1883 during a quarrel over a horse, posed in about 1890 with his friend Frank Wellman. Although Temple was freed by a justice of the peace when no one pressed charges for the killing, he was immortalized as Jim Farrar, murderer of Alessandro (Juan Diego) in Helen Hunt Jackson's Ramona. *Courtesy, Clarence Swift Collection*

hostile environment and were woefully unprotected. Disease and exploitation were daily taking their toll. Their rights to traditional lands were being seriously abridged everywhere. The Indians, Jackson wrote, "ask nothing at the hands of the United States Government now, except that it will protect them in the ownership of their lands—lands which, in many instances, have been in continuous occupation and cultivation by their ancestors for over one hundred years." But one story in particular stung the hardy woman, and continued to bite at her conscience. It had occurred at the Mountain Cahuilla reservation in the San Jacintos only a few weeks before her visit:

A Cahuilla Indian named Juan Diego had built for himself a house and cultivated a small patch of ground on a high mountain ledge a few miles north of the village. Here he lived alone with his wife and baby. He had been for some years what the Indians call a "locoed" Indian, being at times crazy; never dangerous, but yet certainly insane for longer or shorter periods.

Juan Diego came home one evening with a different horse than he had started out on. Elsewhere, Sam Temple, the roisterous lumberjack operating out of Strawberry Creek, found one of his horses had been mysteriously "traded" for another. That night he rode for Juan Diego's home.

[Temple] rode up, and on seeing Juan poured out a volley of oaths, levelled his gun and shot him dead. After Juan had fallen on the ground Temple rode closer and fired three more shots in the body, one in the forehead, one in the cheek, and one in the wrist, the woman looking on.

Temple then rode to Samuel Tripp, justice of the peace, at his ranch in the San Jacinto Valley. He announced that he had killed an Indian in self-defense. Tripp released him. Jackson and Kinney sought to reopen the case, but the district attorney in San Diego refused.

Helen Hunt Jackson retired to write *Ramona*, a

Above: *Many Indian women were claimants to the title of the "real Ramona," the tragic heroine of Helen Hunt Jackson's novel about mistreatment of the California Indian. The most valid claimant, however, would seem to be Ramona Lubo, the Cahuilla wife of Juan Diego. This photograph of Lubo was taken outside a brush ramada in about 1890 by Thomas Millhollin. She died on July 21, 1922, and was buried next to Juan Diego in Cahuilla Cemetery in the San Jacinto Mountains. Courtesy, Clarence Swift Collection*

Right: *In the 1920s Indio was already thriving as the major town in the Coachella Valley, whose desert soils under irrigation were proving to be adaptable to many different kinds of fruits, vegetables, and grain. Although providing abundant harvest of many crops, the area became best known for its most exotic crop—the culture of date varieties imported from the Near East. Courtesy, Lorne Allmon*

romanticized version of Juan Diego's sad story which quickly became one of the best-selling novels of its time and later a popular film. *Ramona* did much to bring attention to the plight of the Indians of Southern Cailfornia. It shared the flaws of other classics such as *Uncle Tom's Cabin* or *Gone With the Wind*—a depiction of a people based mostly on fantasy. Since 1923 the Ramona Pageant, held in an amphitheater set against a rocky hillside in Hemet, has drawn thousands of tourists each year. Conceived by Burdette Raynor, secretary to the Hemet Valley Chamber of Commerce, as a way to "draw a large number of people to our valley at least once a year," one has to wonder how many spectators leave the performance with their understanding of their Indian neighbors appreciably enhanced.

During the 1880s and early 1890s dissatisfaction grew over the long distances settlers were forced to travel to reach their county seats. After the California Southern abandoned its tracks in Temecula Canyon, residents of Temecula, Elsinore, San Jacinto, Hemet, Indio, and part of Banning were forced to go even longer distances to

Top: *Stage driver Ray Forbes takes on passengers outside the luxurious Hotel Hemet on Florida Avenue for the long trip to the mountain resort of Idyllwild. This photograph of the well-known "Owl" stage was taken in 1906 by S.I. White. Courtesy, Clarence Swift Collection*

Bottom: *Banning's most illustrious and powerful citizen throughout much of its history was C.O. Barker, shown here with his wife on the Banning Bench. Arriving in Banning in 1884, he spent his first night in a "flop house." He later taught school, became manager of the Banning Water Company, built the Banning Cannery to handle the Pass's fruit crop, and served as Riverside County's first state assemblyman. It was Barker who led the movement for Highway 99 as the first ocean-to-ocean highway. Courtesy, Leonard McCulloh*

do business in San Diego: a railway journey via Highgrove or Colton, to Santa Ana, then down the coast. The region within San Bernardino County (including Riverside, Corona, Moreno, Beaumont, and the other part of Banning) suffered less from isolation but more from what they considered political oppression. Differences between San Bernardino and Riverside developed from the beginning. San Bernardino County permitted saloons at a low licensing fee; the majority of Riversiders were believers in temperance. There was, as well, San Bernardino's notorious D Street "red light" district—a standard feature in most frontier communities, but unspeakable among Riversiders.

To Luther Ingersoll, Riverside resident and pioneer historian, there was an overall difference in attitude between the cities. In 1904 he wrote:

Riverside grew more rapidly than San Bernardino. Her citizens were largely young men from the East, whose ideas and methods were different from the conservative movements of San Bernardino's solid citizens ... pioneers who had been trained in the school of hard circumstances rather than in the colleges and the rushing business life of eastern cities.

Arguments rose over issues like tax assessment, roads, citrus fairs, and the allocation of dwindling water supplies. In 1887 the towns deadlocked over appropriations and a choice of site for a badly needed new courthouse. Outright agitation for a new county began in earnest. In February 1893, lobbyists for a Riverside County convinced the state senate and assembly to approve twin bills, introduced by Senator Streeter of Riverside and Assemblyman C.O. Barker of Banning, for a new county. A governor's commission supervised an election in which local voters overwhelmingly hailed a new county, 2,277 to 681. Choice of the county seat was equally overwhelming: Riverside 2,140, Menifee 459.

Governor Markham signed the Riverside bills on March 11, 1893. With a total area of 7,090 square miles, it stretched nearly 200 miles from the coast ranges to the Colorado River. Its bulk, all of its desert portions and the San Jacinto-Temecula area, had been carved from San Diego County. An additional 590 square miles left San Bernardino County.

The boom of the eighties performed a sweeping transformation of the Western plains and valleys. Railroad companies, battling to bridge a continent, threw their influence over larger and larger territory, and carried settlement to unimaginable places—hotels and sanatoriums in alpine Idyllwild Village, the steaming desert floor at Indio. Everywhere water was the key. Without it the locomotives could not run and crops could not be sown. Sometimes the railroad found it, as with well-drilling along the Salton Sink, or it found the railroad, as with Hemet Dam. Hand in hand, rivers and rails brought the new county into existence. Still, it was only an imaginary line, shaped somewhat like a key, arbitrarily circumscribing a vast and still largely unoccupied landscape. Its citizens were only momentarily jubilant, and soon returned to their labors. The new county had just a few years left to prepare for a new century.

V Queen of the Colonies

A City Matures in Style

Some mornings in the fall of 1886 Matthew Gage might be seen stepping from the door of his shop on Main Street into the bright early sunlight in Riverside. A somewhat unprepossessing figure, carefully attired, he would peer nervously through his spectacles at his favorite pocket timepiece. The few moments he could spend in the shop lately seemed taken up in restless pacing. His work was falling behind. Matthew Gage was being pressured by time, for the jeweler's great vision, one of the most ambitious land developments in the region, the Gage Canal Company, was already far behind schedule. He could almost hear the soft laughter of Section 30 as it mocked him from Box Springs Mountain several miles away.

In 1881 Matthew Gage, thirty-seven, left Kingston, Ontario, in Canada and followed his friends Joseph Jarvis and William Chaffey to Riverside. They had already purchased twenty acres of fruit trees for him within the "Canadian Tract" along California Avenue. Gage opened a jewelry shop, first in Roe's Drugstore, and later in a shop of his own on Main. Gage spent most of his free time fussing over his grove of trees with an uncharacteristically boyish delight. Like his friend's brother, George Chaffey, Jr., Gage was being wooed by

One of the great busts of the Depression years in Riverside County was the sumptuous and spectacular Lake Norconian Club, built in the 1920s as part of a large resort and subdivision tract in Norco. Guests included many Hollywood stars and other celebrities. During World War II the buildings were converted into the Corona Naval Hospital. Later, the facility was taken over by the California Rehabilitation Center, a state institute for narcotic addicts. This photograph, taken around 1930, shows the resort during its lavish heyday. Courtesy, Lorne Allmon

the magic of water and arid land. From his shop window he watched the busy traffic of the rapidly expanding city—new groves planted and new developments planned each day. Though a man of limited means (his personal worth was estimated at no more than $5,000), the jeweler yearned to take a bigger part in Riverside's boom.

East of the Riverside Colony's Mile Square and Magnolia Avenue lay a great upper plain. Too high to be watered by either of the R L & I canals, the plain—government land and unsold Evans property—was Riverside's barren frontier. It was there in 1882 that Matthew Gage staked out and claimed Section 30, one square mile of government land, under the provisions of the Desert Irrigation Act. It was a vast tract, empty and dry, sloping gently toward the west. Gage could patent his claim only if he could somehow bring water to it within three years. He often rode out to the property. The land, shimmering in the bright sea-salt haze of a Riverside afternoon, seemed to laugh a little as the breeze sifted through the dry brittlebush leaves. It had become a challenge.

The jeweler threw himself into the challenge enthusiastically. He quickly purchased 160 acres in Box Springs Canyon nearby. There, natural springs and stream flow would be, he hoped, enough to irrigate Section 30. After only a little work on the site, Gage ceased operations. It was obvious there wouldn't be enough water. He could easily have let his claim lapse—after all, he stood to lose little money. For a while Gage seemed to do nothing, though at his workbench or in the parlor of his home on Fourteenth Street he would stop periodically and check his timepiece. Section 30 continued to softly chide him. It was a simple matter at its core. The land needed water. Somehow, Matthew Gage would bring it.

The jeweler's thoughts turned to the next possible source of supply: the Santa Ana River. By his calculation the high elevation of Section 30 would require a canal twelve miles long with an intake far upriver, north of present-day Loma Linda. It was a simple matter indeed but it required an en-

Above: *In 1884 Canadian settler Matthew Gage tapped the artesian basin beneath the San Bernardino Valley to launch one of the more ingenious water distribution systems of his time. Gage, standing at the left next to an unidentified man, built a twenty-mile canal that brought water to the undeveloped upper plain of Riverside. Through his skillful development of a new water system, the growth and prosperity of Riverside was assured. Courtesy, Riverside Municipal Museum*

Right: *Corona, known as the "Circle City" of the citrus belt for its huge circular thoroughfare known as Circle Boulevard, began as a colony of the South Riverside Land and Water Company and was incorporated as a city in 1896. Its ornate city hall building, constructed in 1912, reflected the prosperity of one of the major orange-growing communities of the period. Courtesy, Riverside Press-Enterprise Company*

gineering reality that would challenge even the most ambitious developers.

Time was running out. Gage moved quickly. He quietly purchased majority ownership in a small canal company, the Hunt and Cooley Ditch, securing the surface flow of the river near his intended intake. He then secured an option to buy 1,000 acres of artesian basin nearby. Soon after, he invited A.J. Twogood and Stephen Herrick, representatives of the same Iowa land syndicate that developed Corona, to the high mesa north of Riverside where his proposed canal would travel. Herrick and Twogood saw the potential. On behalf of the syndicate they purchased 2,000 acres of land from the Southern Pacific. Then, on August 28, 1885, they contracted with Gage for 335 miner's inches of water from the canal he had promised to build. The price, payable in advance, was

$167,000.

Captain C.C. Miller of Tomah, Wisconsin, had come to Riverside in 1874 to survey S.C. Evans' original canal. For his work Miller was given an empty city block between Sixth and Seventh and Main and Orange streets. There he and his sons built a large adobe adorned with New England-style trappings to house his large family. As their children married, or moved away, the Millers expanded their income by taking in guests in a town where hotel rooms were at a premium. In the meantime, work continued to seek out Captain Miller.

Gage had secured bank loans on the basis of the syndicate's sponsorship. He wrote his Canadian brother-in-law, engineer William Irving, and asked him to hasten to California. In the interim, Gage secured Captain Miller's services to begin

the project. From a distance Gage watched his work crews tackle the most difficult section of the work, the canal's climb up the bluffs near Grand Terrace. A long tunnel pierced the brow of the bluff and, further on, another tunnel was carved out from the granite foot of Mount Sugarloaf.

On November 7, 1886, the canal was completed and its headgates thrown open. Gage planned to turn out the first flow at the end of the line—Section 30—to secure his claim. Herrick looked on as the jeweler and his workers pitched tumbleweeds from the bed of the canal. Against Gage's pleas, he rode upstream, opening and closing successively each lateral gate along his subdivision, to guarantee by law the syndicate's permanent right to Gage water. Beyond, the canal's flow dropped to a trickle. Gage waited anxiously until well after dark, when, by the light of flickering lanterns, he watched the water spill out into the darkness. Doubtless the next morning he returned to seek out the dark stains where the land had swallowed thirstily; to listen quietly, alone, for the soft laughter that no longer came.

Matthew Gage's new canal spurred the boom of the mid-1880s in Riverside. While Herrick's syndicate opened East Riverside, now known as Highgrove, another development rose on the site of John North's old orchard property. Known as White's Addition, it boasted "an ample supply of good, pure spring and artesian water from the Gage water system." Albert White's subdivision soon sported the ornate and commodious homes of well-to-do Victorians. Further south, in 1887, Priestly Hall opened Hall's Addition near Cridge Street. Hall would build an ornate Victorian adobe mansion on a hillside overlooking Tequesquite Arroyo and call it, appropriately, Rockledge. Another developer, John Castleman, subdivided Castleman's Addition just below Gage's own Section 30.

Downtown, too, saw a remarkable transformation between 1885 and 1890, obliterating or obscuring the modest structures of the early colony years. Land sales and citrus harvests created a wealthy banking class who lavished funds on monuments to their success. John Castleman com-

Left: *Chinese provided much of the labor in early Riverside, and all of the citrus belt communities in Southern California had their Chinatowns. The early Chinese settlers in Riverside first accumulated in the mile-square area of downtown, but they were eventually run out by the Anglo merchants. In 1886 they established Chinatown in the Brockton Arroyo between Tequesquite Avenue and Fourteenth Street. Chinatown with its exotic shops and restaurants flourished for several generations until the last shopkeeper closed his doors in 1938. Courtesy, Riverside Municipal Museum*

Above: *Riverside's first daily newspaper was the* Daily Enterprise. *Founded in 1885, the establishment was located in a brick building at Eighth and Orange streets when it was depicted in 1897 by W.J. Miller in this watercolor sketch. Eventually, this newspaper was merged with the* Riverside Press, *which had been founded as a weekly in 1878. The town's first newspaper, the* Riverside News, *begun in 1875, had a checkered existence of about only two years. Courtesy, Riverside Public Library*

pleted a three-story office building at Eighth and Main where, under its huge clock, the new First National Bank opened its doors. Across the street, S.C. Evans began construction of an equally impressive edifice to house his own Riverside National Bank. Completed in 1892, in Romanesque style, it contained arched windows and, for a while, its own stylish tower. (The tower was quiet-

Above: *Riverside's early financial titan, Samuel Cary Evans, Sr., was an old man when the new Victorian style buildings were being erected in the 1890s. In 1892 he completed the most fashionable building of the period, the Evans Building at the northeast corner of Eighth and Main streets, perhaps as a monument to his wealth and power. When the financial panic struck in 1893, he simply liquidated his Riverside National Bank without loss to his depositors and managed to survive the crisis while other wealthy men went under. Courtesy, Riverside Municipal Museum*

Left: *Charles M. Loring, a winter visitor from Minneapolis to Riverside's Glenwood Mission Inn, helped finance the Loring Building so that Riverside could have an opera house. Chicago theater architect J.M. Wood designed the block-long building, which still exists today on the northwest corner of Main and Seventh streets. When it was completed in 1890, it provided the city with one of the most ornate opera houses in Southern California. Courtesy, Riverside Municipal Museum*

ly removed after news reached Riverside of the 1906 San Francisco quake.) The Rubidoux, Hayt, and other buildings also adorned the growing business district.

To the south the community high school took up quarters on the third floor of an imposing three-storied brick building at Fourteenth and Brockton. Today only its iron fountain remains to mark the site outside the later Grant Elementary School. Adding to the city's cultural wealth was (and is) the Loring Building, with its ornate opera

house, opened in January of 1890. Dominating the corner of Seventh and Main, the Loring was a result of cooperation between the city government and Charles Loring, a wealthy winter visitor from Minneapolis. Loring provided the funds for construction and the city repaid him by renting most of its office space, including the second floor for the library and the basement for the jail. Next door, the opera house served as a focus for the self-consciously cultured young community. Over the years many great performers from the turn-of-the-century stage took their bows beneath its arching proscenium—among them Helena Modjeska, Sarah Bernhardt, Alla Nazimova, James O'Neill,

A significant cultural event for all of Southern California was the opening of Riverside's lavish Loring Opera House on January 8, 1890. The opera house was financed by Charles M. Loring, a wealthy flour mill operator from Minneapolis, who spent his winters in Frank Miller's Glenwood Mission Inn. It was here that an aged Sarah Bernhardt gave one of her last performances and Madame Helena Modjeska brought down the house by wrapping herself in an American flag. Courtesy, Tom Patterson

and Isadora Duncan.

The Loring Opera House was equipped with the latest in theatrical devices, which included both gas and, less dependably, electric lights. Since 1888 Riverside had been served by a small hydroelectric plant at the upper canal where it crossed Iowa Avenue. Designed by G.O. Newman, Captain Miller's son-in-law, the plant utilized a drop in the canal to produce (at best) a modest 225 kilowatts. The generators screamed so loudly they could be heard downtown and lights dimmed and went out so often that the plant, long superseded, was little missed when it burned in 1915. More recently, however, its stone and concrete foundations have received their proper glory: historians have discovered that the pioneering little plant was the first hydroelectric in what is now known as Southern California Edison.

The plant provided power for the city's first street lights, a series of blinding arc lamps hung in the center of the business district. It powered as well the first electric streetcars of the Riverside and Arlington Electric Railway, a consolidation of smaller mule- and horse-car companies, and managed by Captain Miller's eldest son, Frank. On April 5, 1899, at 7:10 a.m., the first trolley made its pioneer run down Magnolia from First Street all the way to Van Buren, its bell ringing proudly at

Above: *Riverside's most illustrious citizen for more than a half century was Frank Miller, proprietor and builder of the Glenwood Mission Inn. Miller succeeded in attracting the most famous celebrities of his era to his hotel, and he was the subject of a slavishly admiring biography by novelist Zona Gale. Art and culture were his enthusiasms and he left his stamp on Riverside in many ways. Courtesy, Tom Patterson*

Above, left: *In 1899 the mule-drawn trolley was replaced in Riverside by the electric streetcar, soon to be harnessed into the vast interurban transportation network of Pacific Electric Company, which formed a link between most Southern California communities. Here, one of the new streetcars had been decorated to become part of a Masonic Lodge parade down Main Street. The man astride the horse is believed to be James Boyd, later the city's first historian. Courtesy, the Bordwell Collection, Riverside Municipal Museum*

each intersection.

But young Frank Miller would make another, more substantial, contribution to the city's cultural growth. Frank was seventeen when he accompanied his family to Riverside. With only a grade school education he wandered from one job to another in the new land, from driving a mule cart in the Temescal Tin Mine to growing oranges. For a while it was hoped he would settle down as a merchandiser in his own Blue Front Grocery Store, especially after marriage to a lovely and serious young school teacher, Isabella Hardenburg.

But in 1880 Frank took over his family's hotel, the Glenwood. While maintaining the family traditions of simple, rustic hospitality, he began a modest expansion program. Behind the main house he added a dormitory addition known as "The Barracks," as well as a series of cottages. The cluster of buildings retained a park-like atmosphere of trees and shrubs in the center of the business district, making it a popular stopping

Top: *In 1902 Frank Miller raised the money to rebuild his Glenwood Hotel on a grandiose scale and construction was immediately begun under architect Arthur B. Benton. The new Glenwood Inn, soon referred to internationally as the Mission Inn, opened in January 1903, its prestige assured by the May arrival of President Theodore Roosevelt during his western political tour. Courtesy, Tom Patterson*

Center: *In the horse-and-buggy era, one of the major service industries was the town blacksmith. He not only shod horses, but also functioned as a mechanic, repairing almost anything that used metal. Among the prominent Riverside blacksmiths in 1897 was M.L. Lawrence, whose firm was located at Eighth and Orange streets. Watercolor by W.J. Miller, courtesy, Riverside Public Library*

Bottom: *In 1886 Ed Miller established the Glenwood Stables on Main Street to supply transportation for his brother's Glenwood Mission Inn Hotel and the city as a whole. The firm had two "tally-hos," each with a capacity of fourteen passengers. Courtesy, Riverside Municipal Museum*

place for winter visitors. Indeed, its quaint oddity alone might have kept the Glenwood going well into the twentieth century until sacrificed inevitably to urban expansion. And, were it not for the informal intrusion into Riverside history of one man, a little-known guest of Miller's during the 1880s, the city's growth might have been singularly different.

Wilson Crewdson, wealthy, English, and a former director of Oriental exhibits at the British Museum, came to Riverside for relief for a lung ailment. According to Miller's biographers, Crewdson's casual conversations with the proprietor of the Glenwood Hotel—about art, history, and culture—left an indelible impression on Miller. The erudite and sophisticated Englishman inadvertently broadened the horizons of an energetic but parochially trained young man. Crewdson left Miller with a growing desire to collect, incorporate in the hotel, and dramatize the best of the world's art and spirit. Along the way, Miller almost single-handedly transformed a city's tastes, inspiring it to nearly make itself over. Frank Miller, "Master of the Inn," would leave behind him a grand personal monument— Riverside's Mission Inn.

But the elusive Mr. Crewdson would leave his mark on the city in yet another important way, through Matthew Gage. While the city boomed, Gage's vision grew with equal rapidity. To build

his canal he had already incurred obligations totaling nearly a million dollars. Beyond his canal's
terminus, across the wide Tequesquite Arroyo, lay
3,000 acres of unwatered, unsold land. In June
1887 Gage incurred an even greater obligation by
agreeing to purchase from the Riverside Land
Company all these lands at $75 per acre. William
Irving would supervise the construction of a long
flume across the arroyo and the canal would be
extended another nine miles to these lands. The
jeweler stood ready to repay his debts and reap a
sizable fortune as well.

But in 1888 the boom went bust throughout
the nation. In Southern California a sharp and
prolonged downturn in real estate values left
many ambitious projects high and dry. In Riverside the fanciful Hotel Rubidoux's thick foundations and walls waited half-finished and forlorn
on the mountainside for years.

Gage, too, was unable to continue his development without new backing. With his local resources exhausted, Gage turned frantically to
Wilson Crewdson. The Englishman offered his
influence with associates of the international
accounting firm of Price, Waterhouse & Company, headquartered in London.

Gage wrote Crewdson in 1889, and left soon after for London. He returned as general manager

Above: *Few crops are more temperamental
and more requiring of constant care than citrus. Riverside's citrus growers perfected many
of the horticultural techniques that became established throughout the industry, including
pruning methods. This photograph of a pruning crew with their shears was taken in 1915.
Courtesy, Special Collections Department, Library of the University of California,
Riverside*

Facing page, top: *One of the failures of the
1890s boom was the townsite of Auburndale,
comprising 2,000 acres north of Temescal
Wash in the Corona area. In 1888 W.H.
Jameson and a group of associates built a
$6,000 hotel there and opened a land office,
but it did little business. In the 1920s motorists
crossed the Santa Ana River at Auburndale
by means of a harrowing pontoon bridge.
Courtesy, Lorne Allmon*

Facing page, bottom: *Best known and loved of
Riverside ministers was the eloquent George
H. Deere, who arrived in the community in
1886 and became pastor of the All Souls Uni-
versalist Church. In that same year, he moved
into what he called "Cozy Nook Cottage" on
Seventh Street. In this photograph (circa
1886), Reverend Deere is shown watching his
wife, Louise, tending roses. Courtesy, Riverside
Municipal Museum*

Above: *Riverside's young elite of the 1880s belonged to the Casa Blanca Tennis Club, where they are shown in the new clubhouse sipping tea (a ritual perpetuated by the city's English and Canadian pioneers). One of the members, Grace Gilliland, went on to become the first state champion in women's singles. Courtesy, Riverside Municipal Museum*

Left: *Among the social arbiters of Riverside for several decades beginning in the 1890s were Mr. and Mrs. Robert Bettner, shown here with Ah Sam, cook for more than twenty years at the Riverside Country Club. Bettner was a founder of the Riverside Polo Club in 1892 and known for his fine racing horses. Courtesy, Riverside Municipal Museum*

of the Riverside Trust Company and with more than enough backing to complete his ambitious plans. Early the next year, Gage launched a great new subdivision, Arlington Heights. Salability was enhanced by an elegant avenue landscaped with exotic trees and named for Queen Victoria.

To tie the subdivision more closely to the city, Gage and Irving constructed a long wooden bridge for the avenue across the arroyo. On Thanksgiving Day, 1891, a parade of nearly 200 buggies and carriages and countless pedestrians approached Victoria Bridge from the city. Pausing at its edge, the lively crowd waited until Matthew Gage's mother, eighty-two years old, could be brought forward in her open phaeton. The crowd cheered as a swarm of her grandchildren, grand-nieces, and -nephews took hold of the carriage and pulled it across the bridge.

But while Matthew Gage was celebrating achievements, London's Riverside Trust Company was closing the jeweler out. The Trust began planting more and more of their acreage in oranges and lemons—not for subdivision, but for harvest. At the same time, Gage's financial obligations to the company were called in, and most of his stock repossessed. In 1894 Gage resigned from the company and began a long series of litigations in a fruitless effort to gain the return of his share of the venture. He would never succeed. Much like John North a generation earlier, he would be undone by a tangle of financial commitments, the "necessary evil" of his vision.

Under the name Arlington Heights Company, lands under the Trust came more and more to resemble a colonial plantation such as those the British established throughout their empire. By 1907 the Trust had planted over 5,000 acres in oranges and lemons, retaining a permanent work force of nearly 300, with additional crews at harvest time. The Trust maintained three housing camps: Windsor, Balmoral, and Osborne, along Victoria Avenue. The Trust, and a similar company, the San Jacinto Land Company, were the greatest conduit for an influx of English citizens who would transform society and culture in Riverside. The "English Colony," as it was known, consisted largely of managers and superintendents for the two companies.

After its founding, on the grounds of the Harry Lockwood mansion, the Casa Blanca Tennis Club became the center of activity for Riverside's expanding high society. When Mrs. L.S. Gilliland, an English widow, took over in 1886, she introduced English customs, including tea during breaks in the playing. In 1892 the pioneer Riverside Polo Club was established on Trust property near Jefferson Street. Founders included C.E. Maud, Trust superintendent, G.L. Waring, and San Jacinto Land Company manager William Pedley—all Englishmen. Robert Lee Bettner (whose mansion, built by his mother, is now the city's Heritage House) was one enthusiastic novice.

The tennis and polo clubs competed with many other social activities during the 1890s. The Riverside Wheelmen's Club coordinated bicycle races at Athletic Park on North Hill. Riverside's Racing Association and Driving Association shared the equestrian facilities at Chemawa Park, where the streetcar company had established a zoo and amusement park. Golf, too, was popular, with its most fashionable facilities centered, by 1903, at the newly organized Victoria Country Club.

Riverside's "upper crust" could enjoy more amenities in part because of the ongoing effort of growers city-wide to solve basic problems in the citrus industry. Early on, the most unstable aspects of citrus culture were shipping and marketing practices. Refrigerated cars like the Patent Witcke's Car, first introduced by the Santa Fe Railroad in 1894, helped to nationalize potential markets for perishable fruit. But individual growers, pinched between fluctuating prices and rotting fruit, found themselves at the mercy of distant railroad agents and commission house "middlemen." Complaining of "downright swin-

Above: *Most Southern California towns made contributions to the citrus industry, but none remotely matched Riverside for sheer leadership and technological innovation up into the early 1900s. Two competing mechanical wizards, Fred Stebler and George Parker, produced hundreds of inventions and refinements in citrus packinghouse equipment before their rival firms were finally absorbed into Food Machinery Corporation in 1938. The first successful orange grader was invented in 1887 by J.W. Keeney and by the turn of the century there were highly sophisticated graders in every citrus belt packinghouse. In this 1900 photograph, employees of La Mesa Packing House in Riverside are shown grading oranges and packing them into boxes for shipment. Courtesy, Riverside Municipal Museum*

Left: *The young community of Riverside helped build its reputation as the new orange growing center of California with a series of citrus fairs beginning in 1879. The citrus fair of 1883 (shown here) was one of the most lavish, attracting hundreds of visitors from throughout Southern California. Courtesy, Riverside Public Library*

dling," citrus growers suffered a string of particularly bad years during the late 1880s and early 1890s.

At the same time, however, a few growers in Riverside were developing solutions to the market crunch. In the late 1880s T.H.B. Chamblin brought together ten of his friends and neighbors in a "pool" to market their oranges cooperatively. Calling themselves the Pachappa Orange Growers Association, they contracted as a group with the packing house of F.B. Devine for grading, packing, and shipping. Cooperative, orderly marketing was the key, and the system worked so well that Chamblin was soon assisting in the organization of similar small cooperatives, each in turn to be supervised by a district-wide exchange. Growers throughout Riverside heartily endorsed the plan, and the Riverside Fruit Exchange was born.

On April 4, 1893, Chamblin went before a group of Southern California growers at the Los

Angeles Chamber of Commerce. He explained the factors within his associations that gave them their success and called for a regional network of district exchanges. By August 1893 Chamblin had participated in the formation of seven district exchanges throughout Southern California. These seven, under a board of control, became the Southern California Fruit Exchange, a pioneering organization in the history of agricultural cooperatives. Another Riversider, A.H. Naftzger, became president of the board in 1894. Described as "a forceful character," Naftzger took on the difficult task of establishing allotment procedures as well as bringing older marketing interests, such as cash and consignment operations, into line. The exchange continued to expand its role, promoting new uses for citrus fruit, transforming the orange from an exotic item to a household necessity, and providing ancillary services like box making. By the 1950s, the exchange had assumed its own brand name, so that modern consumers know it simply as "Sunkist."

One explanation for the remarkable success of the Riverside Plan might have been in the type of grower attracted to citrus culture. Irrigated land in Riverside at that time sold for $200 to $400 per

Above: *Prosperous orange grower P.K. Klinefelter poses outside his elegant Victorian home, built shortly before 1890, on Brockton Avenue in Riverside. The house, known as "The Bijou," was one of many fine homes going up in the city whose prosperity rested on the "golden fruit of the Hesperides." Courtesy, Riverside Municipal Museum*

Right, top: *The new Victorian style became part of Riverside's skyline in the late 1880s. One of the ornate buildings of the period, completed in 1886, was the John S. Castleman building, which was three stories high. Housing the First National Bank, it was the leading financial institution in town until the turn of the century. Streetcars were still being drawn by mules until 1899. Courtesy, the Field Collection, Riverside Municipal Museum*

Right, bottom: *One of Riverside's most elegant Victorian homes was the mansion of horticulturist John Jarvis, located at Twelfth and Redwood streets. The house was designed in the English Eastlake Stick Style and had a carriage house at the rear. Members of the Jarvis family are shown here in an 1890 photograph. Courtesy, Riverside Municipal Museum*

acre, a large sum. Citrus historian Harry Lawton described the average citrus growers of the time. They were:

Retired business or professional men from New England and the central states, usually men of intelligence and education...These men had little knowledge of the old world practices of citrus production. Because they were acquainted with other business practices outside of agriculture they were better able to organize an industry along new lines of picking, packing, and marketing fruits—new methods that have since been exploited in other citrus growing regions of the world.

The boom of the late 1880s had given Riverside its solid Victorian base. After the turn of the century, the Mission Revival movement would give the city its unique image and many of its most charming traditions. Frank Miller's brief friendship with Mr. Crewdson had given the hotel keeper a delayed, but powerful, thirst for culture. All Frank Miller needed was a set of traditions and a sense of aesthetics he could call his own. The foundation in 1895 of the Landmarks Club by Southern California publicist Charles Lummis and architect Arthur Benton provided just that— a romanticized revival of the arts and cultures of Southwest Indians and their Spanish conquerors. Miller threw himself into the Mission Revival movement with his characteristically excessive energy. "Dramatize what you do," was one of his favorite sayings, and Miller set about to dramatize what historian Tom Patterson, looking back, called "a past that never was."

Miller befriended a group of artists and writers like Lummis, Helen Hunt Jackson, and Zona Gale. With Arthur Benton as his architect, he set about redesigning the Glenwood Hotel. The old barracks and cottages were discarded. In their place an impressive wing of rooms enclosed a central courtyard. Miller and Benton stripped the New England trappings from the original Miller home and rebuilt it as the "Old Adobe." Beside it

Benton added the Companario, an arched carriage entrance adorned with bells. Renamed the Glenwood Mission Inn, it displayed a growing wealth of art and artifacts as Miller continually expanded his collection. The inn became an attraction of its own—an ever-changing and growing gallery-museum-shrine.

Miller's influence extended throughout the city. He gave his hotel's trademark, the Indian rain cross, to the city for use as its symbol. He urged many civic improvements, and with his encouragement the face of the city was transformed. The year 1903 saw the completion of the Carnegie Library adjacent to the inn, a classic example of

Mission Revival (tragically removed in 1965 to make way for a larger, though entirely unimpressive, new library building). The Loring Building, on the opposite side of the inn, received a facelift to bring it more into line with the new movement. Soon the Union Pacific Depot, with its tile roofline and corner belltowers, would welcome arriving passengers. At Pedley Narrows on the Santa Ana River a massive Mission-style arched bridge conveyed the railroad over seasonal floods. A new Mission-style high school building replaced the Romanesque edifice on Fourteenth and Brockton. Miller was also influential in bringing the Indian Bureau's Sherman Institute to Riverside. Its main buildings were also completed in Mission style.

By 1903 the Mission Inn was known worldwide and the "Master of the Inn" could boast of the friendship of Presidents. On May 7, 1903, "Rough Rider" Teddy Roosevelt stopped in Riverside while campaigning through the West. At Victoria and Myrtle streets he wielded a shovel to plant a palm tree in honor of Queen Victoria. (It is now known as the Roosevelt Tree.) Roosevelt then led a parade to his evening's lodging at the Mission Inn. The following day he assisted the Millers in planting another tree, one of the two parent navel oranges removed from the old Tibbets homestead.

Above: The renowned Gateway Arch in Beaumont separated the western part of Riverside County from the desert at the summit of San Gorgonio Pass on Highway 60 for many years. This familiar landmark disappeared when Highway 60 was elevated to freeway status. Courtesy, Lorne Allmon

Above, left: Riversiders still talk about the great elephant stampede of 1908. On April 16, 1908, the Sells-Floto Circus arrived in the city for its annual one-day stop. Heavy winds fanned a Standard Oil tank wagon that caught fire at Fourth and Commerce streets and embers from the blaze fell on the circus tents located a block away on Third Street near the Southern Pacific tracks. Four elephants stampeded. The troop leader trampled a woman to death on the porch of a house, crashed through the Mission Inn barbershop, and was finally subdued near Seventh Street on Market. The three elephants shown here were rounded up at widely separated points. Courtesy, Lorne Allmon

Far left: The era of the Model T in Riverside was marked in 1922 by the construction of the Mission Boulevard bridge over the Santa Ana River. The bridge formed an ornate western approach to the city from Los Angeles. The Mission Inn influenced the design of the mission-like towers and the inn's symbolic "raincross" design was worked into the balustrades of the approaches. Courtesy, Tom Patterson

Above: *President Benjamin Harrison leads a triumphal procession down Riverside's Main Street in 1891. Although he stopped at the Glenwood Mission Inn, he didn't spend the night there. A few faces of Riverside's earliest black community may be seen in the crowd, which also contains several Chinese onlookers. Courtesy, Riverside Municipal Museum*

Left: *An almost forgotten benefactor of Riverside until recently was John Henry Reed, a citrus grower who formed the Riverside Horticultural Club in 1895 and led club members in conducting the first scientific experiments on frost control through smudging. Reed spearheaded the long battle that led to the founding of the Citrus Experiment Station in Riverside in 1906, lobbied against billboards in the 1890s, and first proposed that palm trees be considered for street trees in Southern California. As Riverside tree warden, he attracted nationwide attention for his remarkable record of planting thousands of trees throughout the city. Courtesy, Special Collections Department, Library of the University of California, Riverside*

It was a fitting memorial to an old century and a new era for Riverside.

Frank Miller would spend the rest of his life expanding the Inn. An inner courtyard, the Cloister Wing, the Saint Francis Chapel, and the unique Rotunda for professional offices would be added. In size alone, however, Miller's greatest project would be a mountain. Part of an unsuccessful real estate development, Mount Rubidoux grew to be-

come a monument to world peace. In partnership with Pacific Electric's Henry Huntington (son of "Big Four" member Collis), Miller began to develop homesites around the base of Mount Rubidoux. As a sales attraction, he constructed a sightseeing road and park overview on the mountain's peak. Though the subdivision was never successful for Miller, Mount Rubidoux became the most beloved of his civic interests and thereby perhaps his single most significant contribution to the people of Riverside. A remarkable road, laid out by the famed engineer, Major Hiram Chittenden, wound its precipitous way to the top where a wooden cross dedicated to Father Serra was erected. Jacob Riis, famed journalist and social worker, spoke at the road's opening in 1907. By

On May 8, 1907, President Theodore Roosevelt transplanted one of the two original parent navel orange trees in front of the "Old Adobe" in the Mission Inn's outer patio in Riverside. The tree died in 1921, but the second parent tree still survives in a small park at the corner of Arlington and Magnolia avenues. Frank and Isabella Hardenburg Miller are shown standing to the left of the President, who also christened the Presidential Suite at the hotel.

tradition it was Riis who first suggested the idea of an annual Easter sunrise service beneath the cross. The first Mount Rubidoux service, held in 1909, sparked a wave of similar sunrise services across the nation. The tradition is maintained on the mountain to this day.

As the years passed Mount Rubidoux would receive new embellishments. Bells and plaques came to adorn the trails. A fountain and wayfarer's rest met the eastward traveler as he entered Riverside across a Mission-style bridge. After 1923, an arched stone bridge and landscaped approach road would guide the traveler past the mountain's northern flank and into Riverside. Then in 1925 friends of the Millers built a stone tower and bridge in their name. Designed by Arthur Benton, the tower bears the symbols of many countries and is dedicated, as Miller was, to world peace. Though changes in civic priorities through the years have left the mountain in an unforgivable state of disrepair, Mount Rubidoux still remains a fitting symbol for a man, a city, and an era.

In the same manner that Riverside growers boldly entered cooperative marketing, growers sought more scientific studies and research into pest and disease control, frost protection, and fruit preservation. On May 13, 1895, pioneer horticulturist John H. Reed organized the Riverside Horticultural Club. Responding to the killer frost of 1892, when half of the local orange crop was lost, club members began a series of experiments in orchard heating. These included burning straw and coal in the groves, and even running hot water in the ditches. Crude oil proved most effective. The era of the "smudge pot" (and air pollution) was born. Another disastrous freeze in 1913—the worst in history—swept Southern California, and the Riverside Sheet Metal Works sold over 140,000 orchard heaters.

Beginning in 1869 cottony cushion citrus scale presented a growing threat to citrus stock. Scientists and growers experimented with hydrocyanic gas released from clay pots beneath the infested trees, as well as with salt, sulphur, and lime sprays. It was not until 1889, when a researcher for the

Periodically, the Santa Ana River has gone on a rampage with its greatest floods occurring in 1862, 1916, and 1938. The 1916 flood wiped out the Santa Ana River bridge between Riverside and Rubidoux, halting all traffic to Los Angeles on the main highway route. The construction of Prado Dam at the entrance to Santa Ana Canyon, and other flood control projects along the river by the U.S. Corps of Army Engineers, is expected to control the unruly river in the future. Courtesy, Lorne Allmon

Department of Agriculture returned from Australia with the scale's natural parasite, the Vedalia (Ladybird) beetle, that the disease was brought under control. Riversiders became strong lobbyists for increasing government-sponsored agricultural research. In 1906 the regents of the University of California authorized the establishment of a Citrus Experiment Station at the base of Mount Rubidoux (now the Department of Agriculture's Salinity Lab). A two-story laboratory building was finished in 1912. Under Professor Ralph E. Smith, early research concentrated on citrus problems such as "mottle leaf" disease. Very quickly, however, under a program of expansion, the state began searching for a new and larger site for an Experiment Station and Graduate School of Tropical Agriculture. Intensive lobbying on the part of communities throughout Southern California made the possibility of relocating within Riverside seem remote. On December 14, 1914, a delegation of prominent Riversiders made a powerful presentation in San Francisco at a Regents' meeting. Soon after, Riverside had secured her new school. When the news reached the city the steam whistle at the electric plant blew steadily for fifteen min-

utes, while Frank Miller rang the bells of the Inn.

The new site consisted of nearly 500 acres of land near the base of Box Springs Mountain. The main buildings, designed by Lester Hibbard, shared elements of Mission and Renaissance styles, with tiled roofs and open connecting archways. Under director Herbert J. Webber, the formal dedication took place on March 27, 1918. The station would be the progenitor of Riverside's University of California campus.

From the courtyard between the buildings visi-

tors look out over a broad expanse of farmland— new varieties of citrus, field, and ornamental crops. Set aside by the state for agricultural research, Section 30 remains a sanctuary within encroaching urbanization. Here, ironically, the original vision of the jeweler has found its ultimate realization. Winding through the center, still an open ribbon of cool blue water, Matthew Gage's Canal serves its highest purpose. Aside from the occasional rumblings of farm machinery, Section 30 remains quiet.

VI Dixie in the Desert

Struggle on an Angry River

The Colorado was the meanest river in the United States. Logs thirty feet long bobbed and floated and disappeared, turning end over end. Sometimes the deep part of the channel would be on one side, sometimes on the other. Sand bars and islands would appear, and I am not talking about big June floods, although I helped fight some of the worst. I am talking now of the everyday Colorado before the dams.

Camiel Dekens, spoke above, in 1962, as he had always acted—with the gruff authority of a pioneer in the Palo Verde Valley. Over the years he faced the river at its angriest and knew its contentious ways. Even today, even after "reclamation," the Colorado retains its powerful option on places like the Palo Verde Valley—the option to destroy.

The lower Colorado emerges from a great chain of canyons—including the Grand—onto a vast expanse of desert. With the easy sinuosity of a snake it twists and turns its way to the delta at the Gulf of California. The region it traverses is unique in the United States—sharing the attributes of the Egyptian Nile Valley. Raw heat dances over a network of sloughs, swamps, and overflows. Nearby, the Yuman tribes played out their campaigns of pride and greed against each other. Here at the Palo Verde Valley the Halchido-

In 1857-1858 the U.S. Army Corps of Topographical Engineers under command of Lieutenant Joseph C. Ives set out to ascertain
whether the Colorado River could be navigated by steamboat. The U.S. Explorer, manufactured in New York in sections, was shipped
west via the Isthmus of Panama and reassem-
bled at the mouth of the river in the Gulf of
California. The expedition successfully reached
Mohave Indian territory north of Fort Yuma,
gathering considerable scientific information
on the region. The Ives expedition helped
pave the way for profitable river transportation that developed up to 1877 when the
Southern Pacific Railroad reached the Colorado River. Courtesy, Special Collections Department, Library of the University of
California, Riverside

mas lost the game and disappeared. Thereafter only the nomadic settlements of the southernmost Chemehuevis knew the valley. It remained a virtual no-man's-land, haunted by the lonely memories of the decimated tribe.

Gold would eventually open the river and bring the outside world to the valley. The California Gold Rush gave Anza's old Gila Trail new life as argonauts made for the diggings by way of the Southern territories. A fort and ferry at the Yuma crossing drew activity and created Arizona City (Yuma's first name). By the late 1850s George Johnson had begun shipping food and mining supplies from the gulf at Port Isabel to Yuma on his 104-foot riverboat, the sidewheeler *General Jesup*. As mining activity increased on the upper reaches of the river, and Mormon settlements approached its canyon walls, the federal government woke to the necessity for upriver exploration. Just how far, mused the War Department, could the cantankerous Colorado be successfully navigated?

Late in 1857, Army Corps of Engineers Lieutenant Joseph Christmas Ives received orders to explore the Colorado from the gulf and establish its limits of navigability. From Yuma Captain Johnson offered his services and the *General Jesup* for the expedition. The lieutenant, convinced that the exploration would launch his career, chose instead to design, build, and ship unassembled a little iron-hulled monstrosity, the *Explorer*.

Snubbed, Johnson outfitted his own expedition. On board the *General Jesup* was a crew of armed men, including the restless Paulino Weaver, vacationing from his rancho at San Gorgonio. On December 31, 1857, Johnson began his exploration of the upper reaches of the river. Johnson was among the few men familiar with the Colorado and the *Jesup* was a sturdy, proven craft. Dogged by increasing sandbars and the constant streamside search for fuel, Captain Johnson nevertheless made good time. Upon reaching the first rapids at

Pyramid Canyon, he decided he'd had enough and turned back. Paulino Weaver passed the Palo Verde Valley twice thereby, and something about the area must have stuck in his mind. Several years later he would return.

Meanwhile Lieutenant Ives departed Port Isabel with the overcrowded *Explorer*. Ives brought with him the accomplished artist Baldwin Mollhausen, who cursed the *Explorer* as a "water-borne wheelbarrow." Indeed, the boat proved uncomfortable, noisy, and unmaneuverable. Lieutenant Ives urged his unhappy crew forward despite the *Explorer's* unquenchable desire to ground on sandbars.

On January 30, the *General Jesup* steamed into view, heading downstream for home. Despite this moderate deflation, Ives pushed harder and actually did manage to ascend farther than Captain Johnson, though his discovery of the head of navigation was somewhat abrupt. It was a submerged rock, which the *Explorer* struck with such force that its boiler and wheelhouse were knocked loose from the hull. Only then did the shaken lieutenant decide to return.

In 1862 Paulino Weaver discovered gold in the placers at La Paz on the Arizona side of the Palo Verde Valley. The resulting rush was responsible for the construction of the first substantial building in the valley. Freighters on the Bradshaw Road built a station at the end of their trail. The building, known as the Old Adobe, was a landmark in ruins for many years. Under Captain Johnson's patronage the port city of Ehrenberg sprang up near La Paz, where his steamboats be-

Travel across the Colorado River between Arizona and California was carried out by the Blythe ferry in the early pioneer days of the Palo Verde Valley. It wasn't until 1928 that a toll bridge was built across the river. Photograph at far left is courtesy Lorne Allmon. Photograph below is courtesy Riverside Municipal Museum

gan to serve the network of diggings, mills, and boom towns that marked the opening of the Southwest mining frontier. Founded in 1866, Ehrenberg served as the main upriver port. Its ragged clusters of adobe huts and arrowweed fences still sported the cosmopolitan veneer of a gold-rush metropolis.

Though the mining excitement around Ehrenberg inevitably faded, steamboats continued to tie up regularly with supplies and passengers. One passenger, an engineer named Oliver Calloway, had little interest in gold. Calloway had recently completed a road from San Diego to Yuma, and was laying out the range and section lines of the land along the river's banks. During this time he saw the Palo Verde Valley, took note of its rich soil, and the unique way the valley actually sloped down *away* from the river. For Calloway all this meant simple gravity irrigation, settlement, and a potential fortune for the developer.

Calloway returned to San Francisco where he sought capital for his project. He found it in Thomas Henry Blythe. Blythe had traveled here from England twice, at least once under an assumed name. His background would always remain shrouded in mystery. He arrived in San Francisco, like so many other fortune seekers, in 1849. He turned a small loan into a fortune in commercial city frontage. By the 1870s he had become a millionaire. Tall, portly, and always immaculately dressed, Blythe was known to indulge himself in food, society, and women. He bred birds, cats, and dogs—it is said he kept an entire chicken ranch on the roof of his San Francisco mansion. Blythe had invested in a mine called the Blue Jacket, near the Colorado, and had established, in partnership with Mexican General Guillermo Andrade, an agricultural colony on the Colorado delta at Lerdo. On the basis of Calloway's maps and his own knowledge of the region, the self-assured investor began to pour thousands of dollars into the Palo Verde project.

Blythe and Calloway quickly filed on and received 40,000 acres of government land in the Palo Verde Valley. Designated Swamp Land Dis-

trict 310, the property extended from present De Frain Boulevard eastward to the curving Colorado River. Supplies and equipment were shipped around the Baja Peninsula, then brought upriver by steamboat to 310 Landing, where Calloway and project manager George Irish established "Blythe City." It is believed that Blythe envisioned a grand canal to water Southern-style plantations growing sugar cane, cotton, and tobacco. When Blythe visited in 1875, the "city" consisted of several tule huts and a few acres of cleared land. Neither Blythe nor Calloway would live to see the City of Blythe.

Things had improved very little five years later. Calloway and Irish were nearing completion of a temporary canal, the headworks blasted from rock outcroppings near Black Point. The canal irrigated a forty-acre experimental farm. "Colorado Colony" land was available for $8 per acre. Belatedly, Calloway turned his attention to the potential dangers from a flooding river. Utilizing Chemehuevi labor at fifty cents a day the engineer began building up levees along its bank. There, on March 28, during an argument with an Indian named "Up and Up," he was stabbed to death by another, known only as "Big Bill."

Calloway was buried in a coffin fashioned from the mahogany fittings of an abandoned Ehrenberg bar. While the army restored order among the Chemehuevi, Irish went to Riverside for a new engineer. He found the ubiquitous C.C. Miller, who was more than willing to leave the tedium of welcoming guests at the Glenwood Hotel. In 1882 Blythe again paid a visit to the project. Pleased with what he saw, Blythe returned to San Francisco, where the following year he, too, abruptly fell dead—of what was described as a "fainting fit."

The high-flown dreams of the mysterious entrepreneur quickly descended into a morass of litigation. While claimants argued in court over their share in the Blythe estate, the property itself sank back into wilderness. Blythe's Mexican empire at Lerdo was lost to Andrade by default. Miller and Irish, despairing that the project in the Palo Verde

Cotton farming began in the Palo Verde Valley about 1910 and soon emerged as the region's major crop. One of the early cotton gins in Blythe, located on Chanslorway between Eucalyptus and Commercial streets, appears in this photograph taken about 1920. Courtesy, Palo Verde Valley Historical Society

Valley would ever be completed, sold all the equipment they could and moved on. The sturdy redwood headgates at Black Point began to break apart under the desert sun and each spring the river swept playfully wherever it chose.

It took eleven years of litigation for the courts to settle on an heir for Thomas Blythe. She was Florence Blythe, an illegitimate daughter ten years old at the time of his death. She inherited very little. By 1894, the Blythe property in the valley was under lease to a rancher named Benton who held an option to buy the property at $4 an acre. South of the estate there were scattered homesteads. At the settlement of Palo Verde, near the southernmost end of the valley, homesteaders had established a post office and a one-room school built of willow poles, arrowweed, and mud, with burlap sacks for its windows and door. Across the river, Ehrenberg was almost a ghost town, though a few saloons still welcomed the occasional prospector. Blythe and the valley remained seventy

miles from the nearest railroad.

In 1904 the Bureau of Reclamation announced plans for the construction of a dam across the Colorado at Laguna, a few miles above Yuma. The era of the steamboat was nearing its end. That same year Frank Murphy, a semi-retired cattleman and grading contractor, saw Blythe for the first time. Benton was giving up his option on the estate and Murphy was considering taking it up under the same terms. Aging and burdened with a large belly, nevertheless Murphy and his friend Ed Williams, another cattleman, spent three days surveying the property, afterwards returning to Los Angeles to seek potential partners. He found them in Oxnard's Hobson brothers, A.L. and John, and in Thomas and Charles Donlan.

Together they formed the Palo Verde Land and Water Company, and planned to rebuild the irrigation system, sell farm plots, and raise cattle on the unsold remainder. Murphy, as a working vice president, established headquarters at the old adobe Ranch House. Under his direction the headgates and canal were deepened, and other workmen began the arduous task of clearing and leveling the land with "Fresno scrapers," the well known and often cursed bulldozer of its day. Prospective settlers arrived daily from Glamis by stage. One of them, Judge Walsh, described the sales pitch he received in 1908:

We were served with a good meal, hearing meanwhile a lot of booster talk for the valley. We were then taken to the Blythe townsite and vicinity. We heard all about the possibilities, the wonderful place Blythe was destined to become. We then returned to the Ranch House for supper, more sales talk and our night's lodging.

Tall, lanky, and strong, Floyd Brown came to Blythe with his wife, Jessie, during its early years while on a prospecting trip. Blythe would become his life's work. The fledgling community hungered for almost everything and, at one time or another, Floyd Brown sought to provide it. His contributions to early Blythe would nearly equal his energy. Brown supervised the reconstruction of the headworks and canal system. His restlessness soon took him into other businesses, including cutting and hauling lumber for the growing settlement. In 1909 he, Jessie, and Camiel Dekens, with a few mules, cleared a road northward to Blythe Junction (later Rice), where the Santa Fe's new Parker Cutoff would soon pass. He and Dekens later strung wire along the road, creating a unique telephone "company" that consisted of three phones—one at his restaurant at Blythe Junction,

one at his barley mill in town, and the third traveling with Dekens' freight team. As a mule-skinner for both Brown and Murphy, Dekens hauled freight over the desert trails eastward to Glamis as well as northward to the Junction. Starting with sixteen mules and two wagons, by 1914 he had mastered the new Best and Holt caterpillars capable of pulling thirty tons of freight.

Brown built a restaurant and hotel at the Junction, Jessie managing. With the arrival of the railroad a rowdy frontier city sprang up around it. "Wingy" Smith, or "Smitty," a one-armed ex-carpenter, opened a saloon and gambling house in a tent with a platform floor. Nearby, another gambler named "Goldie" Williams began operations. Soon the tents of women for hire clustered around the edges of the settlement. The little "Shoe Hill" cemetery nearby did a steady business.

The freewheeling nature of the Junction, its gambling, liquor, and prostitution, was made possible by its isolated location. When deputies from San Bernardino County showed up, citizens insisted it was part of Riverside County. When

Above: *Although there were automobiles on the streets of Blythe when this photograph was taken in 1914, cotton, grain, and hay were still being hauled by mule team to Blythe Junction, and Santa Fe was resisting building a spur line across the forty-two miles between the two points. The following year the farmers of Palo Verde Valley raised a $100,000 subsidy to get the line built. Courtesy, Palo Verde Valley Historical Society*

Facing page: *Palo Verde Valley pioneer Camiel Dekens hauled freight with a mule team between desert towns and from Blythe to Blythe Junction during the early days of development in the valley. His team is shown here in about 1914 outside the Kim Yuen Chinese restaurant in Blythe, located at Main and Hobsonway. Courtesy, Palo Verde Valley Historical Society*

Above: *Conditions were primitive for the early settlers of Palo Verde Valley, but several generations of school children attended the Arrowweed Schoolhouse, made out of arrowweed, poles, and sticks, and daubed with mud. The schoolhouse, shown here about 1906, was located 100 yards east of the Palo Verde Lagoon. Seated fourth from the left in the picture is Edward Hyatt, who was Riverside County superintendent of schools and later California state superintendent of public instruction. Courtesy, Palo Verde Valley Historical Society*

Left: *A stub railway line with a slow-moving tiny steam train inter-connected Riverside and San Bernardino from 1888 to 1892. Known as the California Motor Road, the line was bought out by Southern Pacific as its entryway to the city. Courtesy, Bordwell Collection, Riverside Municipal Museum*

Riverside authorities responded in turn, citizens insisted the reverse. Joint efforts brought an army of lawmen to Blythe Junction on several occasions. One night they swept the town, arresting everyone except the station master. Dekens remembered joining the motley crew in Jessie Brown's basement. Apparently even the incarceration of the whole town made little difference:

They kept the party in the basement for forty-eight hours and then shipped most of them to Riverside. The girls were fined and told to get out and stay out. Jessie and the gamblers and bootleggers were fined, too, but they returned immediately. In the baggage car of the train on which they returned, they had 36 cases of whiskey and 30 barrels of beer.

Settlement in the valley itself was slow but steady. The Census of 1910 set the population at 600. Company land sold for around $70 an acre, though homesteaders to the south were asked to pay $25 per acre for water rights alone—and for all of their acreage at once, no matter how little had been cleared. Accusations arose regularly between company settler and homesteader over stolen cattle. But the conflict did not yet slow development. In 1911, 400 acres were planted in a new crop—cotton—and a growers' association was formed. The association soon had its own cotton gin. In town, the first church, the Methodist Episcopal, offered services out of the new schoolhouse on North Broadway. That year the *Palo Verde Valley Herald* made its first appearance on January 13. Advertisements included the Palo Verde Valley Bank, the Blythe Hotel, and Frank Brown's unique Blythe Auto and Telephone Company.

Were it not for the river, the valley might have amicably settled its differences. After several mass meetings, homesteaders and company settlers were able to form a mutual water company. Ed Williams, Frank Murphy's friend, had early on lost his arm to a mowing machine. Despite this handicap, he was chosen first president of the wa-

ter company, and later headed both the Palo Verde Joint Fence District and the Palo Verde Drainage District. But the river, too, demanded to be heard. Williams estimated that during 1909 and 1910 alone there were six levee breaks. The riverbed, choked with silt, was rising as fast as the levees.

The greatest break up to that time came in 1912. That spring the rampaging river burst through above the town, chewing out a 450-foot opening. Water raced everywhere, filling the old sloughs and spreading out over farmland. Blythe itself became a small island in a giant, murky sea. While volunteers labored without rest in 110-degree heat for a month to close the break, farmers and their families shared the mesa with displaced rattlesnakes and scorpions. The refugees made drinking water by settling the silted floodwater in rows of pans. Supplies, when they could be had, were rowed across the valley from Blythe.

The levee break was bridged by a pile trestle and a long brush mat was dropped against the trestle's riverward side. The first attempt failed and washed a section of trestle away, but the second held. As floodwaters slowly receded, the weary settlers began to rebuild. Floyd Brown invented and installed a series of steel tripods and cables that kept snags and debris away from the levees during high water. The valley's spirit soared when the Santa Fe Railroad accepted a $100,000 subsidy from farmers to build a spur forty-two miles into the Palo Verde Valley. Begun in September 1915 under the California Southern subsidiary, the track was not completed until over a year later. In anticipation, the little town voted to become a city on June 27, 1916. Vital statistics: area—832 acres; population—around 600; budget—$4,000. Soon after, on August 8, 1916, the first steam train reached Blythe. The isolation of the valley had finally been broken.

The railroad brought more than increased commerce, it brought competition as well. Blythe expected to be the railroad's terminus in the valley. A few years later a group of California Southern executives calling themselves the Blythe Construc-

Top: *Railroad crews lay track under a hot desert sun in 1916 for the California Southern Railroad from Blythe Junction on the Parker cutoff to Blythe in the Palo Verde Valley. The trees in the background indicate the photograph was taken near Chanslorway in Blythe. Courtesy, Palo Verde Valley Historical Society*

Center: *In 1920 the Santa Fe Railroad reached its terminus at Ripley, a well-planned community with a town plaza and a new $100,000 hotel. The town never recovered from the disastrous flood of 1922 when the Colorado River overflowed banks and levees and covered the lower half of the Palo Verde Valley. Settlers of the Palo Verde Valley often contended with floods, but the 1922 flood is remembered as the worst disaster in the valley's history. Courtesy, Palo Verde Valley Historical Society*

Bottom: *The days of the Blythe-Ehrenberg ferry between California and Arizona appeared to be over when Floyd Brown built a toll bridge across the Colorado River. Open for four months, the bridge collapsed in the flood of June 1928. It was soon rebuilt as a government project involving both states and is today on the route of U.S. Interstate Highway 10. Courtesy, Palo Verde Valley Historical Society*

tion Company announced plans to build a substantial new town south of the Blythe estate and extend the rails to the center of the valley. This new townsite, named Ripley for an ex-Santa Fe president, was destined to become the trading center for the whole valley.

While Blythe bristled, the homesteaders cheered. Work began in 1920 on the elegant two-story Ripley Hotel. Streets and gutters, a first-rate water system, and even a $70,000 power plant were installed. A school and two cotton gins promised complete independence from Blythe. Residents and developers talked seriously about the relocation of the east-west highway, and the installation of a new ferry service far south of Blythe and Floyd Brown's Ferry. By 1922 citizens of Blythe could watch as trains rumbled past toward a town with 100 homes, fifteen stores and business houses, a lumberyard, hotel, school, railroad station, garages, as well as efficient water and lights.

But on May 1, 1922, the muddy Colorado went on yet another rampage. The full force of the river's flood swept past the northern valley, facilitated, ironically, by Brown's tripod system. Once beyond the tripods the river broke loose with a vengeance, totally submerging the southern end of the valley. Ripley sank into ten feet of muddy water, and this time, the water stayed. Cleanup crews did not enter Ripley until September 1st.

Blythe shed few tears. Camiel Dekens believed he spoke for most Blythe residents when he said: "Even if there was nothing we could have done, a part of the story is that most of us from the north end thought and said among ourselves that they could fight their own flood. They didn't help us in 1912."

But continual battering by the river affected the entire valley. During the 1920s the Palo Verde Valley experienced an overall decline in population. Years of fighting the floods and each other had taken their toll. The Colorado seemed unbeatable. Settlers began to drift away. The City of Blythe and the Palo Verde Valley Irrigation District had exhausted their revenues and stood in default of large sums of money.

By 1930 only massive federal aid could revive the valley. Relief eventually did come. Reorganization under the Reconstruction Finance Corporation allowed the Irrigation District to continue operation. Tax-delinquent lands were sold to finance improvements. Most importantly, though, the inauguration of the Boulder Canyon Project Act on June 25, 1929, and the eventual completion of Hoover Dam would at last put a muzzle on the "meanest river in the United States."

By the mid-1960s Blythe had grown to a city of over 8,000 people. With a junior college and county and federal office buildings, the modern city thrives. It draws on the vast agricultural wealth of the valley, the recreation resources of the Colorado, and a healthy highway trade.

For Ripley, however, the future held no bright hopes. Opened and closed several times over the years, the elegant Ripley Hotel was eventually abandoned. Its fixtures were removed for back taxes. The building was finally bulldozed to complete the work vandals had begun. Vandals also stripped the generators at the power plant for the valuable copper.

Grady Setzler, pioneering Blythe newspaperman, provided the final, sardonic epitaph in 1967: "It is a little hard to steal a slightly used water storage tank, so the stand pipe is still standing. We understand the water works are well guarded by local residents. Nobody knows whatever became of the town's fireplugs."

By the 1970s Ripley had become a rural slum, one of the poorest communities in the United States. Lacking sewer and water facilities, residents, mostly black and Hispanic farm workers, often lived in squalor. If the water tower is still guarded, it is done only symbolically, for it has never worked since the flood. Community leaders point to their once beautiful schoolhouse, rebuilt in 1926 only to be closed by the Palo Verde Valley Unified School District in 1971 and later burned.

In the early 1970s a few old-timers still insisted that someone in Blythe deliberately dynamited the levees in 1922—out of civic jealousy. No matter. Rancher versus homesteader, town versus town—these were all-too-typical rivalries on the American frontier. Add to them the violence of a rampaging river, and the stakes grow very high indeed.

Blythe was still growing up in the 1930s when the city hall also doubled for a fire station. Courtesy, Lorne Allmon

VII Finding the Sun

Of Palms, Presidents, and Paradise

The greater Coachella Valley is the geographical heart of Riverside County. The pass at San Gorgonio serves as a window through which the semiarid environment of coastal Southern California looks out upon a genuine desert. Beyond the pass travelers sense a dimensional change—man, his settlements, his narrow roads shrink under a vastly enlarged sky, a landscape as broad and barren as the moon. Since time immemorial it has been a land to pass through, and a journey more often endured than enjoyed.

Pioneers apply themselves tentatively to environments, seeking first the most familiar climates and topographies. When they approach the desert they do so with trepidation. Small wonder, then, that the Coachella Valley knew delayed settlement. People came here to work the railroad or to cure a ravaged lung. But the sun, drawn so close, had much more to give, as those who stayed learned quickly. The desert is as shy as it is fragile. Those who stayed learned by trial and error. Theirs was a search full of pitfalls and despairing, but it succeeded. The pioneers of the Coachella Valley found that the environment bore as many blessings as it did burdens. From its reclamation of the lower valley, to the celebration of the upper valley, this desert has given abundantly.

The Southern Pacific Railroad first discovered one dimension of the hidden wealth of the Coachella Valley. After surmounting the San Gorgonio Pass in 1875, the railroad skirted the east rim of

Since the 1940s the city of Indio has celebrated the leadership of the Coachella Valley in date-growing with its annual county fair and National Date Festival. Thousands of visitors tour exhibits, watch camel races, and attend the nightly performance of the Arabian Nights Pageant where they may glimpse Queen Scheherazade and her court. Courtesy, Riverside Press-Enterprise Company

the Salton Sink, curving southward toward Yuma and the Colorado. It was a land of barren slopes, blowing sand, and little water. Crews established stations (little more than water tanks and sidings) at Cabazon, Seven Palms, Indian Wells, Walters, and Woodspur, where a siding reached into the mesquite and Indian laborers gathered wood for sale.

At Indian Wells the railroad decreed a division point, installing a wooden roundhouse, tanks, and shops. Nearby, a twelve-room dormitory housed engineers and firemen, and a twenty-four-hour dining hall dubbed "The T-Bone" fed passengers and crews. Later the railroad would sponsor a hotel and hospital here, where the desert's first desperate health seekers gathered. But early conditions at Indian Wells were primitive. Blowing sand clogged the rail switches and chewed through telephone poles. In the summer workmen carried their bedrolls outside, braving rattlesnakes for the cooler evening air. Wagons hauled water from a spring at Twelve Apostle Palms, three miles away. By day the summer sun grew so intense it was said to ignite locomotive coal where it lay heaped in storage, and Indians alone were willing to handle the volatile material.

Trains began service from Indian Wells to Los Angeles on May 29, 1876, Mondays, Wednesdays, and Fridays. As work progressed the rails reached Yuma, and elaborate logistics were developed to keep the thirsty locomotives supplied with water. Trains out of Indian Wells had to pull at least five water cars to tide them over until they reached the Colorado. Emergency water cars were set out on sidings along the way. Meanwhile the railroad company continued to search for ways to expand their water supply. Under contract to the Southern Pacific, the Rose Well Drilling Company began exploratory drilling along the route in 1880. They sank shafts at Indian Wells, Woodspur, and Thermal, with mixed results. At Walters, however, they struck "blue gold" at 1,500 feet—an artesian well with a strong flow. There the railroad built a trestle-and-pipe system capable of filling ten cars at one time by artesian pressure alone.

Nearby, at Salton, the New Liverpool Salt Works began the profitable extraction of surface salt from Lake Cahuilla's dry bed. The company built a spur from the railroad and operated two "donkey" engines to haul salt cars from the sink. At times their dormitories housed upwards of 1,800 men, mostly Indian laborers. For the next twenty years, however, the railroad continued to be the main reason for anyone to brave the valley's heat.

Burly and bewhiskered, A.C. Tingman first came to Indian Wells as a telegrapher and station agent in 1883. With his wife he opened a store near the depot and served as postmaster. In 1894, the same year the railroad discovered its first well, Tingman laid out the townsite for Indio (Spanish for Indian) on his 160-acre claim. There he dug a well and ran a store and livery—the nucleus of early Indio. Throughout the 1890s, homesteaders under the Desert Land Act expanded Indio's settled area, putting down wells and experimenting with new crops such as cantaloupes and onions. In 1897 the Reverend Sylvester Mann began holding Protestant services in the new Indio School District's tent facility. Indio's first child, Cinderella, was born to the Courtney family in 1898, and David Elgin followed a year later, born on his family's homestead west of town. An adobe school was completed near the corner of present-day Fargo and Bliss, and the railroad donated a bell. Settlement expanded along the line. Further east, at Kokell (soon to be Thermal) George Keith opened his general store. Both Thermal and Walters had post offices.

In 1901 J.L. Rector laid out a townsite near Woodspur. At a community meeting the town christened itself "Coachella," a name probably formed from the Spanish "Conchilla," after the proliferation of seashells around the lake's old beaches, and Cahuilla. The Coachella Valley Land and Water Company developed a cantaloupe farm, built an ice house, and organized a cantaloupe growers' association.

That year, 1901, residents' pride in their sub-zero location received nationwide attention when

Randolph Freeman's *Coachella Valley Submarine* began publication in Indio. Early on, pioneers adopted novel means to deal with the strange land. Railroad employees are credited with the development of another "submarine," tin-roofed houses designed to run water continually from the roof and down the sides, creating an evaporative cooling effect.

One of the most pressing problems for farmers was that of salts in the soil. George Leach had come with his parents to the short-lived town of Arabia in 1903. The Leach homestead had burned twice by 1923, and he knew firsthand the rough conditions farmers faced. "You didn't dare let the land lay idle. . . . The area was always salty if you didn't keep farming it, and farmers had to learn how to farm it, and keep farming it, which in effect was leaching the salts down."

In 1903 R. Holtby Myers began development of yet another townsite near the Walters station, where the Caravansary Hotel and Mission

For more than a century, miners have roamed the desert regions of Riverside County seeking gold and other precious ores. This photograph was taken in 1909 of the Iron Chief Mine, a gold mine at Eagle Mountain on the Mojave Desert. The real lode in this area was iron, but it wasn't exploited until Kaiser Steel Company established its mining operations at Eagle Mountain in 1948. Courtesy, Riverside Press-Enterprise Company

Store, with its arched false front, drew prospectors and visitors. That year Myers dubbed the town "Mecca." Myers also helped to promote the development of a crop that would become synonymous with the area: dates. Early on, dates had been tried experimentally, receiving even the interest of Collis P. Huntington of the Southern Pacific, but they didn't fare well. In 1903 Myers sponsored

Bernard Johnson's pioneering trip to Algeria to obtain offshoots of the Deglet Noor variety. That September, Johnson planted them on his own land, near present-day National Avenue and Johnson Street, where they did well. He would return to Algeria in 1908, 1912, and, under the sponsorship of the valley's new Date Growers Association, subsequent trips would net well over 10,000 additional offshoots.

Johnson's activity received a powerful assist from Walter T. Swingle, a scientist for the Department of Agriculture. Swingle was familiar with date culture from his studies in French North Africa. He, too, had planted Algerian offshoots in Arizona in 1900. A year after Johnson's original trip, Swingle convinced the USDA to open a Date Experiment Station in the Coachella Valley. Recognizing Johnson's skill, Swingle leased land nearby, and hired him to care for the gardens. Over the years the station would change sites and expand until, by the 1940s, it consisted of thirty acres on Clinton Street in Indio. Under directors like W.W. Aldrich, Walter Reuther, J.R. Furr, and John Carpenter, the station broadened its research role to include guayule (a hoped-for rubber source) during World War II, and citrus. Scientists provided practical advice to growers on all aspects of cultivation—varieties, irrigation, disease control. The center became an international resource.

With the development of the date and citrus industries, growth in the "submarine" valley appeared assured. But there was a limit to the amount of groundwater available to growers. Beyond the turn of the century, the water table continued to fall as more land came under cultivation. Artesian wells failed. The first hydraulic pump was installed at Indio in 1900, and more and more farmers were resorting to gasoline and electric pumps to draw water. Grower Ben T. Laflin recalled the crisis of the early years of the twentieth century:

We knew we had to do something....There was obviously not enough well water to develop the valley. Imperial Valley had been irrigating from the Colorado River with a canal through Mexico. They were talking about a new high line canal from above Yuma through the sandhills. Folks up here thought that we should bring a canal and deliver water here by gravity.

But early hopes of extending the Imperial Valley system north to the Coachella Valley were dashed by the disastrous floods of 1905, when the whole Salton Sink, including the Coachella Valley, nearly returned to sea bottom. In 1901, under George Chaffey's supervision, the California Development Company diverted water from the river in Mexico and, utilizing the old Alamo overflow channel, delivered it to the Imperial Valley. Colorado River silt soon clogged the channels and lessened the flow. Chaffey must have seen the writing on the wall, for he left the company soon after. Succeeding engineers like C.R. Rockwood carelessly made new cuts in the riverbank to increase flow. Annual floodwaters enlarged the cuts until, in 1905, the entire Colorado River had broken away from the gulf and back into the Salton Sink. Steamboats were left high and dry, while prehistoric Lake Cahuilla was reborn as the Salton Sea. For two years the river flowed unimpeded into the sink. Water lapped at the outskirts of Mecca and threatened to rise even further. The New Liverpool Salt Works disappeared forever under thirty feet of water, along with sixty miles of SP mainline. Only with the full assistance of the railroad were engineers able to close the breach on February 11, 1907.

And so things drifted, the valley's future always uncertain. Indio, Coachella, Thermal, and Mecca adapted themselves to the era of the automobile and electricity. In 1908, the first of three Los Angeles-to-Phoenix auto races passed through the valley, making Barney Oldfield a popular local hero. In 1911, C.P. Rodgers piloted his Wright Brothers biplane over the valley as part of a historic first transcontinental flight. Three years later transmission lines from the Southern Sierras Power Company reached the valley. Otho Moore and E.C. Gillette began offering outdoor picture shows

The desert sands of the Coachella Valley yielded to a prosperous new form of agriculture in 1907 when the U.S. Department of Agriculture established an experimental date garden first in Mecca and later in Indio. The government began experimenting with growing date palms in the southwest in the 1890s by importing offshoots of date palms from the Middle East. The first experimental date palms were planted at the University of California's agricultural experiment station in Pomona. In 1907 this twelve-year-old Nahklet al Pasha date palm variety was moved from Pomona to the Mecca date farm. The date industry was well underway when the Coachella Valley Date Growers Association was organized in 1913. Courtesy, California Museum of Photography, University of California, Riverside

on summer nights.

Meanwhile, farmers reached out farther and dug down deeper for water. In 1917 only 5,552 acres of land were being farmed (compared to over 70,000 in the 1960s). The Coachella Valley had temporarily reached the limits of its growth.

In March of that year, newspapers announced the unveiling of a grand scheme to tap the White-water River and other local sources of water for transport to the suffering Imperial Valley. Colonel William Holabird of El Centro headed the group of Los Angeles and San Diego investors. He planned to deliver enough water by canal and pipeline to irrigate 40,000 acres in the Imperial Valley, leaving only half that amount for Coachella. Growers in the valley were frightened and outraged. Chester Sparey, valley activist, charged that the company was proposing to "sell us our {own} water to save our bacons."

The threat posed by Holabird's impractical scheme served as a catalyst to inspire valley growers. Thomas C. Yager, a lawyer practicing in Coachella, called for a series of meetings to discuss the threat. At his urging, and with Sparey's and Dr. S.S. Jennings' approval, citizens organized the Coachella Valley County Water District to protect their water sources and seek, as well, the development of new supplies.

Under its first engineer, A.L. Sonderegger, the district embarked immediately on groundwater conservation measures. The district also directed Tom Yager to begin agitating at the federal level for the construction of a canal to bring water to both the Imperial and Coachella valleys. Other regional powers and agricultural interests joined with the Coachella District in moving the government toward a comprehensive Colorado River control package, including the construction of a high dam in the canyons for flood control and hydroelectric power, as well as the canal. Yager's lobbying efforts were strongly supported on the home front. One district meeting authorized "purchase of one case of dates from Truman Gridley to be sent to Thomas C. Yager for advertising the Valley among Senators and Congressmen." After ten long years, valley perseverance did indeed bear fruit. On December 21, 1928, President Hoover signed the Boulder Canyon Project Act, allocating $165 million for a dam and an All-American canal.

Today the Coachella Valley prospers. Grapes, citrus, dates, and cotton flourish. The Coachella Valley County Water District operates a modern piped delivery system, computer-monitored, and providing both irrigation and domestic water. In cooperation with the U.S. Salinity Lab, farmers have overcome the soil-salts problem with scientific leaching procedures and careful drainage. An acre of land can produce upwards of $2,000 in crops. A commercial and government center, Indio proudly hosts the county's fair—appropriately called the National Date Festival. The Salton Sea supports lively recreation and, in this energy-conscious age, the valley has become an experimental center for the application of solar and wind power.

The past gives way to the future. In 1982 director John Carpenter oversaw the closing of the Date Experiment Station in Indio, brought on by funding cuts and the changing nature of the date industry. More and more date gardens fall into the hands of management firms that rely less than the small farmer on government assistance. Carpenter could look back with pride on his twenty-eight years with the station. The development of disease-resistant rootstock for citrus, as well as tissue cloning for dates, are milestones that will assure the station's place in agricultural research history.

The words of Leland Yost, longtime grower and Coachella Valley school board trustee, were meant for early pioneers, but apply as well to men like Carpenter who have continued to represent the

Above: *A lofty date palm towers against the Coachella Valley sky. Photo by Darleen DeMason*

Facing page: *The once barren wastes of the Coachella Valley—a part of the great Colorado Desert—have been the center of America's date industry for almost three-quarters of a century. One of the many prosperous date "gardens" is Laflin's Date Gardens at Indio. In the foreground is Professor Darleen DeMason, who specializes in date research at the University of California, Riverside. Photo by Andrew Torres*

"submarine" valley's highest standards:

They were men of character, and many characters.
They possessed strong minds, whether prospectors
or agriculturalists...filled with curiosity, inquiry,
and fascination with the challenges.

The lower Coachella Valley is an anomaly—
only Death Valley approximates such unusual
geographical characteristics within the United
States. Curiously, like the Dutch, who, though under reversed circumstances, have also reclaimed sea
floors, the sub-sea level pioneers of the Coachella
were distinguished by their thrift and their single-
minded determination to make the valley grow.
The settlement of the upper valley was of a completely different nature, as though the invisible
line that on the map marks sea level also divides
settlement patterns and lifestyles.

The upper Coachella Valley lies in the arms of
the San Jacinto, Santa Rosa, and Little San Bernardino Mountains. It is the eastern foot of the
San Gorgonio Pass, where two climates meet and
wind is a frequent companion. Nestled against the
shoulder of Mount San Jacinto are a series of desert "coves" protected somewhat from the violent
blows of the pass. Here, along the alluvial slopes a
network of springs rise up, marked by stands of
native palms. Vast wealth has come to settle
here—dependent not on the desert's reclamation,
but rather on its—and the sun's—very celebration.

John Guthrie McCallum was a successful San
Francisco lawyer during the flush times of that
city's early growth. An influential Republican, he
had participated in the framing of the state constitution in 1879 and had represented consumer interests against the railroad monopoly. But by the
dawn of the 1880s McCallum's son, John, had
contracted tuberculosis. The successful lawyer, secure in his middle age, abandoned San Francisco
in search of the drier air that might save his son.

McCallum first brought John to San Bernardino, where he worked as Indian agent and tended to his son. But the air in San Bernardino was

only semiarid and after two years the boy's doctor
suggested an even drier locale. Guided by an Indian friend, McCallum made the difficult journey to
the palm springs at the Agua Caliente Reservation of the Cahuilla. He stood before the towering
protective escarpment of Mount San Jacinto and
dipped into the acrid mineral springs that gave
the region its name. Few places knew drier, clean-
er air. Brought to the isolated site by a reservation
Indian, in 1884 he assumed the claims of a few
transient ranchers and began to build a house out
of the ruins of an old adobe.

McCallum devoted all of his time and income
to developing the magical location. Walled away
from the rest of the world by wind and drifting
sand, he set about with his Cahuilla employees to

make his "Palm Valley" more habitable for settlers. From the Southern Pacific he and a few partners acquired more property nearby. He would enlarge and tap the water from Tahquitz Canyon. He would build a stone canal from the Whitewater River, sixteen miles away, and set out fruit trees.

McCallum's first neighbors were Dr. and Mrs. Welwood Murray. "Tall, eccentric and colorful," Dr. Murray built a hotel and a sanitorium accommodating twenty-six guests in 1886 and called it "Palm Springs." Around the hotel he planted a grove of ornamental trees. From the railroad station, huddled in the windswept dunes near Seven Palms (later called Garnet), guests began to trickle in, lured by the desert and the hope of greater health. Dr. Murray would eventually entertain

Above: *In 1886 Dr. Wellwood Murray opened his Palm Springs Hotel and sanitarium and gave Palm Springs its name. His cottages held twenty-six guests, who in the community's early days were mostly those recuperating from lung diseases. Photo by C.C. Pierce. Courtesy, Riverside Press-Enterprise Company*

such distinguished and intrepid guests as John Muir, and desert philosopher and publicist George Wharton James.

The boom of the 1880s brought accelerated interest in any land in Southern California. Inspired investors took up railroad land and began subdi-

vision. In the Palm Springs area a syndicate sponsored a major sale at Agua Caliente on November 1, 1887. Excursionists arriving on special trains were greeted by bands and speech makers trying feebly to drown the roar of the wind. Fifty thousand dollars in desert property changed hands that day. It was sun-struck city-booming at its Southern California best. One development, "The Garden of Eden," appeared and disappeared rather quickly. Another was the short-lived Agua Caliente. Yet another investment group, made up of parties from Riverside and San Francisco, and including editor L.M. Holt from the *Riverside Press and Horticulturist,* acquired an option on 2,000 acres. Soon after, on December 24, 1887, Holt published this broadside for the Palm Valley Land Company: "The new company proposes to plant the largest navel orange orchard in California near the new town {Palmdale}, a portion of the trees in this orchard having already been engaged. A railroad will be constructed through Palm Valley, a distance of seven miles to the Southern Pacific."

And, indeed, the unbelievable little railroad to nowhere was built. By late February 1888 work crews had begun grading the roadbed from Seven Palms. Another irrigation ditch snaked away

from the undependable Whitewater River. H.W. Bordwell arrived from Michigan to assume command, bringing with him a railroad car full of possessions, including a prefabricated house. A narrow-gauge line with a "wye" at each end was completed in June. Rolling stock consisted of three flatcars, two bright yellow trolley cars purchased from the San Francisco Street Railway Company, and an aggressive little engine dubbed *Cabazon.* The train ran from July through September 1888, and carried very little. The two carloads of orange trees hailed by Mr. Holt's newspaper did find their way to the siding at Seven Palms, but only half were still alive. Bordwell planted them, but with an insufficient supply of water from the ditch, the rest soon died. By 1892, the entire project had been abandoned. An ex-employee salvaged the *Cabazon* and the flatcars for another development near Bakersfield. The passenger cars were pushed onto their sides. They were eventually torched by surveyors who found them obstructing their line of sight. Finally, in 1916, a flood buried their metal frames and wheels in the sand.

Through the 1880s, McCallum's "Palm Valley" grew steadily. Around the McCallum Ranch, lemon, orange, grapefruit, and apricot trees matured,

Above: *Palm Springs Desert Museum, occupying 75,000 square feet, is Riverside County's largest and most luxurious museum and a home for art, the natural sciences, and the performing arts. Founded in 1932, the museum moved into these new quarters in January 1976. Funds totalling eight million dollars were raised by the community for the building, which was designed by E. Steward Williams and built by Williams, Clark, and Williams of Palm Springs. Courtesy, Palm Springs Desert Museum*

Left: *Palm Springs has from its beginnings been known as an art-conscious community. Since the new Palm Springs Desert Museum opened, it has become increasingly internationally famous as a serious arbiter in the arts. Among its finest acquisitions in the Frank Sinatra Sculpture Court are Henry Moore's "Torso of Woman" and "Reclining Figure." Courtesy, Palm Springs Desert Museum*

Facing page: *Even as late as the 1920s there was nothing fancy about Palm Springs. The desert community, which got its start in the 1890s, still served principally as a small health resort for tuberculosis victims, recluses, and the few who had discovered the joys of desert living. The old Hotel La-Palma (center of the photo) was a predecessor of the plush hostelries that would arise after the discovery of the resort by Hollywood celebrities in the 1920s. Courtesy, Riverside Press-Enterprise Company*

as well as field crops like alfalfa. Dr. Murray enlarged his grove to over twenty different varieties of plants and trees. More and more guests arrived at the hotel, greeted by the tall Scot with his Van Dyck beard and skullcap. But in 1894 drought struck the region. Season after season passed without rain, and more and more crops and trees were abandoned to the sun. McCallum seemed to wither away with his land. In 1897, he died. He had outlived his son, John, by eight years and founded what was to become a remarkable town.

Dr. Murray and his wife watched their business drift away. The old man worried most over his grove of trees. As water grew scarce, the Scotsman argued with the Indians over its allocation. Through ten long years of drought, Dr. Murray struggled to keep his garden alive. The struggle would embitter him. It has often been said that

the indomitable doctor watered his trees with his own tears.

It was a cranky, inhospitable shell of a hotel keeper that greeted Nellie Coffman at his door one windy October evening in 1908. She had knocked, only to have the door slammed in her face. She knocked again.

Soon the door was opened again and there stood a tall, gaunt elderly man about eighty years old, dressed in a long, frock coat, his head surmounted by a skull cap. With a decided Scot accent, he

said, "What do you want?" We humbly told him we wanted accommodations for the night, and we were grudgingly allowed to enter. After a supper of the most meager fare, we were shown to rooms colder than Greenland's icy mountains.

Nellie Coffman, wife of a successful doctor, was in search of a cure for a persistent respiratory affliction. The Palm Springs that she woke to the following day was hardly a town at all. Aside from Dr. Murray's hotel, there was D.M. Blanchard's Feed and Grocery Store, which served as the Post

Above: *The Western White House for President Dwight D. Eisenhower and his wife, Mamie, during the early 1950s was Palm Springs. Here the President could play golf on some of the finest courses in the United States, enjoy privacy on the estates of friends, and find solace in the warm desert sun. Courtesy, Riverside Press-Enterprise Company*

Left: *The Colorado Desert's most unique building is Cabot Yerxa's old Indian pueblo in Desert Hot Springs, formerly the home and art studio of the community's founder and now a museum. Cabot Yerxa, a miner in the Yukon Gold Rush of 1898, first visited the oasis of Desert Hot Springs in 1913, where he homesteaded and dug a well that struck a hot mineral spring. He left in 1914 to join up for World War I and didn't return to the area until 1932, bringing with him developer L.W. Coffee. Coffee formed a land syndicate, built a bathhouse, and offered one-acre lots. As the community developed, Yerxa hurled all of his enthusiasm into constructing an enormous pueblo that soon attracted visitors from around the world. A genial eccentric, he is remembered as the founder of Desert Hot Springs, although it was Coffee that turned it into a popular resort. Courtesy, Lorne Allmon*

Office. On the northern corner of Murray's block was a small wood church and, beyond it a small schoolhouse. But Nellie Coffman had fallen in love with the desert. A year later, in 1909, she returned permanently. In a frame house across from Dr. Murray she founded the Desert Inn by nailing a small, hand-lettered sign to a post on the veranda.

Nellie Coffman singlehandedly brought style and tradition to desert vacationing. Her "boardinghouse," as she referred to it, served as the gathering place for a growing tourist trade. Under her watchful eye, the inn grew from a few rustic shacks accommodating lung patients to a famed hostelry for highbrow vacationers.

Palm Springs, too, began again to grow. Otto Adler opened his Red Front Store and Red Front Hotel. Carl Lykken and J.H. Bartlett took over and expanded Blanchard's merchandise mart opposite Bunker's Garage. Perpetual sunshine was an increasing draw. In the 1920s Hollywood movie makers began utilizing the desert setting as a backdrop for their flickering romances. More and more visitors began to buy acreage to build seasonal homes. Another exclusive hostelry, the Ingleside Inn, a large estate originally built by heirs to the Pierce-Arrow fortune, was destined to become the winter home for the likes of Howard Hughes, Clark Gable, Greta Garbo, and Samuel Goldwyn. By 1924, a paved road finally connected the village with the outside world (in this case, Banning). The Southern Sierras Power Company had begun to furnish electricity and the weekly *Desert Sun* would soon hit the streets.

In 1934 citizens of the village voted 442 to 211 to incorporate. Philip Boyd, chosen from the seven-member city council, served as the town's first mayor. Several years later, Theodore Zchokke, an employee of the Deep Well Ranch, began to lay out a small nature trail to provide visitors with more knowledge of the land around them. Though Zchokke's attempt failed, Carl Lykken rescued the idea, heading up a Desert Museum Committee in 1938. Not until 1947, when the museum was given an old army building, did it find a permanent home.

By the mid-1950s Palm Springs "Village" could, in winter, swell to a population of over 40,000. Stretching out along Highway 111, a series of related "cove" communities had developed, nestled in the interstices of the San Jacinto and Santa Rosa mountains, secure from the desert wind. Cathedral City was named for Colonel Washington's description, in 1852, of a canyon that resembled the ruins of a great cathedral. The city gained impetus by permitting gambling at casinos like The Dunes, built in the early 1930s. Farther south lay Rancho

Mirage, an elegant enclave of country clubs and golf courses, and Palm Desert, where tourists turned south to climb the Pines-to-Palms Highway to Idyllwild.

Indian Wells, west of Palm Desert, was incorporated in 1967. It is the home of the Eldorado Country Club where, behind high security, garden cottages wind through a sprawling golf course dotted with 2,800 fruit trees. Here Dwight Eisenhower established the desert's presidential tradition. Since then, Gerald Ford and Ronald Reagan have frequented the Eldorado. It has become the seasonal home for many influential government and business leaders. In 1982 memberships sold for $40,000. La Quinta, home of the La Quinta Hotel, and youngest of the area's incorporated cities, (April 13, 1982), is also the farthest east of the cove communities. Across the valley, at Desert Hot Springs, health seekers congregate at the mineral baths, and tour Cabot Yerxa's fanciful mansion, built in pueblo style, and now a gallery and museum.

Overall, the greater Coachella Valley contains more than thirty golf courses, and an uncalculated number of swimming pools. Nellie Coffman died in 1950, and the Desert Inn has long since disappeared, replaced by a shopping mall. But the traveler need not worry over lodging. In 1977 Palm Springs had 200 hotels. The median price for a home was the highest in the United States. Visitors now enjoy a breathtaking trip straight up the mountain face from Chino Canyon. The Palm Springs Tramway, one of the highest and longest in the world, was built by helicopter, and opened in 1963. The Desert Museum, sprung from such inauspicious beginnings, now knows a luxurious physical setting and a more than comfortable endowment.

But Palm Springs' remarkable growth was not achieved without conflict. Early struggles over water marred Indian-white relationships. Zoning battles kept the situation unstable. The city itself soon enclosed a great deal of the checkerboard Indian reservation, whose lands were appraised in 1959 at more than $50 million. That year Con-

One of the newer wonders of the Colorado Desert is the Palm Springs Aerial Tramway, constructed during the 1950s, which lofts its riders from the desert floor north of Palm Springs to the 8,000-foot level in the San Jacinto Mountains. From its observation restaurant at the top, tourists can look out over the entire Colorado Desert east toward Mexico. Courtesy, Riverside Press-Enterprise Company

gress passed the Equalization Act in response to a court order requiring the establishment of equal value for each of the forty-seven-acre allotments given to each member of the Agua Caliente band. One hundred four members, of whom about eighty were under twenty-one years of age, held a tremendous fortune in their hands. But for many, the grasp was only momentary.

The Equalization Act instituted a system of guardianship in which trustees, or "conservators," were appointed to handle the financial affairs of Indian minors, and those adults deemed in need of assistance. The conservators were appointed and supervised by the Superior Court at Indio, and were mainly non-Indian businessmen. After five years the Agua Caliente Tribal Council lodged a grievance with the Commission of Indian Affairs, charging conservators with widespread abuse of their appointments.

These abuses included the collection of exorbitant fees, detrimental land sales, and conflict of interest. A series of investigative reports exposing the corruption by *Riverside Press-Enterprise* reporter George Ringwald netted the paper a Pulitzer Prize for meritorious public service. Further investigations by the Department of the Interior corroborated Ringwald's findings. Since then, the guardianship program has been dismantled.

Today Palm Springs and related communities enjoy boundless wealth. Estates like those of presidential confidant Walter Annenberg, with its own private golf course, share a crowded landscape with posh homes and condominiums. It is fitting, if not altogether just, that the Coachella Valley should know such divergence in its development. Below sea level, a once-barren land now nurtures a great harvest. Above, the valley gaily celebrates the sun, the desert, and the exclusive interrelationships of wealth and power. The sun, here so close to the soil, bears many gifts. It is not the fault of the sun that such gifts can exaggerate the disparity between rich and poor, farm laborer and golf enthusiast. Here, the sun, at least, shines bountifully on everyone and everything.

VIII Harvest of the Sun

The Endless Boom

More than anything else, the history of Riverside County is the history of water—the development of its sources, and its division over a fertile but thirsty land. Three of the world's most impressive water transport systems terminate here—at Lake Mathews, Lake Perris, and Lake Cahuilla. Riverside County is bounded on the east by the Santa Ana River, and the west by the Colorado—both of which no longer normally reach the sea, as wells and diversions tap their flow. Southern California could be called a "hydraulic" society. From the great reservoirs in Riverside County, rain and snow from the Rockies and Sierras is distributed throughout the region, making modern metropolitan development—indeed, life itself—possible. The remarkable pioneer agriculturalists of Riverside County settled a desert and made it bear fruit. It remained to the twentieth century to fully reap the long-awaited harvest of the sun.

At the turn of the century the county's development had slowed. Water claims had taxed the Santa Ana River to its limit. Groundwater levels at Coachella and San Jacinto were falling. Silt filled the Colorado River and threatened to inundate the Palo Verde Valley. Drought withered orchards at Palm Springs, and alkali choked them in Temescal Canyon. But no single community could tap the resources necessary to increase their supplies. The twentieth century, as a consequence,

The vast Salton Sea, south of Indio and extending across the Colorado Desert in both
Riverside and Imperial counties, was created in
1905 by a breakthrough of the Colorado River. The lake, which continues to be augmented
by overflow from the Imperial Valley, has become a popular fishing and swimming resort
area. Courtesy, Riverside Press-Enterprise
Company

has witnessed regional, state, and federal agencies taking on expanded roles in the region's development.

Federal participation in local water issues began with one of the Bureau of Reclamation's first projects, the mile-long Laguna Dam across the Colorado above Yuma, completed in 1909. Its construction had one unforeseen effect. Deposition behind the dam was thought to have raised the riverbed as far north as the Palo Verde Valley. The valley's irrigation district joined a growing block of interested groups in the agitation for a high dam in Boulder Canyon—a dam which would regulate floodwaters and prevent silting.

The Imperial Irrigation District began lobbying for a high dam soon after its formation in 1916. The district coupled its endorsement with a proposal for a federally financed "All-American" canal to replace the old diversions in Mexico that nearly drowned the Coachella and Imperial valleys in 1905. The City of Los Angeles entered the crusade in 1920, with the intention of utilizing the hydroelectric power a high dam would produce. The Coachella Valley County Water District also monitored the lobbying activities of the high-dam group. As interest in the regulation of the lower Colorado grew, so did the scope of proposals. Los Angeles joined with several neighboring communities in the creation of the Metropolitan Water District in 1927. This district began implementing plans for another large-scale diversion of water from the Colorado, 260 miles away, to serve coastal cities.

Though all parties agreed on a high dam in Boulder Canyon, their unity ceased there. In 1921 Coachella lodged a protest against the City of Los Angeles, claiming that use of water for power alone would interfere with the needs of irrigators. The Coachella District studied the possibilities of its own canal with an intake at the northern end of the Palo Verde Valley. In 1923 district engineer W.P. Rowe surveyed a route from Blythe through the Chuckwalla Valley to the foothills north of

Indio. The district also considered the possibility of constructing another canal north of the proposed All-American intake.

Activities accelerated throughout the 1920s as lobbying turned into crusade. Desert farmers in Riverside, Imperial, and San Diego counties charged San Diego's incumbent congressman with foot-dragging on the Colorado issue. Pledging to work for the high dam, El Centro attorney Phillip Swing launched his own campaign. Former Coachella Water District President Richard Blackburn recalled Swing's campaign caravan to the Riverside Courthouse: "We had a frame erected on one Model T on which we placed a swing and Mary Bundshuh would swing back and forth while a banner proclaimed, 'Swing with Swing for Congress' and it drew a lot of attention."

Swing's campaign bid succeeded and the Boulder Canyon Project Act was signed into law on December 12, 1928. Two years later Coachella District Board members Blackburn, Sparey, Clay, and Yager set out to survey the proposed canal's route, and make off-road vehicle history. According to Blackburn, field engineer Rowe devised a unique tread apparatus for the dunes:

We bought two Fords, one for $75 and one for $125. We took the fenders off them, took a twelve-inch belt and put blocks underneath so we could bolt the belts to the wheels...We ran as close as

Above: *The Alberhill region north of Elsinore has been renowned for its superior clays since before the turn of the century, and by the 1920s 90 percent of all clays shipped to Los Angeles came from that vicinity. In 1918 the Los Angeles Pressed Brick Company built a modern clay producing plant at Alberhill to furnish large quantities of fire brick, hollow building tile, and face brick. Courtesy, Lorne Allmon*

Facing page, top: *In the early nineteenth century settlers of Agua Mansa and La Placita northwest of Riverside began exploiting the great mass of limestone that lay at the eastern end of the Jurupa Mountains to make whitewash for their adobe houses. In 1907 developer William G. Henshaw, namesake of Lake Henshaw in San Diego County, incorporated a cement company with six kilns. The present Crestmore plant of the Riverside Cement Company, shown here in the 1930s, became one of the major industries of Riverside County with the growing need for cement in the new building technology that employed a combination of cement and reinforcing steel. Courtesy, Lorne Allmon*

Facing page, bottom: *Riverside's Fire Department entered the motorized era in 1909 with the purchase of a Seagrave Company Motor Propelled Combo Hose Wagon and Chemical Engine. The old fire horses were put out to pasture for this noisy, smoke-belching truck. Courtesy, Riverside Municipal Museum*

we could to the actual canal site-route and followed it over the dunes. We'd race along at a pretty good clip but when we came to the edge of some and looked down, some of those drops were twenty-thirty feet. It made the trip pretty interesting.

In 1931 citizens of the City of Riverside held a plebiscite to decide on membership in the Metropolitan Water District. Riverside County as a whole stood to gain a great deal from the Colorado Aqueduct. Most of its 260 miles would lie within the county, providing potential jobs, improved roads, and supplemental water. For more incentive M.W.D. engineers implied that another route, through San Bernardino County, would be adopted if the city didn't join. But the city's long and painful battles to secure its water rights to the Santa Ana River had fostered a strong tradition of independence and local control. With local water sources now secured, there seemed little reason to take on a new tax burden, especially during the Depression. In addition, Colorado River water would go primarily toward the opening of new, competitive agricultural acreage. Depending on where their water came from, and how much came, the county was divided. Opponents cited the profit made by San Fernando Valley landowners when Owens Valley water reached Los Angeles in 1913. Riverside grower Burdette Marvin declared against the Aqueduct unless "dryland owners give me a juicy cut." On March 31, city voters turned down M.W.D. membership by a ratio of more than four to one.

But the Great Depression would forcibly alter Riverside's aversion to regional and federal interference in local affairs. WPA sidewalks began to appear throughout the city as civic leaders sought to relieve growing unemployment. Moreover, Juan Bautista de Anza would receive his rightful recognition in a statue created by Sherry Peticolas and funded by WPA and Riverside Art Association grants. From his island park on Fourteenth Street and Magnolia Avenue, the great explorer evokes two disparate eras—the Spanish and the New Deal.

A construction consortium organized in part by Henry Kaiser and known as the Six Companies completed Hoover Dam (in Black Canyon, rather than Boulder) in 1935. At the time it was the world's highest dam and, behind it, Lake Mead would soon be the world's largest reservoir. Parker Dam, the point of diversion for the Colorado Aqueduct, was completed by the Six Companies three years later, and only after sparking a little-known "Water War." In 1934, the governor of Arizona ordered the river ferryboat *Julia B.,* manned by members of the state's national guard, to the isolated construction site in an effort to block California's appropriation of Colorado water. Actual bloodshed was prevented only after Congress stepped in to mediate the dispute.

Working from far-flung camps, 35,000 men drawn from the ranks of the Great Depression's unemployed labored through desert heat and cold to complete the aqueduct. From pumping plants above Parker Dam, at an elevation of only 450 feet, the aqueduct touches Riverside County west of Rice. Another pumping plant lifts the water to Iron Mountain Tunnel. The aqueduct again enters Riverside County east of the Coxcomb

Mountains. Two more pumping plants, at Eagle Mountain and Hayfield, raise the water to an elevation of 1,807 feet. At Cabazon, a private contractor began work on a tunnel thirteen miles long, straight through the heart of Mount San Jacinto, but was unable to complete the project. M.W.D. workers finished the difficult task. On the Perris Plain the aqueduct crosses Cajalco Basin and reaches its terminus at Lake Mathews. The Colorado Aqueduct was designed to deliver 1,500 cubic feet of water per second. From the lake, capable of storing 225,000 acre-feet of water, feeder lines reach as far away as Palos Verdes and San Diego.

In contrast, the All-American Canal needed no pumping plants or siphons. From Imperial Dam, seventeen miles north of Yuma, water first reached Holtville in the Imperial Valley in 1940. Coachella District representatives dutifully attend-

Above: The All-American Canal snakes across the desolate reaches of the Colorado Desert to bring precious water from the Colorado River to farms in the Coachella Valley. In the distance in this 1950 photograph may be seen the Salton Sea. Courtesy, Riverside Press-Enterprise Company

Far left: In the 1930s the Metropolitan Water District began construction of an aqueduct from the Colorado River across 260 miles of desert and mountains to Lake Mathews, which it reached in 1939. The most difficult phase of the nine-year project was construction of the San Jacinto Mountains tunnel (shown here). This massive water promised a new source of water for the arid southland. Courtesy, Metropolitan Water District

ed the ceremony even though the Coachella Branch, 123 miles long, was only one-third completed. A year later, work was further delayed by an event, occurring thousands of miles away, that would drastically alter and increase the federal government's impact on the county: Pearl Harbor.

Riverside County's modern military presence began in 1918 with a small dirt airstrip near the abandoned townsite of Alessandro, on the Santa Fe Railroad, south of Box Springs Mountain. Barnstormers sometimes took shelter here during their cross-country flights. The air was clear, the winds dependable, and the surrounding dry plain free of trees and other obstructions.

When the First World War began in 1917, Congress appropriated funds for the expansion of the army's small Air Service and the establishment of new airfields throughout the country. Arthur Sweet was a member of the Riverside Chamber of

Commerce and an observer for the Aero Club of America. Sweet spearheaded a drive by the Chamber to locate an airbase at Alessandro. Dedicated lobbying succeeded, and by February 1918 plans had been laid for the establishment of a U.S. Aviation Training School. Riversiders staged a celebratory parade on February 9, led by captain and attorney Miguel Estudillo on his white horse.

Soon after, Major Theodore McCauley, from San Diego's Rockwell Field, led the advanced contingent, consisting of four men and a 1917 Model T truck, to the field. They bivouacked in the barley stubble across from the railroad station. On the morning of February 26, 1918, the men raised a wind sock on a bamboo pole and spread a strip of bunting on the ground to mark the landing strip. March Field, named for fallen pilot Peyton C. March, was officially open.

It took only sixty days to erect twelve huge hangars, six barracks, mess halls, and the base exchange. Five training squadrons, flying venerable Curtis JN-4Ds, called "Jennys," were stationed there. The base could turn out 750 aviators every three months, and could house 2,000 support personnel. The First World War ended in 1919. By 1924 only two people occupied the windswept base, a caretaker and his mother. One of the hangars was removed to Hemet for a girls' gymnasium, another for a new home for St. Francis de Sales Church in Riverside.

In 1926, the Army Air Service split from the

Above: *Six Thunderbird jets come to a precision formation halt on the runway at March Air Force Base, currently headquarters of the Fifteenth Air Force. Established in 1918, MAFB is a showplace installation and the oldest air force facility on the West Coast. Courtesy, Riverside Press-Enterprise Company*

Left: *Colonel H.H. (Hap) Arnold, commanding officer of March Field, is shown seated in a 1914 Wright Pusher airplane about to take off from the tiny U.S. Army landing strip. An instructor is in the foreground. Arnold became one of the great names of military aviation in World War II. Courtesy, Riverside Press-Enterprise Company*

Facing page, top: *World War I flying ace Roman Warren circles the Mount Rubidoux Peace Tower, built in 1925 through the efforts of Frank Miller of the Mission Inn. Warren acquired local fame soon after the war by flying under the low Highway 60 bridge between Riverside and Rubidoux. He later served on the Riverside County Board of Supervisors. Courtesy, Riverside Municipal Museum*

Facing page, bottom: *Mobilization for World War I got underway in Banning in 1917. The first recruit was Sergeant Paul Smith, who was killed in action in Europe the following year. This photograph was taken of the mobilization of Banning recruits in 1917 for Company M of the 160th Infantry of the National Guard. Courtesy, Leonard McCulloh*

Signal Corps and became the Army Air Corps. March Field was reactivated as a bomber base. Under Colonel William C. Gardenhire, the wooden buildings of the World War I era were replaced. Spread out in a triangular pattern, new quarters arose in Mission Revival style, and a new flight line emerged. The City of Riverside donated over 200 palm trees for landscaping. As the home of the first Bomb Wing, the base would know stellar airmen like Curtis LeMay and Henry "Hap" Arnold. (The need for expanded air defense was brought home to residents of San Jacinto when, in 1937, a Soviet ANT-25 with three crew members performed an emergency landing in a nearby cow pasture while attempting to reach San Francisco from Moscow!)

But World War II would mobilize the nation as never before. Because of its isolation yet close

proximity to the coastline, Riverside County became an important staging ground for the Pacific campaign, and the impact of the military's presence would alter the county's growth and the lives of its people. In 1940, personnel at March Field doubled to 3,600 enlisted men. Across the highway Camp Haan sprang into being, a $6 million antiaircraft training facility, built over a few short months by 5,000 construction workers. To the west, the Army Quartermaster Corps occupied their Mira Loma Depot, an endless landscape of long wooden warehouses and rail sidings. South of Riverside, the army occupied another 1,000 acres at Van Buren and Arlington avenues. Camp Anza was a staging area for soldiers departing to, and returning from, overseas. Train after train rounded the long railroad spur until a grand total of over 600,000 individual soldiers' assignments were processed here.

Riverside County could provide the armed forces at least one other unique resource—luxury hotels at bargain prices. North Corona, or "Norco," had long before failed as a citrus subdivision. In December 1920 Rex B. Clark purchased 5,000 acres of land in Norco. Clark completed the street layout and water system, built Acacia School (now the community center) and a hotel/general store on Old Hamner Avenue. But Clark's most impressive achievement was the Lake Norconian Club, opened in 1928. Spun from his discovery of a hot sulphur spring while drilling for irrigation water, Clark's "World Resort Supreme"

Above: *The slow moving tenor of life in the citrus belt changed drastically with World War II and the construction of Camp Haan across Highway 395 from March Field in 1940. At its peak, Camp Haan was the base for as many as 80,000 men, both in the barracks and at training locations on the Mojave Desert. For the first time, Riverside had a fast-paced nightlife. Civilians were encouraged to invite servicemen on weekend passes to their homes for dinner, the USO flourished downtown in both the YMCA and YWCA buildings, and Municipal Auditorium became a weekend dance hall. Courtesy, Lorne Allmon*

Facing page, top: *In 1922 the U.S. Army sent its first dirigible on a cross-country flight from the east to California. Crowds filled the streets of downtown Banning as the dirigible entered the San Gorgonio Pass. Courtesy, Leonard McCulloh*

Facing page, bottom: *Founded in 1918, March Field languished for many years as a small U.S. Army Air Force Base and was deactivated with the building of new hangers of reinforced concrete. This photograph was taken sometime in the 1930s. During World War II March Air Force Base would emerge as one of the great military air force bases in the United States. Courtesy, Riverside Press-Enterprise Company*

came very near to being just that. The Lake Norconian Club at one time covered over 700 acres, and included a large lake graced by an elegant ballroom pavillion, a marina, an airfield, a double Olympic-sized pool, and stables. Crowning the hill overlooking it all was a giant hotel. Under its red-tiled roof, the many rooms contained carved furniture and imported tilework. Manicured lawns, lush gardens, and waterfalls enclosed the plush pleasure palace.

Unfortunately, Clark's timing was very bad. For a while, the club enjoyed the patronage of movie stars and the well-to-do, but the Great Depression sent its profits plummeting. By the beginning of World War II, it was simply the "Rex Clark Hotel," and had ceased to function as a "resort supreme." In 1942 the property passed to the U.S. Navy, who established a hospital on the grounds. At the same time, in Palm Springs, the army purchased the equally impressive El Mirador Hotel for $425,000 and began its expansion as Torney General Hospital.

Torney Hospital was a small part of what was to be the largest military installation in the county (and possibly the nation): the Army's Desert

Right, top: Southern Californians had a saying that the temperate and wealthy orange-growing city of Riverside "always rolled its streets up at dusk." All of this changed when World War II inundated the streets with military personnel from March Air Force Base, Camp Haan, and Camp Anza on weekend passes. The USO flourished, nightclubs mushroomed, and the Riverside Fox Theatre hospitably permitted soldiers to sleep in its lobby any evening after the late show ended. Courtesy, Riverside Press-Enterprise Company

Right, bottom: Food Machinery Corporation, later FMC Corporation, was the world's largest producer of citrus packinghouse equipment. It geared up for World War II by producing the Water Buffalo tank and other amphibious vehicles. The tanks were tested in Riverside's Lake Evans in Fairmount Park. In 1950 during the Korean War, FMC was involved in reconditioning amphibious vehicles, one of which is shown here in a test. Courtesy, Riverside Press-Enterprise Company

Below: During World War II thousands of injured navy veterans were treated or went through convalescence at the U.S. Naval Hospital at Norco. The hospital facility was originally the old Lake Norconian Club, a plush resort built in the 1920s that failed to weather the Depression years. Courtesy, Lorne Allmon

training here. In all, thirteen armored divisions and nearly all infantry divisions were tested on "The Desert." It would take a decade after the war for bomb squads to find and deactivate all unexploded shells.

Within Riverside County cities, troops outnumbered everyone else. Passes were restricted to Riverside and San Bernardino counties. With a population of only 4,000, Blythe alone entertained 1,000 soldiers every weekend. Palm Springs was a "sea of khaki." Though at first the influx gave rise to fear among some residents, the county soon threw its support wholeheartedly behind the GIs. At Riverside, the headquarters of the Fourth Air Force occupied the old Post Office building at Seventh and Orange streets (now the Municipal Museum). With no other place to sleep, many soldiers camped on the lobby carpet at the Fox Theatre on Market Street, and were roused in the morning according to the marks they had chalked on the soles of their shoes. The hastily formed Riverside Housing Authority attempted to keep pace with the swollen population by building several housing units, including one in the orange groves at Blaine and Canyon Crest.

The war stimulated local industry as well. Years before, two brothers, Joseph and Ed Hunter, took over their father's Riverside Foundry and began manufacturing venetian blinds. By 1942, as Hunter-Douglas, their company had begun wartime production of machine tools and aluminum aviation parts. At the same time, the Food Machinery Corporation began production of the famed "Water Buffalo" ("Landing Vehicle, Tracked") for use in the Pacific. Evans Lake in Riverside's sedate Fairmont Park served as their testing ground.

Rapid demobilization followed the end of the war in 1945. Within five years the county would recover from a short postwar slump and, as a charter member in the nation's "Sunbelt," embark on a boom that seems, still today, virtually endless. It has been marked by the transition from agriculture to industry, from railroad to automobile, from urban centralization to "suburban" sprawl. Cities like Riverside would treble in population

Training Center. From its permanently temporary headquarters near Cottonwood Springs and Chiriaco Summit, the Training Center spread out over 55,000 square miles, touched three states, and included at its heart almost all the unoccupied desert areas of Riverside County. There was also a substantial airbase on the mesa west of Blythe, and a communications center at Banning. West of the Chocolate Mountains and north of the Salton Sea were headquarters for the Quartermaster, Medical, Ordnance, Engineering, and Signal Corps.

First to command here would be General George Patton, followed by General Walton "Johnnie" Walker. The Third and Fifth Armored divisions, along with the Sixth and Seventh Motorized Infantry Divisions, took part in grueling combat

over the next twenty years, diversify their economic base, and face up to growing urban challenges in planning and social services.

Of the many military installations in Riverside County, only March Air Force Base and the Naval Hospital continued an active military role. The 22nd Bomb Wing, utilizing B-29 Superfortresses, participated in the Korean War. Later, as an important link in the SAC network, and as headquarters for the 15th Air Force, the base continues to expand. The Naval Hospital at Norco was reactivated for the Korean War, and then closed permanently. The Naval Ordnance Laboratory began operations within the compound and, in 1962, the State of California took over the remaining facilities as a statewide narcotics rehabilitation center.

Immediately following the end of military activities in the desert, Henry Kaiser took over an old Southern Pacific claim to iron ore deposits at Eagle Mountain. By 1948, the Kaiser Steel Company had completed a fifty-two-mile railroad spur from the Salton Sea to the mine site north of Desert Center. The facilities at Eagle Mountain could

Above: In 1984 University of California staff and other local citizens launched a drive for an archaeological study of Riverside's old Chinatown site, a vacant lot of about four-and-a-half acres owned by the County Board of Education and scheduled to be paved over for a parking lot. The county, city, and Board of Education swung behind the movement and funding was raised for the Great Basin Foundation of San Diego to study what had become the last remaining whole Chinatown site in California. The Chinatown site, dating back to 1885, proved to be the richest Chinese historical site ever excavated in California. Courtesy, University of California, Riverside

Facing page: In 1948 the Kaiser Steel Company took over an old Southern Pacific Railroad claim to iron ores at Eagle Mountain on the Mojave Desert. A railroad spur was built by the steel company across fifty-two miles of desert to a Southern Pacific siding near the Salton Sea. From here iron ore was shipped to Kaiser's steel plant in Fontana, northwest of Riverside. Courtesy, Riverside Press-Enterprise Company

Above: *In 1917 the Citrus Experiment Station was moved from its earlier site at the foot of Mount Rubidoux to a new site at the foot of the Box Springs Mountains, where it is today part of the University of California campus at Riverside. In this 1917 photograph, taken shortly before the dedication of the laboratory main building and its south wing the following year, a woman operates a tractor in a cultivation demonstration. Courtesy, Special Collections Department, Library of the University of California, Riverside*

Below: *Hollywood in the 1930s discovered that "how it plays in Riverside" and not Peoria was the key to a film's success. The Riverside Fox Theatre became a center for sneak previews and premieres with film celebrities on hand. The circular drive-in restaurant with car hops had become a new craze in Riverside, and for theater-goers every film ended with a mandatory trip to Ruby's Drive-In. Both the theater and drive-in were located on Market Street. Courtesy, Riverside Press-Enterprise Company*

Facing page, bottom: *One of Riverside's best known celebrities in the 1930s and 1940s was dog trainer Lee Duncan, who brought the original Rin Tin Tin back with him from Germany after World War I. During the years he trained at least five successors to Rin Tin Tin for the popular motion picture series. Courtesy, Riverside Municipal Museum*

process as many as thirty carloads of iron ore a day, transshipped to the steel plant at Fontana. Elsewhere in the county military facilities quickly reverted to civilian use. Blythe inherited an especially fine airfield. Rohr Corporation took over part of Camp Anza in Riverside for the assembly of jet aircraft power units. Similarly, the Mira Loma Depot eventually became the Mira Loma Space Center, where various industrial concerns utilize the vast storage facilities. Other large employers participating in the postwar boom included Bourns Incorporated, a manufacturer of high-technology instruments, and Lily Tulip Cup Company. The Hunter brothers' operations went through several corporate transformations, becoming AMAX, Hunter Engineering, and Toro's Moist-O-Matic Division.

Riverside's Citrus Experiment Station and School of Tropical Agriculture underwent significant expansion as well. In 1947 the State Legislature approved the development of a liberal arts college at the Riverside site. The new school, the University of California at Riverside, opened in February of 1954. Gordon Watkins served as first provost. As statewide projections for college attendance expanded through the postwar years, the role of the Riverside campus changed as well. Originally planned to accept no more than 1,500 students, the limit was soon raised to 25,000. By

1960, under Herman Spieth, a graduate division was under way. At the same time, under Alfred Boyce, the Citrus Experiment Station emerged as the Citrus Research Center and Agricultural Experiment Station. University expansion utilized, for married students, the World War II housing tract at Canyon Crest.

The 1950s and 1960s saw dramatic changes in the county's urban living patterns. Under the Eisenhower administration, the Interstate Highway System spurred rapid development of freeways throughout the nation. The City of Riverside would eventually be drawn, north and south, by State Highway 91, and quartered, east and west, by State Highway 60—the Riverside and Pomona Freeways. To the east, Highway 60 joins Interstate 10 near Beaumont, traverses San Gorgonio Pass, skirts Indio, and bisects Blythe on its way to Phoenix. The county's latest interstates, 15 and 215, are replacing in piecemeal fashion Highway 395 along the Perris Plain, and will follow a north-south route through Norco, Corona, Temescal Canyon, and Temecula.

Freeway construction stimulated several new trends in urban geography in Riverside County. Suburban expansion followed the freeway. Throughout the 1950s Riverside's population center moved southward as housing developments mushroomed along the Magnolia Avenue corri-

Above: *The last flare-up of the old west in Riverside County was the Willie Boy manhunt of 1909. Posses from both Riverside and San Bernardino counties pursued a twenty-six-year-old Paiute Indian across more than 500 miles of desert in the two counties before he shot himself when surrounded. One of the legendary stories of the region, the manhunt has been the subject of books, articles, and finally the 1970 motion picture* Tell Them Willie Boy Is Here. *Courtesy, Harry W. Lawton*

dor. Elsewhere freeways skirted downtown areas and a new phenomenon, the shopping mall, siphoned commercial business away from the traditional Main Street. In Riverside, the "Plaza Mall" pioneered in Magnolia Center, opening in 1956. It was followed in 1970 by the Tyler Mall at the southern end of the city. Similarly, the cities of Banning, Beaumont, and Corona saw the deterioration of downtown areas as their respective freeways swept patrons by. The automobile contributed another uncomfortable factor—photochemical air pollution. As Southern California grew, so did the "smog" problem, from a minor nuisance to the eye to a major health hazard. Appropriately, a statewide air-pollution research center at the Riverside campus leads the research effort to improve air quality.

Local government agencies were faced with a broad spectrum of problems incurred by growth. In 1965 Lowell Elementary School, at Victoria and Cridge streets in Riverside, was burned. Lowell

School became a symbol for growing educational segregation within the city, and its torching helped focus attention on one more insidious factor in urban change. Minority leaders challenged the Riverside Unified School District to implement desegregation. Encouraged in part by forward-looking sociologists and educators from UCR, the School Board under Arthur L. Littleworth instituted a sweeping desegregation plan in 1967. The pioneering plan, observed throughout the nation, consisted of closing the most segregated schools and beginning an equalized busing program. The plan succeeded with little strife.

Similarly, Indian/white relationships in the county have often been characterized by extremes.

Against the violence of a Sam Temple in the nineteenth century, there rose the poignant expression of empathy and indignation provided by Helen Hunt Jackson's novel, *Ramona,* and her documentary study, *A Century of Dishonor.* In the twentieth century, activists like Banning's Harry James and Los Angeles writer Edwin Corle continued to bring the Southern California Indian's struggles to public attention. Corle's *Fig Tree John,* published in 1935 and partially based on the life of a well-known Cahuilla leader, has been recognized as one of the best books on the modern Indian written by a white man. The turbulent sixties accelerated this tradition. Harry Lawton's historical reconstruction, *Willie Boy: A Desert Manhunt,* drawn from his research as a reporter in the Banning-Beaumont area and published in 1960, received equal critical acclaim, and became the basis for a popular movie, *Tell Them Willie Boy is Here.* Four years later, Morongo Indian Reservation activists and supporters launched the Malki Museum, the first public museum ever established on a Southern California Indian reservation. Since that time, Indian scholars like Katherine Siva Saubel have expanded the museum's role and Indian participation overall in the community.

During the 1960s, Riverside took steps to counteract continuing urban decay. Under a Redevelopment Agency, downtown began a transformation in 1966 with the closing of five blocks on Main and Ninth streets for the construction of

a pedestrian shoppers' mall. Riverside's downtown continues to revive in its new role as financial and cultural center with the construction of high-rise office buildings, a new City Hall and Convention Center, as well as the new fourteen-floor County Administrative Center, completed in 1975. The Mission Inn, too, at times facing demolition, was preserved and reopened by the city. Other cities, like Banning and Corona, have followed Riverside's footsteps in urban redevelopment with the construction of malls and new administrative centers.

But through all the growth and challenges brought on by an endless boom, water has been the vital prerequisite—the key. After World War II, a new generation of civic leaders had reconsidered Riverside's options for growth. The city threw in with development, abandoned its policies of local control and local water sources, to join the Metropolitan Water District in 1955, along with Corona, and Elsinore. The Coachella Canal had been completed since 1949, and thirty years later a new reservoir at the canal's terminus near La Quinta was opened by the county for recreation. It was named (one hopes not prophetically) Lake Cahuilla.

But the boom had only just begun. In 1956, California embarked on one of the most ambitious, costly, and far-flung water projects in the world. Today, the California State Water Project begins at Oroville Dam on the Feather River, and

Left: *Riverside's annual Eastern Sunrise Service on Mount Rubidoux was launched in 1909 by Frank Miller of the Mission Inn after social reformer Jacob Riis urged him to organize an annual ceremonial or pilgrimage similar to the Danish Christmas Eve torchlight processions. The service, shown here in about 1915, has been widely imitated across the United States, particularly after the idea spread to the Hollywood Bowl. During World War II the ceremony was cancelled because of blackouts. Courtesy, Riverside Municipal Museum*

Facing page, top: *One of the major cultural events of Southern California for more than a half century has been the annual Ramona Pageant, which was launched in 1923 under the sponsorship of the Hemet-San Jacinto Chamber of Commerce. The script, based on Helen Hunt Jackson's novel* Ramona, *was written by Garnet Holme. The traditional event is staged in a natural amphitheater, the Ramona Bowl, and each year attracts thousands of visitors. Noted actors have played title roles in the pageant, but the cast includes representatives from the Soboba Indian Reservation and many other citizens of the San Jacinto Valley, some of whom have played their parts for many years. Courtesy, Lorne Allmon*

Facing page, bottom: *Katherine Siva Saubel, Cahuilla Indian president of Malki Museum, shows some of the artifacts housed in the small adobe museum on the Morongo Indian Reservation near Banning. A non-profit institution, Malki Museum was built by Indian volunteers from many Southern California reservations. Lacking rich donors, the museum has survived by developing the most ambitious publications program of any small museum in America—more than thirty scholarly and popular books on California Indians published since its founding in 1964. The museum also publishes the prestigious* Journal of California and Great Basin Anthropology *in cooperation with the University of California, Riverside. The museum's goal is to preserve the heritage of California Indians for both Indians and non-Indians. Courtesy, Riverside Press-Enterprise Company*

California Governor Ronald Reagan was the guest of honor at the dedication of the Lake Perris Reservoir Dam in 1970. Here a Pony Express-type rider presents Reagan with a canteen of water carried across the state from Northern California. The dedication marked the nearing of completion of the California State Water Project that would bring water south from Oroville Dam to meet the water needs of Southern California. Courtesy, Riverside Press-Enterprise Company

utilizes the Sacramento River and Delta to supply a canal that, via several large pumping plants, climbs along the west side of the Central Valley, over the San Gabriel and San Bernardino mountains, terminating—where else?—near Riverside, in the Bernasconi Hills.

History can be many things—a good story, a tradition to be revered, a lesson to be learned. And, though nothing ever "justifies" a flat tire, history sometimes helps put it into perspective.

One windswept afternoon, while speeding along the Ramona Expressway between one forgotten task and another, this writer experienced just such an occasion. At the crest of Bernasconi Pass, between Nuevo and Lakeview, I heard the telltale thump-thump, cursed, and pulled over to the side of the road. After I'd changed the tire (thankfully, the spare had air), I stood up and took in the view—which struck me with unexpected force.

Through the low opening between two granite outcroppings, where I have so often sped by, Captain Juan Bautista de Anza led his weary colonial procession of soldiers, wives, children, and cattle toward settlement at San Francisco Bay in 1776. At the same time, I became aware that beneath my feet rumbled 1,500 cubic feet of water *per second*—the Colorado Aqueduct on its way to someone's sink somewhere, possibly mine. Immediately northwest, Indian women, emerging from childhood, once raced each other to those rocks

where they painted curious diamond-shaped patterns to mark their passage. There now loomed the long earth-fill dam of Lake Perris. Behind its two-mile brow sits 131,000 acre-feet of Sierra snowmelt.

Beyond me, the once sleepy little towns of Sunnymead, Edgemont, and Moreno were cloning themselves into a vast suburban city—"Moreno Valley," second largest and newest in the county, sprung full grown, like Athena, from the head of Orange County. Elsewhere, Mira Loma, Jurupa, Corona, and La Sierra were following suit. The City of Riverside threatens to reach 200,000 by 1988. Together with San Bernardino County, Riverside in 1981 constituted the fifth largest population area in the state, and the twenty-fourth in the entire nation. And by 1984 it was deemed the fastest-growing area in the United States. The population in-rush dwarfs the booms of the 1880s, 1920s, and 1950s. Western Riverside County has become a world of strangers, where being a "native" is both a source of pride and isolation. The once familiar landscape changes constantly.

I stood there and pondered: we drink from the far-flung Rockies, the Sierras, the Cascades—but we reap the harvest of *this* sun.

That day, in Riverside County, the sky was blue.

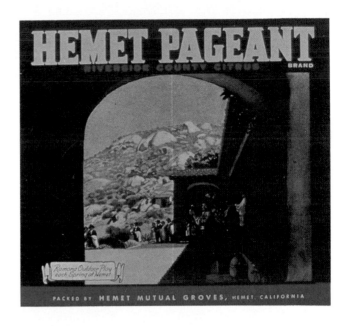

A major factor in promoting California citrus was the orange crate label, which originated with the Riverside Board of Trade printing and offering labels to growers in 1889. By the 1890s the colorful labels had become synonymous with California's pride in its golden fruit. Crate labels mirror a great diversity of subject matter, including flowery, sentimental Victorian art, animals, events, and scenic Southern California landscapes. The label pictured below is the world's largest.

Pictured here are more examples of the fine art of crate label illustration. The beauty and detail of these labels helped to make Riverside County's citrus industry so successful.

Above: *Each spring brings an outburst of wildflowers from the Santa Ana River in the west to the eastern reaches of the Colorado Desert. Photo by John Kleinman*

Top: *These sheep graze the brush-covered terrain of the Gavilan Hills. Photo by John Kleinman*

Above right: *The harvest of the sun lies stored in a rustic barn near Riverside. Photo by John Kleinman*

Right: *This young grove of citrus trees is seen against the rolling hills in the community of Sage. Photo by John Kleinman*

Above: *Lofty Mount San Jacinto towers above the Colorado Desert floor. In the foreground is the Whitewater River wash, which flows southward from Mount San Gorgonio. Photo by John Kleinman*

Above right: *Luiseño Indians once inhabited the banks of Riverside County's Lake Elsinore. Beginning in the 1880s the lake became a noted recreational resort that still attracts tourists today. Photo by John Kleinman*

Right: *The community of Idyllwild is shown here in a blanket of snow. Photo by John Kleinman*

Above: *This new orange grove in the Wood-crest area of Riverside County overlooks the distant San Bernardino Mountains. Photo by Robert Platt*

Left: *Two Riverside mounted police enjoy a leisurely patrol around Lake Evans in Riverside's Fairmount Park. Photo by John Kleinman*

Far left: *These two hikers rest in a lush forest of the San Jacinto Mountains near Black Mountain. Photo by John Kleinman*

Bottom left: *The distant lights of a recreational wharf cast an enchanting spell at twilight on the Lake Perris Dam Reservoir. Photo by John Kleinman*

Top right: *The Santa Ana River flows across western Riverside County from out of the San Bernardino Mountains. Photo by John Kleinman*

Bottom right: *Fairmount Park continues to be Riverside's most popular recreational area. Two boats sail Lake Evans against a distant backdrop of the San Gabriel Mountains. Photo by John Kleinman*

Above: *In the 1930s noted architect G. Stanley Wilson designed and supervised construction of the Mission Inn's famous St. Francis Chapel and its finest courtyard, the St. Francis Atrio, which includes a copy of the Bacchus fountain in Prato, Italy. Photo by Michael J. Elderman*

Top left: *Riverside colonists drained a swamp in about 1884 to create the city's first park, White Park, which has become a popular gathering place for many groups, particularly senior citizens. Courtesy, Riverside Municipal Garden*

Bottom left: *Riverside's Heritage House, administered by Riverside Municipal Museum, is one of the cultural highlights of the city. Courtesy, Riverside Municipal Museum*

Top right: *One of the showpieces of Riverside's Mission Inn is the marriage altar in St. Francis Chapel, which was built in 1763 by Spanish workmen for the private chapel of the Marquis de Rayas of Guanajuato, Mexico. Photo by Michael J. Elderman*

Bottom right: *Among many art treasures of Riverside's Mission Inn is the carrara marble statue of Pomona, the Roman goddess of harvests, which is mounted in an alcove in the Spanish Gallery. Photo by Michael J. Elderman*

Above: *The Riverside County Courthouse, with its Roman Imperial columns and vaulted roof, was designed by the Los Angeles firm of Burnham & Bliesner in 1904 under the supervision of Chicago architect Franklin Pierce Burnham. The design was a virtual copy, reduced in scale, of the facade of the 1900 Paris Exposition Fine Arts Building. Courtesy, Riverside Municipal Museum*

Left: *In 1919 former Riversider Charles Williston Benedict returned from the east a wealthy man. He erected a Spanish-style castle in 1931, which he called the Castillo Isabella. Called Benedict Castle, it now houses Teen Challenge, which works with troubled young people. Courtesy, Riverside Municipal Museum*

Above: *The most conspicuous landmark in Riverside is Mount Rubidoux, where a cross dedicated to Father Junipero Serra, founder of the Spanish missions, was erected in 1907 by Frank Miller. Courtesy, Riverside Municipal Museum*

Right: *First Congregational Church at Seventh and Lemon streets has become one of the many landmark structures in Riverside that are regularly shown on tours of the city. Photo by Michael J. Elderman*

Above: *Students from the University of California, Riverside, have thronged to the University Commons since the early 1970s to hear the Wednesday "nooners" featuring well-known rock, jazz, or pop bands. Photo by Michael J. Elderman*

Left: *Now a National Historic Landmark, Riverside's Mission Inn has entertained and lodged thousands of distinguished visitors and celebrities since it opened as the Glenwood Cottage in 1876. Photo by Michael J. Elderman*

Top right: *Riverside Community Hospital enjoys a beautiful view of the surrounding mountains. Photo by John Kleinman*

Right: *The magnificent five-block Riverside Mall is graced by this nineteenth-century Seth Thomas hand-wound clock, which was installed in 1921 by Fisher's Jewelry. Courtesy, Riverside Municipal Museum*

Far Right: *The first Spanish trailblazer to cross Riverside County, Juan Bautista de Anza, is commemorated by this statue in Newman Park on Magnolia near Fourteenth Street. A project of the Riverside Art Association, the statue was designed by artist Sherry Petecolas and completed by the Federal Works Project Administration in Los Angeles. It was dedicated on May 19, 1940. Photo by Michael J. Elderman*

Above: *The Riverside County Administrative Office on Lemon Street was built in two phases—the top ten floors were added in 1975. Photo by Michael J. Elderman*

Left: *Riverside's new city hall was completed in 1975 fronting the Tenth Street entrance to the Riverside City Mall on Main Street. Courtesy, Riverside Chamber of Commerce*

Facing page, top: *Riverside Municipal Museum was constructed in 1935 to house the Riverside post office. Courtesy, Riverside Municipal Museum*

Facing page, bottom: *New houses stretch out in the Moreno Valley against a hilly backdrop and blue skies. Photo by John Kleinman*

183

IX Partners In Progress

Corporate Biographies

Through the early morning light, Riverside's downtown skyline stands out against the darkness of the Box Springs Mountains to the east. The skyscrapers erected in the past two decades—and those still going up—have introduced striking changes to the city. The view is from the top of Mount Rubidoux. Courtesy, Riverside Chamber of Commerce

What has marked the economic development of Riverside County has been the resolute, adventurous spirit of its people. In a vast area, greater than the size of Rhode Island and Connecticut combined, spanning elevations from over 10,000 feet to below sea level, entrepreneurs who have had the vision and courage to see its potential have found this region a land of richly diverse opportunity.

Its economic base has traditionally been agricultural with early land grants raising sheep, cattle, and grain. With the advent of the railroad in the 1870s, access to the area increased, bringing the first influx of new settlers and a wide variety of new commercial enterprises.

Characteristic of these pioneers was the willingness to boldly venture into the risky business of experimentation, trying new crops in a new area. Cattle on the Jurupa Rancho gave way to mulberry trees and silkworms in 1869 and, when the profitable scheme collapsed the next year, the town of Jurupa (Riverside) was laid out by Judge J.W. North to be financed by the commercial planting of the new navel orange.

As water became more available, fruit growing encroached on dry farming. Banning became famous for its almonds, Beaumont for cherries and apples, Blythe for pecans, Elsinore for walnuts and olives, Coachella Valley for dates and grapefruit, Hemet for apricots, San Jacinto for citrus, Corona for lemons, and Riverside for navel oranges and citrus.

Agriculture alone did not draw people. In the first four decades of this century one of the major attractions was health. Sun and dry air, which the region had in abundance, was considered the best cure for tuberculosis and other diseases. The area boasted such famous resorts as Palm Springs' Desert Inn, Murietta Hot Springs, Soboba Hot Springs, and Gilman Hot Springs.

Only a few visionaries recognized the impact that World War II would have on the county and its economy. With March Air Field and Camp Hahn in the Riverside area and General Patton's troops at Desert Center, large numbers of service personnel were introduced to the county.

After the war not only did many servicemen and their families return to this part of the Sun-belt, but increased ease of traveling and desirability of the area for vacationing and retirement added to its popularity and growth. Overnight bulldozers began uprooting orchards and groves for subdivisions. New industry chose Riverside County in the late 1940s and 1950s to get away from more congested metropolitan areas.

By the 1970s and 1980s a second building boom occurred. The latest surge of population growth is filling communities such as Rancho California and Sunnymead. Overflowing the high-priced Los Angeles and Orange counties' housing markets, they come in search of the more reasonably priced housing in Riverside County.

All of this growth, which shows little sign of slowing before the next century, has brought dramatic change. But, even though high technology has become a major part of the county's economy, agriculture continues to be an important economic base. Judge North might not recognize the agricultural town of Riverside that he founded, but he would be proud of the dynamic area that has emerged in the past 100 years. What he would recognize is the spirit of the generations of people who have brought this change to Riverside County.

The organizations you will meet on the following pages have chosen to support this important literary and civic event. They illustrate the variety of ways in which individuals and their businesses have contributed to the county's growth and development. The civic involvement of Riverside County's businesses, institutions of learning, and local government, in cooperation with its citizens, has made the area an exceptional place in which to live and work.

RIVERSIDE COUNTY HISTORICAL COMMISSION

A historical committee for the Riverside County Board of Supervisors was created in April 1966 to plan commemorative activities for the county's seventy-fifth anniversary and, according to former commission member Francis Johnston, to conceptualize how such a group could best promote the county's history. "Out of that committee grew the basic purpose to locate, document, and mark areas in the county of historic importance," comments Johnston.

The board of supervisors officially established in May 1968 a permanent Riverside County Historical Commission to consist of nine members. Ole Nordland of Indio was chosen as its first chairman, and he served for many years.

At first the commission was assigned to the county's Department of Development but had only a small budget and no staff. The number of tasks they could undertake was therefore limited, and they settled on identifying and marking State Points of Historical Interest. "We had a pretty broad brush in those early years," recalls Nordland.

In 1969 the County Parks Department assumed the administrative responsibilities of the Riverside County Historical Commission. This was to be an important move for the commission, for by 1973 the department had hired its first professional historian, William Ray, to guide the commission's progress. Ray began by researching sites for various landmark designations.

He was followed in July 1974 by John Brumgardt. During Brumgardt's five years as historian, the commission began a publications program that now includes eight titles and is supported by proceeds from book sales. Also during this period, an indepth study was conducted to identify historic sites for acquisition as historic parks. Selected were the Gilman Ranch in Banning, the Trujillo Adobe in north Riverside, and the Jensen-Alvarado Ranch in

Rubidoux.

Stephen Becker became the third county historian in 1979; under him the entire Jensen-Alvarado Ranch Historic Park was acquired and, with donations and grant funding, restoration began at both the Jensen and Gilman historic parks. The hiring of a full-time curator of history in 1984 marked the first step to establishing historical museum programs at each park.

Since 1980 the commission has also undertaken the Historic Resources Inventory, which has marked a shift from commemorative landmarking to a policy of preservation. Conducted with the volunteer help of local historical societies, the survey includes over 5,000 nominations to the California Inventory of Historic Resources, and has allowed for a new emphasis on advising local communities and individuals on historic preservation.

Over the years the commission has continually broadened its perspective to meet the needs of the county, and it has proven itself to be a vital and important part of county government.

Ole Nordland (right), the first chairman of the Riverside County Historical Commission, with Don Mitchell, manager of the California Date Corporation, at the unveiling of the historical marker for the birthplace of the date industry, December 12, 1973.

DEUTSCH ELECTRONIC COMPONENTS DIVISION

In 1938 the nation was on the brink of war and emerging from the Great Depression. This didn't deter Alex Deutsch from opening a new machine shop in a rented Los Angeles building. With a handful of employees, he operated the machines at night and delivered parts in the daytime.

From this inauspicious beginning, Deutsch rapidly progressed to become a large metal job shop, and a leading supplier of component parts for military aircraft during World War II. The year 1946 not only marked the end of the war, but also the conversion of Deutsch from defense and military production to consumer goods, including ballpoint pens, cigarette lighters, and deluxe outdoor furniture.

In a planned step toward diversification and growth, in 1954 the company purchased the Mono-Watt Connector Division of General Electric. The new Deutsch Connector Division moved to Huntington Park in 1956. By 1957 the division had outgrown the capacity of the Huntington Park facility, and Alex Deutsch made a bold decision: to locate the new assembly and administrative facilities away from the manufacturing center.

The San Gorgonio Pass area was selected, and a fledgling operation, Beaumont Electronics, was relocated in a former lace factory adjacent to the Ring Ranch in Beaumont. For two years the twenty-eight employees of Beaumont Electronics produced electronic connectors for the expanding aerospace and defense markets. Don Lea, president of Deutsch Electronic Components Division, recalls the unique shipping process: "We would go down to the Greyhound Bus Terminal every night on our way home from work, and we would put all the parts on the bus and send them to Beaumont. On the way to work in the morning, we would stop

The current offices of the Deutsch Electronic Components Division are situated next to the Banning Airport.

at Greyhound and pick up the shipment of the prior day's production from Beaumont."

Deutsch officially opened its new 30,000-square-foot plant adjacent to the Banning Airport in September

Shown here at the groundbreaking ceremonies for the new plant in 1959 are (left to right) John Ratz, mayor of Banning; Ed Jones, general manager; and Lester Deutsch.

1959. With its philosophy of dedication to delivering the finest-quality product, on time, at a fair and proper price, the company has grown beyond expectations.

As one of the largest employers in Riverside County, with several plants in the Pass area and Hemet Valley, the Deutsch Electronic Components Division has maintained a firm belief that building good employee relations can lead to a family-type atmosphere and rewarding experience and this will be the key to its future growth.

LOMA LINDA FOODS

What would the average American household do without graham crackers, oatmeal, cornflakes, peanut butter, and granola? These well-known products were the foundation of Loma Linda Foods.

Developed in the latter half of the nineteenth century by Dr. John Harvey Kellogg to improve the diet of his Battle Creek Sanitarium patients and fellow Seventh-day Adventists, these products became the staples of Kellogg's brother Will's famous company, Kellogg Toasted Corn Flake Company, as well as other Battle Creek, Michigan, multi-million-dollar food corporations. Dr. Kellogg also created the first vegetable protein sources for meat analogs and artificial milk from powdered nuts and soybeans.

In the early 1900s Southern and Northern California Seventh-day Adventists were actively working in the areas of diet and health. Some of their efforts resulted in the formation of the Loma Linda Sanitarium and Loma Linda College of Medical Evangelists.

Loma Linda Foods began in 1906, supplying bakery goods for the sanitarium, the college, and the small community of Loma Linda. It made a variety of baked stone-ground, whole-wheat breads, health cookies, and fruit crackers.

Demands from residents for the bakery goods grew quickly. They liked the life-style and diet and came to rely on the company for its products. By 1907 increased production required the construction of a separate building, a small white-frame structure located on Anderson Street across from the railroad station in Loma Linda.

Now there was room for the production of foods similar to Dr. Kellogg's original line of foods as well as experimentation with new lines.

The original building and staff in 1925.

Breakfast cereals, meat analogs from soybean and wheat, soy milk, and canned tofu were added, and bakery items became less important over the years.

In 1933 the name was officially changed to Loma Linda Foods and by 1935 delivery routes brought the firm's products to stores within a 125-mile radius. Since working space was cramped and Loma Linda Foods wanted to concentrate on production of the breakfast cereal, Ruskets, the decision was made to relocate. The company opted for a site next to La Sierra Junior College near Riverside, with the promise of student employment cinching the move.

In November 1938 the first section of the present plant began operation with its unique three-story Ruskets oven. In that first year the firm employed fifty students and paid eighteen cents an hour.

Before the relocation sales had totaled $60,000 a year. Sales increased

Today Loma Linda Foods occupies this facility at 11503 Pierce Street, Riverside.

rapidly during World War II, almost doubling during the first six months of 1943. Annual sales now total several million dollars with distribution through regional distributors, health food stores and grocery chains, and Seventh-day Adventist camp meetings, local conference bookstores, and schools.

Loma Linda Foods' association with Dr. Harry Miller provided a major impact on its growth. In January 1951 the company took over his International Nutrition Laboratories, Inc., in Mt. Vernon, Ohio. Dr. Miller donated the sales profit to form the International Nutrition Research Foundation at the Arlington plant near Riverside. Under his direction the foundation did much to establish soy foods as a scientifically recognized source of superior vegetable protein for human needs.

Dr. Miller had been groomed by Dr. Kellogg to be his protégé. He graduated from the Battle Creek Medical School in 1901, married a classmate, went to China for the next forty-five years, and developed a soy milk infant formula from the staple of the Chinese diet—soybeans. When the Japanese overran Mainland China, Miller returned to the United States to establish his soy milk factory in Ohio. Upon the sale of the factory, he returned to Hong Kong for another twenty years, rejoining the research group at Loma Linda Foods only when he was in his nineties.

By 1966 the company was producing six types of soy milk, which now accounts for 70 percent of its market.

In the late 1960s Loma Linda Foods adopted a further innovation in the vegetarian protein foods field—spun protein fiber, which it now manufactures. Each year new products have been added to the line and the textures and flavors of established foods have been improved.

From humble beginnings Loma Linda Foods has now grown to employ 250 people in its two plants and to carry a line of seventy products. The future will see a diversification of the product line. According to Dr. Oliver Miller, vice-president of research and development, "Loma Linda Foods must address itself to the market of advocates of healthful life-styles. We've been a kind of sleeping giant. Things that seem new in the marketplace, such as tofu, Harry Miller experimented with seventy-five years ago, and we've been marketing for forty years. It doesn't seem new around here." The future product line may include fresh and dried fruits, vegetarian convenience foods and nuts, grains, and beans for the health food market.

Loma Linda Foods began with the intention of joining other Seventh-day Adventist hospitals, colleges, and food factories to raise the world's health standards and it moves forward with that goal firmly in place.

PRESS-ENTERPRISE

The local roots of the *Press-Enterprise* go back 106 years, when the *Press* began as a weekly in 1878. The *Enterprise* was started in 1885 and the two were combined in 1932 with the *Press* ownership predominant.

As competitors they had agreed on at least one matter—the creation of Riverside County, in 1893. The county constitutes the *Press-Enterprise* circulation and news coverage area, all 7,500 square miles of it, from Mira Loma to Blythe and from Highgrove to Temecula.

James Roe, druggist, teacher, land owner, and civic leader, founded the *Press* at the urging of other leading citizens including those of conflicting views on the major local issue of the day—control of the water supply. That issue was settled by the much-applauded "Holt Compromise," engineered by the *Press'* second owner, Luther M. Holt, who also promoted scientific research and boosted the town on the basis of its culture of the Riverside-introduced navel orange, an economic triumph.

Dr. E.P. Clarke became editor and president in 1896, since which time the changes have been evolutionary. Howard H Hays, Sr., became vice-president in 1928 and was president until his death in 1969. Arthur A. Culver joined the management in 1937, became general manager in 1949, and later president and co-pub-

The Riverside Press, *circa 1908, complete with job presses, a news press with locomotive-style wheel and drive shaft, and a stove pipe growing to the ceiling. By then it was one of the town's foremost businesses, with twenty-nine people on the payroll.*

lisher. He retired in 1984. Howard H Hays Jr., educated in law as well as journalism, became assistant editor in 1946, editor in 1949, co-publisher with Culver in 1965, and president, editor, and publisher in 1984.

Under the Hays editorship the *Press-Enterprise* developed metropolitan character and completeness in world and local coverage, including news and feature material from political, economic, recreational, entertainment, and social life. No longer was it necessary or customary for Riverside County people to supplement the local news by subscribing to a Los Angeles newspaper.

In 1940 the circulation of the two newspapers (which were basically morning and afternoon editions of the same paper) was 12,057. During the 1960s circulation growth exceeded 66 percent. By late 1984 the circulation was approaching 120,000 daily and 124,000 on Sunday.

Quality of the paper has been indicated by numerous prizes, including the prestigious Pulitzer Prize for Meritorious Service in 1968.

Physical growth has been continuous. The present building at Fourteenth and Orange Grove streets, occupied in 1955, was repeatedly expanded and the printing facilities were correspondingly enlarged and updated. News bureaus were established in Washington and Sacramento to supplement the wire news services with news of particular local interest. Company offices for news and business were opened in Banning, Corona, Hemet, Indio, Palm Springs, and Sun City. Six regionalized editions were established.

Responding to a nationwide preference by readers, the *Press-Enterprise* in 1983 became solely a morning publication. In the process the news staff and coverage were enlarged. Circulation has continued to increase.

Today's Press-Enterprise *is the result of the merger of the two newspapers in 1932. Still one of Riverside's foremost businesses, the paper now employs more than 850.*

RUBIDOUX MOTOR COMPANY

You would expect to find Rubidoux Motor Company in Rubidoux, but it has never been located there. When Fred Schweitzer started his Buick dealership in 1924 in Riverside, there was no community of Rubidoux, only West Riverside.

By the early 1930s Schweitzer bought the Cadillac, Oldsmobile, GMC Truck franchise, moved to Sixth and Market, and continued the name of Rubidoux Motor Company.

In 1936 Charles "Woody" Dutton, Sr., and Edgar L. McCoubrey were working for General Motors Acceptance Corporation, GM's financing division, when they heard of the availability of the Riverside dealership. Jumping at the opportunity, they mortgaged everything to purchase the agency. Since the area could only support one of them, McCoubrey became the active dealer and Dutton remained at his position of branch manager of GMAC in Hollywood.

Riverside's economy dipped in 1938 due to a poor citrus crop. Suddenly handling a surplus of Cadillacs, McCoubrey got the bright idea to sell them in Palm Springs, which was a flourishing winter resort. He rented a garage in the newly constructed Plaza, called it Plaza Motors, and sold the remaining inventory.

Charles Woodard "Bud" Dutton, Jr. (right), chairman of the board, and Edgar L. McCoubrey, member of the board and one of the original founders of Rubidoux Motor Company.

Rubidoux Motor Company is located on Riverside's Auto Drive, in the Riverside Auto Center.

In 1948 McCoubrey commuted to Palm Springs to manage Plaza Motors. When Dutton returned from World War II he established residency in Riverside and ran Rubidoux Motor Company. To familiarize himself with the dealership, Dutton had the invaluable help of Brick McKee, sales manager for the company since 1924.

In 1958 Dutton and George Reade, Sr., De Anza Chevrolet dealer, determined that their facilities were inadequate and inappropriate for ex-

pansion. They proposed to the other dealers the idea of the world's first auto center. By 1963 the proposal became reality with sixty acres on the "outskirts" of Riverside. In October 1964 Rubidoux Motor Company moved into its new 4.5-acre facility where it is now located as the cornerstone of the center.

Four years before, Dutton's son, Charles "Bud" Dutton, Jr., had joined the business at his father's request. Except for the years Bud had studied business at the University of California at Berkeley, the dealership had been his only employer while growing up, so he knew the business well. When the agency moved to the Auto Center, he became general manager and in the late 1960s, a dealer and partner. By 1973 he was president, and upon his father's death in the late 1970s he became chairman of the board. Ed McCoubrey remained a stockholder and an active member of the board.

Looking to future needs, Rubidoux Motor Company has now expanded to 6.5 acres. "It is our policy to provide the highest-quality service possible in the Riverside/San Bernardino metropolitan area," comments Bud Dutton.

HUNTER ENGINEERING COMPANY, INC.

Hunter as it now stands, just across from Hunter Park in Riverside.

In the early 1950s Joseph L. Hunter tinkered in a small machine shop set in the middle of a large citrus ranch on the northern edge of Riverside. It was a period of corporate hiatus for Joe Hunter, since he had just divested himself of his interest in Hunter-Douglas Corporation, the outgrowth of a business started in 1932.

But it was a period of personal accomplishment for Hunter, as he set about converting imaginative ideas into prototypes of new and improved machinery.

Hunter's impact on the industrial scene started with a powered hacksaw, which was developed by his original company, Riverside Foundry and Pattern.

By 1935 Hunter's genius for invention had put him in the forefront of the venetian blind industry. His developments provided automation in an industry that had been highly labor intensive. By the end of the decade Hunter Engineering Company, incorporated under that name in 1937, was building 90 percent of the equipment used in venetian blind production.

With the start of World War II Hunter retooled and for the next few years produced machine products that were vital to the war effort. Then, in 1946, an alliance that had first been formed in the mid years of

the war took shape. Hunter merged with a New York company to form Hunter-Douglas Corporation.

A new period of intense research began. Much of it was directed at the development of machinery to produce aluminum sheet as a replacement for wood in blinds and other building products.

One development of great significance occurred early in this period, when Hunter built the industry's first machine for painting metal in continuous coil. Eventually, more than 70 percent of the metal sheet used in product manufacturing would be painted in continuous coil.

Prior to the merger with Douglas, Hunter activities had been confined to the manufacture of machinery. Now the company began using its own machines to create a fast-growing line of aluminum products.

In 1954 Hunter-Douglas' U.S. operations were acquired by Bridgeport Brass. Joe Hunter retained rights to the machinery activities, which he then placed in a reactivated Hunter Engineering Company.

In the following months a breakthrough occurred that, according to trade publications, revolutionized the

production of aluminum. The Hunter Continuous Caster, which cast molten metal directly into wide sheets, was patented and put into commercial operation in a new plant just across Columbia Avenue from the research center. The caster anchored a facility that was equipped almost entirely with machinery designed and built by Hunter.

Olin-Mathieson Chemical Corporation joined forces with Hunter in 1956. Together they organized the firm into two divisons: Mill Products, which manufactured aluminum sheet and foil, and Machinery, which built machinery for the production of aluminum. Mill Products became a showplace for the machines that were designed and built by the Machinery Division.

With cast sheet making a significant impact on the economics of aluminum production, and machine developments gaining worldwide recognition, Hunter grew rapidly in the late 1950s and early 1960s. A third division, Building Products, was created by the acquisition of a number of

Joseph Hunter, founder of Hunter Engineering Company, Inc., shown with the Continuous Strip Casting Machine he invented.

small firms. Then, in 1963, in a move spearheaded by Richard S. Brill, who had succeeded Joe Hunter as president in 1959, Hunter was sold to American Metals Climax (AMAX) of New York.

That same year marked the death of Joe Hunter at the age of fifty-four. Although he had already received wide acclaim as an inventor, the full commercial success of his contributions to metal processing was still to come.

As Hunter had left his mark on the world of industry so had he on the local community of Riverside. Long a supporter of the California Agricultural Extension College, which later became the University of California at Riverside, he established and funded the Hunter Foundation to aid students in the fields of science, engineering, and agriculture.

At his home ranch, which became widely known as "the Foundation," Hunter built motel-type housing for students and subsidized them with part-time jobs on the ranch.

Another example of Hunter's generosity is a 35-acre, palm-studded park across the street from the present Hunter headquarters plant which he donated to the City of Riverside.

Joseph Hunter's home with orange groves, the site of Hunter Park, and the cottages for scholarship students, machine shop, storage building, and horse barn.

As a result of a lifelong affinity for railroading, Hunter equipped the park with a miniature steam railroad. Today on warm, sunny days, it still carries noisy young passengers through the tunnel, between the palms, and around the park.

In 1966 Amax separated aluminum production from machinery manufacturing, and Hunter, now located in a new facility that had been built alongside the existing plant, was once again concerned solely with designing and building machinery.

Amax sold Hunter to an independent group in 1970 and S.J. "Tom" Collins became president.

During the next decade, Hunter's marketing direction gradually shifted from domestic to international. Complete plants and other major machinery installations were built by Hunter for metal producers on five continents.

In 1978 Paul Hoboy succeeded Collins as president. As the former director of technical services for Alumax, Inc. (formerly the Aluminum Division of Amax), Hoboy had long been responsible for Alumax purchases of Hunter machinery. In 1979

Hunter underwent still another change in ownership. Dr. Hans Niederer became owner and chairman.

Under the new leadership, Hunter has continued its penetration of the international market. More than 50 percent of the company's business is now in export.

To better accommodate growth and acquisition, Hoboy reorganized Hunter into four divisions operating under a common banner as The Hunter Companies. Included in the group is Hunter Engineering Company, Inc., and Hunter Manufacturing Company, both headquartered in Riverside, Hunter Engineering (Canada) Ltd., Mississauga, Ontario, Canada, and N-Tech Systems of Boardman, Ohio.

Today Hunter is the world's most diversified designer of metal processing equipment. Among both foreign and U.S. machinery suppliers, Hunter alone manufactures melting, casting, rolling, leveling, coil coating, slitting, and cut-to-length systems, all of the major machinery needed to produce aluminum sheet and foil.

The same spirit of inventiveness that produced so many of the metal industry's most significant machinery developments is still evident as Hunter enters its second half-century of contributions to the advancing technology of metal processing.

PARKVIEW COMMUNITY HOSPITAL

With long lines rounding the block from Jackson to Magnolia, the small Parkview Memorial Hospital opened on November 4, 1958, to an overwhelmingly enthusiastic response from Riverside's Arlington community. *The Arlington Times* called it "the most significant step in the advancement of medicine and hospital facilities in the Arlington area."

The 48-bed hospital had been the project of five family-practice physicians who felt a growing need in the greater Riverside area for additional hospital facilities. Dee Lansing, Franklin Dailey, Carl Eckhardt, Charles Field, and Robert Zweig met in 1956 to begin planning for the hospital.

Dr. Lansing had arrived in Southern California in 1940 to take his medical training at Loma Linda University and had been practicing in Arlington since 1947. In 1960 he left the area for further training and returned in 1967 with a specialty in obstetrics and gynecology. After years of serving as chairman of the board of directors of the hospital and as temporary administrator of Parkview during interim periods, Dr. Lansing gave up his private practice in 1977 to become one of the few physicians in the country to be a full-time administrator. As Dr. Lansing explains, "I had grown up with the hospital and I knew it well."

Franklin Dailey, a graduate of St. Louis University, began private practice as a family physician in Arlington in 1952. He was asked to assume the position of emergency services director at Parkview in 1975 and, in order to do so, gave up his private practice.

Carl Eckhardt came to the Arlington area shortly after World War II. He remained in private practice in Arlington until he retired in the early 1970s, five years before his death.

A Loma Linda University graduate, Dr. Field practiced medicine in

The first frame and stucco hospital building opened in November 1958.

Missouri before moving to the Arlington area in 1957. He retired in 1981 and passed away the following year.

Robert Zweig, an activist in environmental issues, came from the East in 1953 to settle in the Arlington area. A longtime member of the Parkview Hospital Foundation board

With the addition of a three-story tower, Parkview Community Hospital now has a 156-bed capacity; and an ancillary addition in 1977-1978 provided a new lobby, admissions, a gift shop, X-ray facilities, and laboratories.

of directors, Dr. Zweig has maintained a close affiliation with the hospital over the years.

By 1958 these five doctors had purchased fifteen acres, built the first frame and stucco single-story structure, and leased the facility to an operating company composed of

twenty-five Riverside and Corona physicians. Hoping to be a nonprofit organization, but finding such financing unavailable in 1958, the group chose a proprietary operation.

Dr. Zweig recalled the hectic excitement of the opening days. The hospital had its first patient, a maternity case of Dr. Zweig's, before it officially opened. "We didn't even have diapers. A nurse went to the drugstore and bought some," reminisces Zweig. The $500,000 hospital formally began operation the following day with 16,000 square feet, three operating rooms, fifty-eight staff doctors, and 120 employees. Pharmacist Jack Bobbitt remembers starting the pharmacy in a closet-size room and running it for the first five years with the help of only one part-time pharmacist. By the late 1970s he had three full-time and two part-time pharmacists to help him.

The demand for occupancy increased so rapidly that by 1962 the hospital was enlarged to ninety-nine beds and 44,000 square feet. There was no doubt by now of the important place Parkview held in the community. Recognizing this, a group was formed from the community in 1967 to purchase the hospital business and create a nonprofit entity. In 1971 the Arlington Community Hospital Corporation purchased the buildings from the original shareholders. Since the 1967 formation of Parkview Community Hospital the facility has operated so efficiently that fund raising has not been a critical factor in its maintenance and growth.

By 1973 the hospital boasted 156

The alternative birth center, the first in the area, is family oriented in a homelike setting.

beds, with the addition of a three-story building supported by municipal bonds. In 1977-1978 services were again expanded to include an ancillary facility housing a lobby, admissions, a gift shop, X-ray equipment, and laboratories.

Parkview Community Hospital has maintained a reputation in the medical community for its close relationship between administration and medical staff, encouraging a sense of harmony rather than competition. The hospital's continuing high esteem in the greater Riverside area is based on its friendly, service-oriented, self-sufficient character. Over the years the hospital has become well known for the special services it offers the community: An alternative birth center, the first in the area, was added in 1979; the Intercept Program

for alcoholism treatment was added in 1981; and arthroscopy, an orthopedic microsurgical service, was added in 1984.

Having grown from fifty-eight physicians in 1958 to a medical staff of 204 in 1984, Parkview Community Hospital has experienced tremendous growth and looks forward to a continuing expansive trend. The future holds plans for a further increase in the number of beds, a skilled nursing facility, and a retirement village for the elderly.

In order to meet the changing health delivery system trend and in order to be more flexible to changing economic needs, the board of directors of Parkview Community Hospital restructured the organization by creating a holding corporation separate from the hospital in 1980, named Arlington Health Services Corporation.

Further reorganization occurred on April 1, 1985, when separate boards for the hospital and the holding company were implemented along with separate administrators.

D. Mark Rankin became president of the hospital board at that time and J. Dee Lansing, M.D., became president of Arlington Health Services Corporation. This reorganization is expected to result in greater capability to serve the medical needs of people of the hospital service area.

The hospital offers the latest in medical technology such as this laminar flow surgery room.

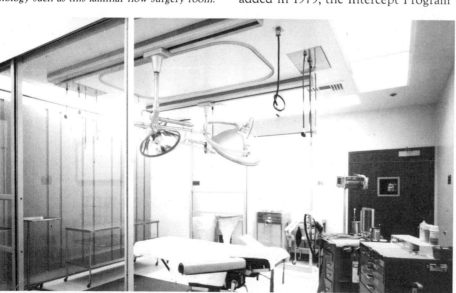

RIVERSIDE INTERNATIONAL RACEWAY

The year was 1957, and the growing popularity of sports car racing had created a strong demand for specially constructed, privately owned road-racing circuits to replace the many temporary courses in use at the time, usually at municipally owned venues.

In Southern California, which had been without a major motor-racing facility since the demise of the old Ascot Speedway in the 1930s, the demand was especially heavy, for this was the heartland of sports car sales and competition, a market heavily populated with foreign car dealers anxious to boost the sale of their sportiest models by demonstrating their prowess in actual road-racing activity, and with a wealth of budding race car drivers to do the racing.

The inevitable result was the birth of Riverside International Raceway, a privately constructed road course that was carved out of a 600-acre site in western Riverside County, just south of U.S. 60 and only ten minutes from downtown Riverside.

The man who bulldozed the original nine-turn, 3.3-mile Grand Prix course was Los Angeles restaurateur and racing enthusiast Rudy Cleye, who secured the help of engineer-race driver Jim Petersen and the financial backing of John Edgar, wealthy sportsman and sports car owner who helped develop such great drivers as Dan Gurney and Carroll Shelby, among others.

At the time, it is doubtful if either Cleye or Edgar foresaw a long-term future for the raceway, or the tremendous success and worldwide notoriety it would eventually achieve, to say nothing of its eventual economic impact on both the city and county of Riverside.

In twenty-five years the raceway went through five ownership changes and survived some turbulent times, financially and otherwise, including competition from the $25-

The Los Angeles Times *Grand Prix began in 1958 and featured exotic sports cars of the Can-Am series shown here "threading the needle" through Riverside's famed "esses." Photo by Sam Spina, Riverside* Press-Enterprise

million Ontario Motor Speedway, which was constructed in 1968 just twenty miles away. In 1974, however, those problems were stabilized under the new ownership of Fritz L. Duda, a Dallas-based real estate developer, and by the sure-handed guidance of Les Richter, a former all-pro linebacker with the Los Angeles Rams who served as the raceway's president from 1963 through 1983, when the raceway progressed from little more than a ribbon of asphalt, with a chain-link fence around it, to one of the most successful and best-known circuits in the world.

Today it is recognized as a multipurpose facility, busy more than 250 days each year with various testing, new-car introductions, RV shows, television and motion picture filming, and an annual schedule of major racing events that includes everything from traditional sports car competition to Winston Cup stock cars, Indy cars, drags, motorcycles,

off-road vehicles, and formula cars.

All of this activity annually brings thousands of visitors to the Riverside area, including race fans, racing teams, and a wide variety of high-level corporate executives from many of the nation's top companies, automotive oriented and otherwise.

As a result, the raceway's economic impact on its market is exceptionally strong. A 1983 study shows the Riverside International Raceway as one of the major contributors to the economy of Riverside County, while, around the world, the Riverside dateline is as well known as Indianapolis or Daytona.

Annually hosting the Budweiser 400 and the Winston Western 500, Riverside Raceway is the only road-racing course on the $10-million Winston Cup Grand National stock car circuit.

JOHNSON TRACTOR CO.

When Jim Freeland decided to take over part of a Caterpillar Tractor dealer's area, he was motivated by poor health and the vision of the Inland Empire's expanding citrus groves and vineyards. The year was 1928. Freeland had been an accountant with Price Waterhouse before setting up his Freeland Tractor & Equipment Co. on Seventh Street in Riverside.

His sales and service to the agricultural market grew rapidly, so that in 1937 the dealership moved to larger quarters on Eighth Street.

By 1940 Freeland was ready to retire. W. Ruel Johnson, a Caterpillar finance man, was fascinated with the idea of owning a dealership. In December 1940 he saw a golden opportunity and purchased the firm with its fifteen employees and guaranteed service to the orange growers, viticulturists, and dry farmers of the Inland Empire.

A year later the United States entered World War II, and Johnson found himself with parts in short supply, new equipment unavailable, and skilled mechanics enlisted in the war effort. With only six employees, he assembled machines out of parts. The company continued to grow, and by 1945 had moved to new facilities on Seventh Street and added stores in Coachella and Ontario.

Revolutionary changes occurred in all types of machinery after the war. Caterpillar had moved into the heavy-duty earth-moving equipment and engine power fields. It was none too soon for the Inland Empire. Large numbers of military personnel stationed in the area during the war returned to create a population boom that needed homes, businesses, major thoroughfares, and a new water system. The mountains and desert were rich in ores and minerals and their extraction also demanded heavy equipment. Johnson Tractor Co. found itself in the hub of activity, in

This 1942 photo shows the Johnson Tractor Co. service shop.

the fastest-growing area in California; it was ready to meet the challenge. In 1963 W. Ruel Johnson chose a 48-acre site on the corner of La Cadena and Citrus for the location of his fourth plant.

Johnson retired in 1969. He had worked seven days a week for twenty-nine years. He had treated his customers and employees with honesty and integrity and his business had thrived on his goodwill. Now he passed it on to his son, who had been working in the business since age thirteen.

Bill Johnson took over a concern in which agricultural tractors then represented only one percent of its business. The area had changed and so had Johnson Tractor. In 1976 the firm began to add other lines of equipment, including forklifts and hydraulic cranes.

The future holds yet further changes for this forward-looking enterprise. New machinery designed for refurbishing crumbling metropolitan infrastructures, and for maintaining highways and recycling materials, will eventually be added to Johnson Tractor's growing inventory.

Freeland Tractor & Equipment Co. moved to this Eighth Street store in 1937. The firm was purchased by W. Ruel Johnson in 1940.

SHADOW MOUNTAIN RESORT AND RACQUET CLUB

Shadow Mountain Resort and Racquet Club's figure-eight, Olympic-size swimming pool was the first of its kind in the area. The Top of the Court Restaurant is in the background.

Clifford W. Henderson spearheaded the development of Palm Desert, boasting an hour more sun each day than Palm Springs, with Shadow Mountain Club as the focus of the new post-World War II community.

Henderson, who had been associated with the National Air Races, was the first director of Los Angeles' Department of Airports and later, with his brother Phil, developed the Pan Pacific Auditorium in Los Angeles. He fell in love with the desert while recuperating after World War II, in the exact area that he and his older brother, Randall, editor of *Desert Magazine,* had discussed for a new community to be named Palm Desert.

He approached his Pan Pacific associates, men well known in Los Angeles' financial and entertainment communities, to back the new project. Early in 1945 Cliff and Phil formed the Palm Desert Corporation to develop the townsite.

Central to the development was the Shadow Mountain Club, the creation of Cliff and Leonard Firestone. A tennis enthusiast, Cliff planned to make tennis the new local sport and built the tennis court first, then the figure-eight pool (still the largest in the Coachella Valley). The million-dollar clubhouse was lavish for a site with cactus as its sole landscaping. Its opening in 1948 was a major event that lured Hollywood stars and affluent visitors.

When completed, Shadow Mountain Club included an artificial lake, the swimming pool with Olympic diving boards, a golf course, a clubhouse, and cottages. The clubhouse sported a bar with its own waterfall.

Through the 1960s the club remained the focal point for local gatherings with activities for all ages: Easter egg hunts and parades, movies for children, and church services for equestrians. The first Christmas Henderson invited all the local children for a toy, expecting a maximum attendance of 100. When 400 youngsters arrived, his staff frantically raided nearby stores for additional presents.

Members of the golf club eventually purchased a portion of the club in order to create a private organization. In 1972, when Lowe Enterprises bought Shadow Mountain, the racquet club consisted of twenty acres, the major portion of the clubhouse, seventy hotel rooms, the pool, seven tennis courts, and a two-story tennis shop and restaurant complex. Bob Lowe, the developer, envisioned condominiums. He started by converting the hotel rooms and using the profits from their sale for continued development. By 1979 Shadow Mountain Resort and Racquet Club had been totally developed with 167 condominiums, four swimming pools, four spas, sixteen tennis courts, two paddle courts, and conference facilities. Condominium rentals are now managed by Destination Resort Management Company. With its many greenbelts and outdoor activities, the club has maintained its tradition of being a family-oriented resort.

ERNST & WHINNEY

Located in the rapidly growing downtown area of Riverside, the Ernst & Whinney office stands out, marked by a prominent sign, a first for the firm in an industry that, for years, did not advertise. Founded by brothers A.C. and Theodore Ernst in Cleveland, Ohio, in July 1903, the enterprise has been a pioneer in the field of public accounting and ranks high among the big eight firms internationally. With over 300 offices and 22,000 employees in seventy-five countries, Ernst & Whinney specializes in accounting, auditing, tax, management-consulting, employee benefits, and special services to smaller, privately owned businesses.

In the first decade of this century, however, the field of accounting was in its fledgling stages and very few businesses had adequate accounting records. In 1906, at age twenty-five, A.C. Ernst found himself the sole partner of Ernst & Ernst. Undaunted and guided by clear vision, within two years he opened his first branch office in Chicago, increasing the number to ten by 1917. He developed in these early years the procedure he called "system work," the initial establishment of the field of management-consulting services.

Even after his death in 1948, many of Ernst's early policies and directions continued to guide the firm in its remarkable growth. In 1974 Ernst & Ernst merged with the English accounting practice of Whinney, making it an international firm.

As Ernst & Whinney, the firm expanded into the rapidly evolving Inland Empire in August 1982 through its merger with a local accounting firm founded by Donald Ecker and Jerry Bigbie. Ecker, a California State Polytechnic University at Pomona graduate, moved to Riverside in 1969. Bigbie, an Oklahoma Baptist University graduate, came to Riverside from Alaska in 1967. The two formed a partnership in the mid-1970s and ag-

gressively built their firm into one of the largest local practices. They also became very active in civic affairs. With the merger, Ecker became managing partner and Bigbie became partner in charge of the privately owned business practice.

In the fall of 1982 Joseph Barr, a fifteen-year veteran of Ernst & Whinney's Cleveland headquarters, joined the Riverside office to become partner in charge of audit. Following Barr, Chuck White, previously an attorney and managing partner of Best, Best & Krieger in Riverside, joined Ernst & Whinney as principal in charge of tax. Since the merger, the local office has increased from twenty-one to sixty-five employees, re-

The downtown Riverside office of Ernst & Whinney.

flecting not only the rapid growth of the firm, but also the tremendous support from Inland Empire businesses and organizations.

Ernst & Whinney looks to the future with the same winning principles originally laid down by A.C. Ernst in the early part of the century. "If we are unique," says one inside observer, "it is because we are aggressive and innovative, promoting within our firm the philosophy of giving back to one's community through a commitment to community development."

RIVERSIDE COMMUNITY HOSPITAL-MEDICAL CENTER

In 1901, thirty-one years after the founding of Riverside, Dr. Cary Gill and a few other local physicians created the community's first hospital with an investment of a few hundred dollars. Located on Eleventh and Orange streets, the facility consisted of a small, remodeled cottage. "Up until that time," states Mrs. Aileen Boylan, historian for the Riverside County Medical Association, "most physicians transported their patients into Los Angeles by railroad." Mrs. Boylan continues, "In addition to being one of the primary founders of the hospital, he was one of the individuals responsible for routing the Security Pacific Railroad through Riverside."

Dr. Gill had moved to Riverside in 1876 at the age of forty to pioneer a medical practice in the new settlement. Within a short period of time he became active in the community and helped to shape its rapid growth.

By 1903 the expanding community needed a larger hospital. A small group of physicians and concerned citizens raised $21,335 for a new 25-bed facility on Twelfth and Walnut (now Brockton) streets.

Since Riverside City Hospital was privately owned and operated, it was subject to the direction of its owners. By 1920, when the hospital had again outgrown its quarters, the board of directors refused to invest in expansion. With foresight, one board member, Dr. C. Van Zwalenburg, moved to create a nonprofit institution that would be responsive to the community's needs. "Several things have happened to interfere, especially the war," wrote Van Zwalenburg. "But after several conversations the thought was to raise a sum of money and buy up the stockholders who demanded it and take the rest of the money and build a hospital for the benefit of the public and not for revenue."

Subsequently, the stock in the hospital was cancelled and a $250,000

Riverside physician, Dr. Cary Gill, established the community's first hospital in 1901.

building fund campaign was begun in 1922. The hospital's *Health Tidings* announced in December of that year that 230 babies had been born in the past two years and that "all the babies lived and thrived. What is that worth to you?" Donations were critical since the hospital operated on patient fees and a private room in 1922 cost fifty dollars per week; an operating room for major surgery cost $12.50.

The new hospital opened March 6, 1925, at its present location on Fourteenth and Magnolia streets. The first patient was a woman who was moved from the old building the day before she gave birth to a son.

The following year sixty women formed the hospital's first auxiliary. Volunteers were the backbone of the expanded facility. They did much of the original landscaping; a sewing committee made four dozen surgical gowns, eighteen dozen towels, 100 tray cloths, two dozen napkins, and sixteen sheets in the hospital's first year; the Jams, Jellies and Vegetable committee produced sixty-eight quarts of fruit, forty glasses of jelly, four dozen eggs, and one can of coffee. The auxiliary's first financial pledge was for $6,000; by 1985, with 335 members, it had given such significant donations as $44,000 for the Cardiac Care Unit.

Additions and building programs characterized the years following World War II. The baby boom had its own effect; a 32-bed maternity ward had to be added in 1950 to keep up with Riverside's growing population. A three-year fund drive reached fruition in 1956 with the erection of a three-story, $1.25-mil-

lion addition. Yet, only ten years later, the hospital again broke ground for a six-story wing. This $5.5-million project was financed by community donations and borrowed monies and created an area medical center.

The hospital's expansion program continued through the 1970s with

David W. Patton, president of Riverside Community Hospital.

the opening of the Rehabilitation Unit. In 1973 the Riverside Community Hospital established a foundation as a separate corporation for fund-raising purposes. Since its inception over five million dollars has been raised. In 1981 the Golden Staff Society, a 52-member physician donor support group, was formed as an offshoot of the foundation and they have raised $95,000.

Alongside these three developments, the 1970s and early 1980s saw expansion of the Coronary Care Unit in 1974; construction of the Professional Building in 1975; completion of the Family Practice Group in 1976; the merger and acquisition of Knollwood Center, which houses the Alcoholic Treatment Center in

1978; construction of the Outpatient Surgery Unit in 1980; and completion of the Mental Health Unit in 1982.

In May 1984 David W. Patton joined Riverside Community Hospital as president. He foresees the hospital continuing to provide technologically advanced programs and services of high quality in support of inpatient care, but at the same time broadening the scope of services in ambulatory care. An inpatient diabetic treatment center was recently established, and a facilities development program to upgrade surgery and intensive care is under study. New ambulatory care programs include a home health care service, a gastrointestinal laboratory, and new

The thirty-bed Riverside Hospital (inset), at Twelfth and Walnut (Brockton), was opened in 1903 and was the forerunner of Riverside Community Hospital-Medical Center.

outpatient surgery capabilities. The concept of a diagnostic, ambulatory care "shopping mall" is under study.

"The future of the community hospital is tied closely to the reimbursement system," states Patton. "Health care consumers are looking for a quality product, competitively priced, and they will shop the marketplace to find that product. The health care consumer is more than likely the one responsible for paying the bill, and that means that business and industry are influencing care choices as never before."

ALFRED M. LEWIS, INC.

Alfred M. Lewis, Inc., records its history from the year 1905, when Alfred M. Lewis ventured into the retail grocery store business in Riverside.

In 1918 Lewis bought out his partner and named the small group of grocery stores the Alfred M. Lewis Company. At about that time he chanced to buy seventy-five cases of soap, which he sold to neighboring store owners at cost plus a small handling charge of seven cents per case. Lewis originally intended to be in the retail business only, but with the volume soap purchase he became a wholesaler as well.

By the late 1920s the retail multiple-store operation developed into a local wholesale enterprise, which was incorporated in 1933. Today the firm is engaged principally in the purchasing of merchandise in large quantities from hundreds of manufacturers, processors, and other vendors, and then warehousing and distributing these products. Delivery occurs from five major distributing centers (Riverside, San Diego, and Northridge, California; Phoenix, Arizona; and Las Vegas, Nevada) to approximately 3,700 retail stores ranging in size from small convenience stores to supermarkets in California, Arizona,

Nevada, New Mexico, Colorado, and Utah. Also serviced by Alfred M. Lewis, Inc., are 104 military exchanges and commissaries, and food-service facilities such as restaurants and hotels. Efficient warehousing methods and a modern truck fleet assure rapid assembly and delivery of products to customers in a prompt and dependable manner.

The year 1933 was also the beginning of the company's cash-and-carry operation, initiated with a small wholesale warehouse in Riverside to meet the needs of smaller independent store owners. Today Alfred M. Lewis, Inc., provides food products, general merchandise, small appliances, janitorial and paper supplies, and associated items for 5,000 small retailers, distributed through thirty-eight strategically located cash-and-

carry outlets in the Southwest.

In 1983 Alfred M. Lewis, Inc., launched its sponsorship of some thirty IGA stores in Southern California. IGA, the Chicago-based Independent Grocers' Alliance, is the third-largest food retailing organization in the nation. Full-line services, including private-label merchandise and cooperative advertising, are offered through the local wholesale supplier to the grocery retailer. Thus, Alfred M. Lewis, Inc., is expanding its eighty-year business now to provide services to small Southwest retailers usually available only to large chain supermarkets.

Alfred M. Lewis offered home delivery for customers of his 1912 retail grocery store business.

A modern fleet of trucks assures rapid delivery of products to Lewis customers throughout the Southwest.

CORONA COMMUNITY HOSPITAL

Returning from medical missionary service in Argentina in 1929, Dr. Henry Herman recognized an urgent need for a maternity home in his new community. Corona then had only four physicians, a few dentists, and one small hospital. He opened the El Nido Maternity Home in 1933 after purchasing and remodeling an existing rooming house at 812 Main Street.

The facility accommodated three patients and was quickly expanded to nine beds by 1935, making it a licensed, full-scale maternity hospital.

Both Dr. Herman and his wife, Alma, worked long hours to meet the growing demands for services. By 1940 they were licensed to operate as a general hospital with twenty-one medical/surgical beds and three obstetrical beds. By the end of the decade the hospital, which had physically expanded in every direction, had grown to thirty-one beds.

What had started as a skeleton staff in the 1930s had grown by 1962 to fifty-six employees, handling 1,756 patients. The need for a new, larger hospital was all too evident. The following year Dr. Herman purchased the adjacent American Red Cross building. Shortly thereafter, he donated the hospital to Loma Linda University which transferred the facility to Associated Medical Institutions, Inc. (now known as VERSA-CARE), to operate as a nonprofit entity. Founded in 1951 as a private, nonprofit corporation, VERSA-CARE has been committed to the development of an individual's maximum spiritual, physical, and emotional potential.

To meet this goal VERSACARE immediately undertook expansion of

the hospital, and by April 29, 1965, opened a new $1.2-million, two-story facility adjacent to the old one. In 1968 a third-floor addition brought the total bed capacity to 148. Since then, the hospital has broadened its capabilities to include neurological rehabilitation, eating disorders, cancer treatment, and treatment of premenstrual syndrome. The hospital has also invested nearly one million dollars to open the area's first permanent C-T scanner.

The hospital has the only Southern California hospital-based fitness center, a 15,000-square-foot facility known as the Total Health System.

In addition, Corona Community Hospital sponsors a home health care agency, a hospice program, and a site for the county's senior nutrition program. In 1983 it donated adjoining land for a 36-unit senior citizen

Corona Community Hospital, and its affiliated corporations, began as a maternity home under the guidance of Henry Herman, M.D., in 1933.

housing project. To supplement this, the county's first adult day health care center opened in 1984 as the initial phase of the Corona Community Care Center, a ten-acre complex with a skilled nursing facility soon to be available.

As Byron Streifling, president, has commented, "... we have implemented a number of ways to deliver better care requiring shorter stays in the hospital as well as innovative programs to improve the general health and well-being of our community." It is this commitment and its "whole person" health care approach that keeps Corona Community Hospital in the forefront of the community.

Construction on the hospital's expansion will conclude in 1986. The new wing will not add beds, but the $11-million project will help to improve the hospital's outpatient services—an area that has experienced dramatic growth.

BLUE BANNER COMPANY, INC.

Citrus packinghouses liberally dotted the Riverside area in the 1930s and 1940s. Most were fairly small, family-run operations. Fred Krinard and his son Russell started their own packinghouse during these turbulent years.

Among their employees was an ambitious, hard-working man who knew the business well: W.J. Mazzetti. Mazzetti had learned from his Italian parents that hard work, long hours, and integrity would bring success in life.

His parents came to the United States in the early 1900s. They worked for the Arlington Heights Fruit Company, which planted Riverside's greenbelt of citrus. When the firm went bankrupt in 1926 and sold its holdings, the Mazzettis were able to purchase their first grove.

Born and raised in Riverside, W.J. grew up with the citrus industry as a central part of his life. Before joining Krinard Packing Company, he had worked for Arlington Heights Fruit Company.

By the early 1950s Mazzetti was a partner in Krinard Packing. When the Krinards decided to sell the business, their partner was the major buyer. In 1951 Mazzetti incorporated the packinghouse as Blue Banner Company, Inc. The plant was located on Fourth Street, one and one-half blocks from its present site. In 1965 he purchased and remodeled the old Cresmer Manufacturing plant,

Blue Banner Company, Inc., is located at 2601 Third Street, Riverside.

which had been constructed in 1918. Mazzetti then had a 70,000-square-foot citrus packinghouse, a truck maintenance shop, a carton storage shed, and an office.

In 1964 Mazzetti's son, Tom, came to work full time after receiving his degree in business from San Jose State University. He had been working summers and vacations on the 250-acre citrus farms his father had been acquiring over the years. When his father passed away in 1972, Tom became president of Blue Banner.

Since then he has made major changes in the family business. Citrus farming has increased to 800

Checking the quality of fruit in the field are (left to right) Daniel Sandoval, Charles Browning of the field department, a grove worker, president Tom Mazzetti, and another grove worker.

acres in four counties. Blue Banner has stayed in the forefront of the industry by continuously modernizing its operations. These innovations have increased the firm's volume from 800,000 boxes of oranges, mandarins, and grapefruit annually in the 1950s to three million in the 1980s. As a licensed Sunkist packinghouse, Blue Banner now ranks fourth to fifth in size of Sunkist's sixty U.S. packinghouses.

Tom Mazzetti and Blue Banner have long been involved in community service. Mazzetti has made it a policy to support local community activities, such as church bazaars, athletic teams, and youth clubs.

It is clear from the solid reputation that Blue Banner has acquired in the Riverside area that hard work, long hours, and integrity have indeed paid off for the Mazzettis.

SAN GORGONIO PASS MEMORIAL HOSPITAL

San Gorgonio Pass Memorial Hospital in Banning is surrounded by two rows of mature trees—a part of the living memorial to those who gave their lives or health in world wars I and II. In August 1944, with the country still engaged in war, a great many Banning and Beaumont citizens expressed their desire for a tribute in the form of a hospital. Howard Osborn and Dr. Charles E. McClean publicly advocated a hospital memorial in September 1944 and in the following election the electorate mandated twelve to one the formation of a hospital district, and four to one the formation of the hospital.

Early in 1947 the Beaumont Kiwanis began a campaign to promote the district hospital. Subsequently,

San Gorgonio Pass Memorial Hospital was dedicated on March 4, 1951. The institution has since undergone two major expansions, in 1973 and 1980.

the Beaumont and Banning hospital committees met together. They formed one body, the San Gorgonio Pass Memorial Hospital Central Committee, with five members from each committee appointed by the city councils: Ray F. Allen, Leonard Dovert, Charles T. Poole, Mrs. Capitola Crosby, Mrs. Genevieve Morse, Dr. David C. Williams, Mrs. Hildred Crawford, Fred Roberge,

Today San Gorgonio Pass Memorial Hospital is a 78,000-square-foot, 68-bed, general and acute care, state-of-the-art medical center.

Fred Herfurth, and Carl Barkow.

After four years of diligent problem solving, the committee concluded its work and was superseded by a five-member board of directors appointed at the time of the district formation by the county board of supervisors. Fred Roberge, William King, Frank Stowell, Sydney Bridges, and Jesse Price comprised the board.

Their work culminated in the March 4, 1951, dedication of the San Gorgonio Pass Memorial Hospital. The new facility had thirty-four medical-surgical and ten maternity beds.

Since that time the hospital has undergone two major expansions, in 1973 and 1980. It is now a 78,000-square-foot, 68-bed, general and acute care, state-of-the-art hospital. The medical staff has grown to number seventy-seven, with 240 employees operating the hospital. It serves a population area of 35,000 including Banning, Beaumont, Cabazon, Calimesa, Cherry Valley, Whitewater, and part of Yucaipa.

The Pass Hospital is in the process of a major corporate restructuring to meet the needs of the communities and the future changes in the health care industry. The district hospital will become the organizational framework for a nonprofit community institution.

In addition, the hospital is looking to structure a total health care system. The first step has been the formation of Real Pass. This district-owned subsidiary functions to attract capital for the construction of a medical office building. The board foresees a continuing-care retirement center for which the hospital has acquired fourteen adjacent acres to build an initial 100 units. The future also holds plans for a skilled nursing facility and home health service to complement the present acute care services. Thus will San Gorgonio Pass Memorial Hospital continue to serve as a living memorial.

CENTRE BRANDS, INC.

Harry E. and Mary Roberts had started their venture, Butcher Boy Foods, with the theory that if you provide customers with what they request, business will thrive. And thrive it did. Starting in January 1950 in a small rented Riverside building, the Robertses ran a locker plant with six employees, cutting and wrapping beef for customers. Expansion began after receiving a contract for beef patties from the original local McDonald's Drive-in in 1952.

For four years the Robertses remained content with the steady growth spurred by the McDonald's contract. In 1956, however, they perceived the great potential of Mexican foods and introduced frozen burritos. At the same time they also supplied a line of frozen meat and barbecue products. Sales were made from several refrigerated route trucks providing service throughout the state of California, offering products to small "mom and pop" shops and restaurants. Their son, Duane, broke into the business at age eighteen, driving the most demanding route through the desert from early morning to late at night.

By 1960 Harry Roberts realized that greater opportunity and profit were in processing, rather than distribution. Thus, the firm built its first facility, only 5,000 square feet, on Main Street in Riverside. Eight years later Butcher Boy Foods was unquestionably one of the largest frozen-food processors in California.

Acquisition of Western Taco Co., processor of the Carmen Brand, was one of several influences on the 1969 decision to divest the company of its distribution division and concentrate solely on food processing. Further acquisitions, such as Lolita Mexican Foods in 1972, and Markes Foods in 1979, only cemented this commitment.

In 1980 Central Soya Company, Inc., purchased Butcher Boy Foods. Duane Roberts was then president. By that time Butcher Boy had an estimated 40 percent of the frozen Mexican foods market. About 80 percent of sales were in the food-service division, both commercial and noncommercial segments of the industry. Sales to supermarkets and military exchanges comprised the firm's second market under the Marquez and Little Juan labels.

By 1984 the company, renamed Centre Brands, Inc., had processing plants in Riverside, Montebello, and Santa Ana, California, and in Albuquerque, New Mexico. The Riverside plant had been expanded from 8,000 square feet to 73,000 square feet with additional acreage available for further expansion.

Centre Brands' future promises boundless opportunity as the company continues to lead the way with innovation in the fast-growing Mexican food segment. Consumers everywhere are discovering and requesting more and more eating experiences as provided by Centre Brands' products.

THE AMES GROUP

In 1914 E.B. Ames sold his Highland Park grocery store and set out with his wife, Cordelia, for Mecca on a new adventure. He purchased eighty acres from the Southern Pacific Railroad, gradually cleared the land, and became, by the mid-1920s, one of the Coachella Valley's most highly successful and regarded farmers. Unfortunately, he was not so astute at other investments and, when he purchased a Durant auto agency in Riverside just in time for the 1929 stock market crash, his business career ended.

His son, George, took over the ranch then in 1930. A veteran of World War I, he had returned to work with his father on the ranch and sold real estate on the side. His success came not from the methodical, painstaking practices of his father, but from his creativity. He invented the concept and technology of icing sweet corn to ensure its freshness. Along with this he also pioneered several direct-marketing techniques. Whereas E.B. Ames had marketed his produce door to door in Riverside in the 1920s, George leased a stall at the then-new Los Angeles Farmers Market at Third and Fairfax in the 1930s. He survived the Depression in this desert land by growing and marketing fruits and vegetables under the trade logo— "From the Devil's Bowl." In 1942, tir-

The Ames management team in 1965.

ed of farming, he sold both the ranch and his produce business to join the war effort.

George's son, Paul, had been born and reared on the Mecca ranch and had studied at UCLA and UC Davis, graduating with a B.S. in plant science. After service in World War II Paul decided to return to the Coachella Valley. He tried his luck with a crop with which his father had been successful: sweet potatoes. He designed new machinery for their harvesting and packaging and had captured the early Los Angeles market when someone developed a better sweet potato that would not grow in the valley.

With quick foresight Paul moved on to ranch development and management. The Ames Group has since expanded to include not only Ames Management Service Inc. and Green End Development Co., Inc., but also Ames Real Estate Inc. and Mecca Farms, Inc., comprised of his own ranches.

Among other properties now owned by Paul is the original Ames Ranch, which he bought back in 1968 and has planted to Ruby Blush grapefruit and spectacular Red Flame seedless grapes. He is also a pioneer and leader in the production of exceptionally high-quality Valencia oranges.

Paul, like his grandfather, is highly respected as an agribusinessman but like his father, he is also an inventor.

Paul Ames poses with a four-foot, two-way plow in 1957.

He has pioneered and conceived many new techniques for the expanded production necessary in the postwar years. He built the first reservoir for overnight water storage and produced a plastic membrane lining to prevent water seepage.

Paul Ames has maintained the independent, pioneer spirit of his grandfather and father before him. It is probably the combination of qualities inherited from both his father and grandfather that is making this third-generation Coachella Valleyite finally successful in subduing the desert. With this as the underlying strength of The Ames Group, the firm has been a major force in the development of the Coachella Valley and will continue to be in the years to come.

LOMA LINDA UNIVERSITY, LA SIERRA CAMPUS

With the explosion of metropolitan Los Angeles following World War I, Southern California Seventh-day Adventists feared the urbanization of their San Fernando Academy. They felt an urgent need for a rural boarding school with acreage for a farm and campus. In 1922 the Southeastern California Conference purchased a 330-acre portion of Rancho La Sierra, south of Riverside, from W.J. Hole, who remained a strong financial supporter until his death.

The school opened on October 3, 1922, with only two buildings partially completed. The faculty consisted of six members. James I. Robison, the first president of La Sierra Academy and Normal School, later recalled that faith, courage, and loyal cooperation saw them through the first years. Over 100 students enrolled in the first year and overlooked such inconveniences as only four washbasins for the entire student body and no electricity for the first two months. Students worked twelve hours a week in these early years to offset their school expenses of thirty-five dollars a month.

The student body expanded rapid-

The school library in the 1930s.

ly and created new demands on the physical plant. Despite the original hardships, the school became so prominent that it was elevated to junior college status in 1927 with an enrollment in the junior college grades of fifty-four students.

By the next year eighty-seven students were enrolled and the school was renamed Southern California Junior College. Enrollment remained constant through the Depression, but by 1932 a fourth building, later named San Fernando Hall, eased the

By 1934 the college was accredited and pre-dentistry, -nursing, and -med programs had been added. This is the student body of that era.

The interior of Matheson Chapel.

crowded conditions.

Several changes had occurred by 1934. The school was accredited and pre-dentistry, -nursing, and -med programs had been added. By the end of the 1930s the physical plant had been expanded to house a student body of 400. La Sierra College was now an accredited three-year school.

With the outbreak of World War II, the campus and farm were briefly considered for a military training camp and hospital but the school's contribution to the war effort took

the form of the La Sierra Medical Cadet Corps for noncombatant military training.

In May 1942 fifteen students received the first bachelor of science degrees to be conferred by the school. In 1945 the first bachelor of arts degrees were given to another fifteen students out of a graduating

The new library was built in 1973.

Completed in 1982, E.E. Cossentine Hall was named in honor of a former president of the school.

class of fifty-seven. The following year La Sierra College became a fully accredited, four-year school.

The postwar years were marked by increased enrollment with the return of veterans and great physical growth for the campus. By 1954 La Sierra Academy, which had been housed in the basement of one building, separated itself from the college and moved off campus.

Several men had served as president of the college during these years of growth. Erwin E. Cossentine became president of Southern California Junior College in 1930, and during his twelve-year administration saw the school become La Sierra College. Lowell R. Rasmussen was president from 1942 to 1946, and Godfrey T. Anderson from 1946 to 1954. Norval F. Pease, a Bible teacher who had pastored the College Church, followed Anderson; in 1960 William Landeen took over the presidency, to be succeeded in 1962 by Fabian Meier. He died one year later and was replaced by David Bieber.

By 1960 enrollment had reached 999 but students still experienced a personal relationship with teachers since the faculty was still less special-ized and often taught several subjects. That year was a landmark in the school's history for the introduction of three master's degree programs. The 1960s were also marked by much building on campus.

The most significant event, however, occurred in 1967 when La Sierra College merged with Loma Linda University, the medical school in nearby Loma Linda, forming the largest Seventh-day Adventist educational institution. The concept of merger was not new; it had been proposed as early as the 1930s. But the Western Association of Schools and Colleges' limitation of accreditation to institutions with full liberal arts programs had necessitated the move. With the formation of the La Sierra Campus, Loma Linda University now had a liberal arts college. David Bieber, La Sierra's president, took over administration of both campuses and V. Norskov Olsen became La Sierra Campus provost in 1972, later to be made president.

Expansion and growth have continued to be the keystones of the La Sierra Campus. Through the 1970s and early 1980s the physical plant was renovated and enlarged. The student body, many of whom have been foreign students, also grew, reaching a peak of almost 2,600 in 1978. The School of Education, which was formed in 1968, offered the first doctoral degree in 1981.

There are now on the La Sierra Campus twenty-one departments offering over 100 majors, with a faculty of approximately 168 full-time instructors.

Within the next five to ten years the university will spend ten to fifteen million dollars on building projects. Whereas the sciences attracted large numbers of students in earlier years, now business and economics have the greatest draw and will be needing expanded facilities.

As a community of both faith and learning, Loma Linda University continues to be dedicated to education "to make man whole," to help its students and teachers reach their highest potential in education, research, and service.

LA QUINTA HOTEL

With grace, charm, and dignity La Quinta Hotel has reigned over the Coachella Valley since 1926 as a refuge in the quiet of the Santa Rosa Mountains. Through time and several changes of ownership, La Quinta Hotel has grown from six original cottages to a hotel of 268 rooms and suites. The commitment to the privacy and comfort of the guests, a legacy of graciousness given to the hotel by its original owner Walter H. Morgan, has continued.

This 1937 photograph shows La Quinta Hotel's casitas. The hotel, which opened in 1926, has entertained many celebrated guests.

Born in San Francisco in 1874, Morgan was the youngest son of wealthy Morgan Oyster Company owner John S. Morgan. He came to the desert in 1921 for his health and purchased 1,400 acres. He named his secluded retreat La Quinta after a Mexican hacienda of that name.

To help him turn his dreams into reality, Morgan hired budding Pasadena architect Gordon Kaufman in 1925. Kaufman not only designed the buildings and landscaping, but the furniture and lighting as well. The Mexican laborers crafted from the site more than 100,000 adobe bricks, 60,000 roof tiles, and 5,000 floor tiles for an estimated construction cost of $150,000. Also included was a nine-

hole golf course designed by golfer Norman Beth.

La Quinta Hotel first opened during the Christmas holiday in 1926, entertaining such guests as President William Howard Taft's brother, and the William Crockers of San Francisco. After a successful first season Morgan made his hotel a social "must" by inviting Hollywood celebrities.

Walter H. Morgan died in 1931. The hotel closed that fifth season in financial turmoil. The courts appointed B.J. Bradner, an investor in Morgan's dream, as receiver and he exercised control until 1945.

The Hollywood stars continued their interest in the property as well. "I'm off to La Quinta," Bette Davis told newspaper reporters on the set of *Jezebel,* and she was but one of many who came.

In the spring of 1942 the hotel closed for the duration of World War II except for reports of General George Patton's staff using some of the facilities.

In 1945 Chicagoan John Balaban purchased the hotel. In the late 1950s he sold it to Chicago attorney Leonard Ettleson. It was Ettleson who brought golf back to La Quinta. He not only created La Quinta Country Club in 1957, but hired golf professionals Ernie Vossler and Joe Walser, Jr., in 1972 as consultants on a new golf course.

Vossler and Walser, senior vice-presidents of Landmark Land Company, Inc., also recognized the potential of the underdeveloped land that stretched from the hotel into the hillsides. In July 1977 the company purchased Ettleson's interest in the property, including La Quinta Hotel.

The hotel's golf club opened in 1980, followed in 1981 by the hotel's tennis club, under the tutorship of eleven top tennis professionals.

Through careful additions, the charm and grace that made La Quinta Hotel famous in the past have been enhanced to make it famous today.

The entrance of La Quinta Hotel, 1984.

WASHBURN & SONS

Located in a small building designed to be movable—but never moved since its construction in Highgrove in 1952—Washburn & Sons started in the citrus pest-control business in 1921. The family, however, traces its beginnings in citrus farming back to 1885 when A.C. Thomson planted citrus on his Duarte ranch. He also owned a citrus packinghouse and nursery, which he used to plant his second ranch in Glendora. The trees planted were the successful Thomson Improved Navel Orange, which Thomson named in 1891.

One of his eight children, Jessie, married Clyde Washburn, who ran a fumigation crew for Custer and Watterbury Pest Controllers in Glendora around 1910. His son Archie and friend Gordon Bell found the work agreeable and, for one year following high school, joined Archie's father on a crew.

On August 6, 1921, young Washburn and Bell opened their own pest-control business in Glendora, offering H.C.N. gas fumigation and oil spraying services in Riverside, San Bernardino, and Los Angeles counties. Washburn & Bell quickly became one of the largest in the industry and found it necessary to open another office in Riverside. Dressed in brown riding boots, jodhpurs, and felt hat, Washburn was easily identifiable when he moved his family to Riverside in 1928 and operated an office out of his house until 1939.

Pests were primarily controlled by cyanide fumigation until 1950, when parathion was introduced. The gas was pumped under tents placed over individual trees. A good four-man crew could fumigate ten acres, consisting of 1,000 trees, in one night. Washburn & Bell was chosen to conduct experimental work in parathion use from 1948 to 1950 for the University of California at Riverside.

Archie's son, Phil, started working

Three generations of the Washburn family (left to right), David, Dennis, Alan, Phil, and Archie A., are all involved in the diverse interests of Washburn & Sons.

part time in the business in 1944 at the age of thirteen. He attended local schools and in 1948-1949 went to California State Polytechnic University at Pomona to study citrus production and pest control. Phil then joined the firm on a full-time basis.

Gordon Bell remained a partner until his death in 1958. Washburn closed the Glendora office and created Washburn & Sons. He then retired and sold the business to Phil in 1967. In 1975 Phil sold portions to his sons, Alan, Dennis, and David.

Washburn & Sons is now the largest citrus pest-control firm in Southern California, operating in five counties and two states on about 6,000 acres. Alan shares the business responsibilities with his father and they have expanded into mechanical tree topping and hedging of citrus trees.

David and Dennis now operate the family's grapefruit ranches in

In the 1930s cyanide and tents was the method used to fumigate citrus groves.

Hemet. The initial 160 acres purchased in 1945 have now expanded to 400 acres of grapefruit. It is this diversification of interests that they feel will ensure the future success of the Washburn family business.

UNIVERSITY OF CALIFORNIA, RIVERSIDE

The University of California first came to Riverside in response to a need for citrus research. A UC outpost—established in 1906 in the form of a two-man, 23-acre Citrus Experiment Station—planted the seeds from which sprang UC Riverside, a campus that today is spread over 1,200 acres and educates nearly 5,000 undergraduate and graduate students each year.

As the premier research institution of higher education in the region, UCR is uniquely equipped to serve the Inland Empire in its economic, social, and cultural development as the campus forwards the university's missions of teaching, research, and public service for the state and nation.

With its world-renowned faculty conducting research at the forefront of knowledge, UCR provides a foundation for economic development of the Inland Empire. The future of high technology in the nation is based on the advanced scientific information that emerges from university classrooms and laboratories and on the educated men and women prepared for significant roles in industry and business. Partnership opportunities mutually beneficial to UCR and the Inland Empire abound.

A broad-based general campus in the University of California system, UCR provides undergraduate and graduate education in the sciences, arts, humanities, and professional fields through its College of Natural and Agricultural Sciences, College of Humanities and Social Sciences, School of Education, Graduate School of Management, Graduate Division, and Summer Sessions. The faculty and staff numbered more than 3,600 in 1985.

Given the importance of research

The architecture and landscaping of the Humanities Building and Plaza are characteristic of the campus at UC Riverside.

The Citrus Experiment Station, shown in this 1920s photograph, began the University of California presence in Riverside. A liberal arts campus for undergraduates was opened on surrounding land in 1954; expansion to a general campus of undergraduate and graduate education came in 1959.

conducted on the campus, UCR not unexpectedly is the site of several special facilities, unique in the world or the nation, as well as a number of formally established research units. In addition to the Citrus Research Center and Agricultural Experiment Station, research units located on campus include the Center for Social and Behavioral Science Research, Dry Lands Research Institute, Institute of Geophysics and Planetary Physics, Statewide Air Pollution Research Center, and seven sites in the UC Natural Land and Water Reserve System, including the Philip L. Boyd Desert Center. The campus also is the home of the regional headquar-

ters of Cooperative Extension and a branch of University Extension, which enrolls thousands of area residents in its wide-ranging curricular offerings each year.

An educational institution's effect on the surrounding community is almost beyond measure in many areas—intellectual, economic, social, and cultural. The presence of a university deepens and enriches the cultural environment. Each year classical and contemporary entertainment is brought by some of the world's finest performing artists. In addition, conferences, symposia, and other special events regularly draw top scholars in various fields for an exchange of the most up-to-date knowledge.

Among UCR's special attractions is the California Museum of Photography, one of the most important centers in the nation for the study of photography. The museum is host to a collection of 12,000 prints, 4,000 pieces of apparatus and cameras, and

an unparalleled selection of several hundred thousand early stereographs.

Visitors to UCR are struck by the visual and aural beauty of its Carillon Tower, set in the center of the campus. Raised in the tower, 161 feet above the ground, the carillon consists of forty-eight bronze bells, ranging in weight from a manageable twenty-eight pounds to a gargantuan 5,100. The sound of UCR's musical instrument can be heard across campus on the hour and in special concerts.

The UCR Botanic Gardens comprise both the landscaped campus and thirty-seven acres of gardens along its eastern borders. The gardens were established primarily for teaching purposes and serve not only UCR faculty and students but other educational institutions and the general public as well.

UCR's origin as the Citrus Experiment Station was in answer to a plea to state government from Southern California citrus growers for a research facility. Since those early years the Citrus Experiment Station has provided both basic and applied agricultural information and quick aid to California agriculture in times of emergency. Because the facility's work grew over time to encompass some 150 crop commodities, its name was changed in 1961 to the Citrus Research Center and Agricultural Experiment Station. Today about 20

percent of its projects involve citrus crops.

The presence of the experiment station provided the impetus for the establishment of a campus of the University of California in Riverside. UC Riverside received its first 130 undergraduate students in February 1954 with its innovative College of Letters and Science. The academic program placed emphasis on excellence in teaching. As a measure of its rapid success, UCR was listed in a 1956 *Chicago Tribune* survey as one of the ten best undergraduate colleges in the nation. By 1959 its enrollment had exceeded 1,200 students.

UCR underwent a fundamental change in 1959 when, because of increased demands on the state's educational system, the UC Regents made it a general UC campus with an expanding enrollment, specialized departments, and graduate and professional schools.

As UC Riverside begins its fourth decade—and the Citrus Experiment Station nears its eighth—the impact of the campus is felt not only in the Inland Empire but beyond state and national borders as it fulfills the university's missions of teaching, research, and public service.

Chemistry professor Charles L. Wilkins works with graduate students Carolyn Johlman and John Cooper in a laboratory at UC Riverside.

ROHR INDUSTRIES, INC.

In a period of military buildup in Europe in the summer of 1940, five men met to realize a dream. On August 5, 1940, in San Diego, Fred Rohr and four others began the procedure to incorporate Rohr Aircraft Corporation.

Rohr had worked for five years as factory manager at Ryan Aeronautical Company and was eager to start his own subcontracting firm, which would specialize in structural components. He was a born mechanical genius who had grown up in his family's heating and air conditioning business, giving him an expertise with sheet metal. In an era when aircraft had recently advanced from fabric-covered skins to sheet metal exteriors, Rohr's training gave him a distinct advantage. He later invented equipment for forming sheet metal.

As the company's first temporary headquarters, Rohr's garage was filled with drawing tables. He had been promised subcontracts by Consolidated Aircraft Corporation and Lockheed if and when he formed his own company, so the garage hummed with immediate work. However, with a backlog of work there was no room to do more than draw plans. Rohr needed a factory with at least ten acres. He preferred Chula Vista on lower San Diego Bay so a search for a site commenced.

In the interim, Rohr leased in San Diego a three-story brick building which had been a cabinetmaker's factory and was not a fully adequate space. The firm's first employee recalled, "I was hired probably because I had my own tools, and my first job was to put the toilets in working order and clean up chunks of varnish left on the floor by cabinetmakers." The company's growth was mind boggling. By October it had sixty-four employees with many working eighteen- and twenty-hour days for the first four months to meet deadlines.

That month Rohr was able to purchase ten acres with an option on an additional ten of Santa Fe Land Improvement Company property in Chula Vista. A 37,500-square-foot plant was completed by February 1941. The space proved too small to enable the company to meet wartime contracts and by June the firm had another 125,000 square feet of factory space and 12,000 square feet of office space.

By July 31, less than a year from incorporation, the work force had reached 865 and the first year's sales, $1,493,488. With a contract to install Sperry bombsights in LB-30 bombers and other military contracts, sales peaked in 1944 at seventy million dollars.

Rohr quickly became known for its specialty—ready-to-install power packages for airplanes—but after the war, sales dropped to six million dollars in 1946. This trend lasted only a short time and by 1954 sales topped $100 million.

In the meantime, Rohr had become a subsidiary of International Detrola Corporation in 1945. Four years later Rohr officers and directors repurchased the company in order to gain a firmer control over its direction.

Thrust reverser assembly for a modern airliner nacelle.

With the onset of the Korean War, a new plant was located in the Riverside area in 1952. Boeing Aircraft had offered a substantial contract, which created the need for a new facility. The federal government had been encouraging the dispersal of

Numerically controlled filament winding of composite nacelle components.

aircraft production and with an increase in defense orders, a separate plant location looked quite desirable.

In the spring of 1952 the company, with Air Force approval, settled on eighty acres with 110,000 square feet of existing buildings in Anza Village in Arlington. Groundbreaking for additional factory space was held quietly in July 1952. The acreage not under cement was sown in wheat, and its harvest netted the first ninety-dollar profit from the Riverside site.

Employees were drawn primarily from the area, and within six months Rohr shipped in record time the first Riverside-produced power packages to Boeing. Building continued through 1955, by which time the work force had increased to 4,000 with Rohr then the largest employer in the county.

By the 1960s the firm began to diversify out of concern for the cyclical nature of the aircraft industry. In the 1960s and early 1970s, it ventured into modular housing, large solid rocket motors, steerable space antennae, high-speed rail transit cars, city transit buses, marine construction, automated warehousing, and several other areas. The Riverside plant, however, remained tooled for aircraft structural components and did not participate directly in Rohr's diversification.

Rohr disposed of its nonaircraft operations by the mid-1970s because of heavy losses. Through the years the Riverside plant became more and more involved with bonded and nonmetallic components. Additional satellite facilities, one of which had been a motor home production plant, were leased in the 1970s to meet increasing production demands.

The company encountered serious production problems with a major increase in orders in 1979 and 1980. This was, at least in part, because of undercapitalization resulting from losses associated with diversification efforts.

In 1980 Harry W. Todd, who had been with Rockwell International for many years, became president. He later became chairman and chief executive officer.

Over the next four years Todd instituted a major turnaround in the firm's performance and earnings, placing Rohr in a strong position for further expansion in the commercial aircraft market. This market will represent 60 percent of the company's future business. "Our technology advancements," stated Todd in 1984, "have enabled Rohr in recent years to establish relationships directly with engine builders and to engage

The 100-acre Rohr Industries plant on Arlington Avenue.

as partners in research and development joint ventures with the major airframe and engine companies."

It had been Fred Rohr's insistence in the firm's early years that had kept it solely a subcontractor of structural components, and it will be this continuing expertise that makes Rohr Industries unique in the future of the aerospace industry.

An employee works on a nose cowl for the new Boeing 737-300.

LVW BROWN ESTATE

On January 2, 1922, after his first day in office as mayor of the City of Riverside, Lyman Van Wickle Brown was tragically killed in a trolley collision. The community mourned this man who had been such an active participant in its affairs as well as a foremost citrus grower in the county. He had made a lasting imprint on Riverside, one his family would carry on through their citrus business.

Born in Belle Plaine, Iowa, in 1870, Brown moved with his parents to the newly formed Southern California Colony Association's Riverside lands in May 1871. His father, E.G. Brown, became one of the area's early successful citrus growers and his holdings were later augmented by his son.

Lyman Brown attended local

Lyman Van Wickle Brown, 1870-1922.

schools and later attended the University of the Pacific, the first class at Stanford University, and Cornell University, graduating in agriculture and entomology. Following the death of his father, he returned to Riverside and assumed control of the family business.

He became a major developer of citrus groves, reclaiming a total of 2,000 acres in the Highgrove area, 1,200 of which were planted to oranges and the rest developed as a reservoir. In 1906 Brown purchased a packinghouse on Center Street in Highgrove. The packinghouse is still in the same location, although it had to be rebuilt in 1927 after a fire. The production line developed by Brown is still being used to process fruit.

To aid the war effort during World War I, Brown grew cotton in Arizona and shortly before his death he became involved in the fledgling date industry in the Coachella Valley.

Among the properties he developed was the 197-acre Sunny Mountain Ranch in Highgrove. Here he created his own nursery and reservoir and kept a team of horses to plant his groves.

Brown was a man who was not afraid to try anything. From operating a schooner between Laguna Beach and Catalina Island during his school days to being the first to promote new experimental varieties of fruit in the county, his drive and creative vision motivated those around him. He had been chairman of the committee that brought the Citrus Experiment Station to Riverside. He was always one of the first to use new cultural methods on his groves.

One benefactor of his dedication and enthusiasm was his wife, Theresa, whom he married in 1896. Upon his death, she took over the family enterprise. She had good business acumen and was respected by her staff and associates. Under her ownership,

Lyman Brown with daughter Charlotte in front of their Russell Street home. Today this is the intersection of the I-215, 91, and 60 freeways.

the packinghouse became a member of the Sunkist marketing organization in 1928.

By the 1940s LVW Brown Estate had become one of the largest citrus-growing, -packing, and -marketing organizations in the county; it handled 1,000 acres of fruit from not only its own groves but from others as well, and packed these under the

Mahala and Sunny Mountain brands.

In the late 1930s and early 1940s Mrs. Brown's two daughters, Charlotte and Sara, married and their husbands became active in the business as co-managers. Upon Mrs. Brown's death in 1952, Charlotte Stevning and Sara Holman became co-owners and they continued to run the firm until 1972 when Sara passed away.

Her sister, Charlotte, bought out her interest and in 1979, upon her death, the children of Barbara Stevning assumed control of LVW Brown Estate. Don Stevning continued to manage the company until his retirement in 1982. One of the keys to the success of LVW Brown Estate has been the commitment of

its employees. Many have been with the business for thirty to fifty years.

LVW Brown Estate is now operated by Lyman Dean Stevning and Barbara Ann Stevning Branstetter's husband, Gary. Dean grew up in nearby Redlands and graduated in agribusiness from California State Polytechnic University, Pomona. After working for Security Pacific Bank and owning a western wear store in Colorado, Stevning returned to Riverside with his family in 1980 to run LVW Brown Estate.

Gary Branstetter was raised in the San Diego area and attended California State University, San Diego, graduating with a degree in economics and geography. He taught for fourteen years in Redlands while

working during the summers at the packinghouse. In 1979 he received his master's degree in education from Azusa Pacific University. One year later he joined Dean in the full-time operation of LVW Brown Estate.

In the tradition of Lyman Brown, the current generation has incorporated new farming ideas and preventive maintenance to produce remarkable growth and improved efficiency in the past four years. They foresee LVW Brown Estate's continued growth in Riverside County's citrus industry.

Theresa Brown (center), Lyman Brown's wife, with daughters Sara Barbara (left) and Charlotte (right).

KAISER DEVELOPMENT COMPANY/ CALIFORNIA RANCHO

Rolling hills, broad valleys, mountain meadows, running streams, and sunshine had lured many prospectors, adventurers, and cattlemen to the Temecula Valley and one in particular, Walter L. Vail, had left his mark.

A little over a century after the area's Spanish land grants had passed to private ownership, Temecula Valley, with its new community of Rancho California, is seen as a land of opportunity for new western settlers fleeing modern smog, traffic congestion, and urban sprawl.

Walter Vail had made the journey west as a young man, settled in eastern Arizona, and established the Empire Ranch. By the 1880s he was a force with which to be reckoned. He increased his holdings in the early 1900s with California grazing lands such as Santa Rosa Island. In 1904 he purchased from the San Francisco Savings Union 87,500 acres comprising four Spanish land grants and many lots in the town of Temecula. Temecula was completely surrounded by grazing lands pasturing his HEART brand cattle.

At fifty-four Walter Vail was killed by a trolley car in Los Angeles in 1906. The Vail Ranch became the responsibility of his seventeen-year-old son, Mahlon, who loved this land the best of all his father's holdings. Mahlon began planting portions of the ranch in feed crops to supplement the grasslands. With the irrigation of crops, water became a major issue for the owner of Vail Ranch, and for most of his adult life Vail fought for and guarded the ranch's water rights. Both he and his father had dreamed of damming the Temecula River and he realized the dream in 1948 when the million-dollar structure created Vail Lake. Ten miles of pipeline finally irrigated permanent pastures and fields of feed crops.

By the 1950s, however, the ranch raised no cattle but rather fattened

Jeffrey Minkler, vice-president of Kaiser Development Company and general manager of Rancho California.

beef cattle for the Los Angeles slaughterhouses. In spite of the ranch's adoption of current technology, Mahlon Vail managed to preserve an empire of untouched acreage. When asked if urban sprawl or mounting taxes would ever cause him to dispose of his massive ranch, he vehemently replied, "I will never sell! At least, I won't sell until taxes get me."

Why he sold in the end is history. On December 4, 1964, a joint venture of Kaiser Aluminum & Chemical Corporation, Kaiser Industries,

and the Macco Corporation, purchased the 87,500-acre Vail Ranch for twenty-one million dollars and named it Rancho California.

It had been Henry Kaiser's dream to enter the field of real estate. His company's first endeavor was during World War II in the Southern California housing market. Only later did Kaiser Aluminum expand to large-scale community planning and development in California and Hawaii.

Rancho California operated as a joint venture until August 1969 when Macco's one-third interest was purchased by Kaiser Aetna, a joint real estate venture between Kaiser Aluminum and Aetna Life and Ca-

The Vail Ranch was a working cattle-raising operation until the 1950s and fattened beef cattle for market until 1964, when Rancho California purchased the land for twenty-one million dollars.

sualty Company. In 1977 Kaiser Aetna dissolved and Kaiser retained Rancho California. KACOR Development Company was formed as a wholly owned subsidiary to consolidate all of Kaiser's real estate holdings. Its name changed in 1982 to Kaiser Development Company but Rancho California still remained one of its four basic operating divisions.

One year after Kaiser Aetna assumed control, 10,000 acres were added from four separate purchases,

The wine industry has been revitalized in Southern California with nine wineries operating in Rancho California.

increasing the total acreage of Rancho California to 97,500, two and one-half times the size of the city and county of San Francisco. All of it had been undeveloped, vacant land ready for the stamp of the planners and architects, a project the scope of which was truly exciting.

The final master plan called for a population of 100,000 for this 153-square-mile property. The site was chosen because development could occur along Highway 395, which was to be upgraded to a major artery— I-15. Planners originally predicted a ten to fifteen-year growth period. However, I-15 did not materialize as quickly as anticipated and the growth of Rancho California has been slower. With a current population of 11,000, the updated forecast for build-out will be the year 2000. It is, however, expected to become the fastest-growing area in Southern Cal-

Rancho California Business Park

ifornia.

The first phase of Rancho California's development provided for the sales of large acreage. Between 1965 and 1967 some 6,000 acres were sold to Boise Cascade, which in turn created five-and twenty-acre parcel subdivisions. Another 6,000 acres in two areas were sold to Palomar Land Company, a wholly owned subsidiary of Arco, which subdivided and sold the property, except for one 2,100-acre piece, 640 acres of which was sold to Jack Nicklaus and developed as Bear Creek Golf and Country Club in 1983. From the impetus of the early years, 63,000 acres have been sold for agricultural, recreational, and low-density residential purposes.

In 1968 the first test grove of avocados was planted in the section of Rancho California nearest the ocean. It was widely held that the fruit could not grow so far north, and so with later success Kaiser began to sell twenty- and forty-acre planted avocado ranches in 1972 in the rugged Santa Rosa south area. By 1976 the firm decided to offer just raw land for avocado production, and today some 10,000 acres have been planted. Attesting to the significance of Santa Rosa south for growing avocados is Calavo's decision to build a new packinghouse in Rancho California.

Citrus has also been successful in Rancho California. First planted in

1965, groves now cover 2,000 acres of the hilly Rancho Pauba area.

The other success story among Rancho California's agricultural interests has been the wine industry. The area's suitability for wine grapes was noted perhaps as early as 1853 when the father of California's wine industry, Louis Vignes, purchased Rancho Pauba, one of the four Spanish land grants to comprise the Vail Ranch. In 1913 Joe Moramarco, ninth-generation viticulturist, praised the higher elevations of the Pauba Ranch as an ideal wine-growing area. The first vineyard plantings, however, had to wait until 1967. Since then ten wineries have been active in Rancho California. The area has so revitalized the industry in Southern California that it has come to be known as "Napa Valley South," producing approximately 140,000 cases annually.

The first viticulturists in the Temecula Valley were with Brookside Wineries. The son of Joe Moramarco had joined Brookside vineyards in 1968. That same year the Cilurzo family planted their first grapes on their 52-acre ranch. In 1969 two wineries, Callaway and Mount Palomar, planted their initial vineyards.

The majority of the land not sold in the formative years was designated in the master plan as three core areas: Rancho Villages with 10,000 acres, 8,000-acre Santa Rosa Springs, and 8,000-acre Vail Lake Properties. These were most conducive to industrial, commercial, or residential development.

Rancho Villages was the first, and as yet only, core area under development. In 1967 construction got under way with the first phase of the Plaza on the east side of I-15. This shopping area was developed to provide necessities and services. It set the architectural plan for Rancho California with its combination of California ranch and Spanish revival styles and its heavy reliance on wood and stucco to blend with the western frontier and Spanish historical influences on the area. The Plaza immediately became a popular attraction as soon as the western boardwalks were in place. Since then plaza expansion has been continuous with a motel in 1969, its first medical group in 1972, and later a professional center, county library, Safeway supermarket, savings and loan institutions, and banks, and, in 1983, twenty-two new tenants including Mann Twin Theaters.

Between 1968 and 1970 the infrastructure was laid for the first residential improvements. Construction started on the first single-family housing. The master plan called for the 8,000-acre Rancho Villages and 10,000 acres of several self-contained villages, each with its own school and shopping area to be zoned for residential development. The population when completed would be approximately 50,000.

The first residential development was called Country Community. It was supplemented in 1970 with the first apartment complex. In a separate area called Valle de los Caballos, forty-acre horse ranch parcels were developed around a thoroughbred track and training center.

To date Kaiser has been the primary residential builder at Rancho California, but with the successes recorded in 1984 by Kaiser with its Starlight Ridge Development and the Alcor Group with its Rainbow Canyon Village Homes, it is expected that several other builders will be participating in 1985. When Kaiser

Recreational activities abound. Here golfers tee off at Rainbow Canyon Golf Resort.

opened its first 66-unit phase of Starlight Ridge, an affordably priced neighborhood at $59,900 to $100,000, it was sold out during its grand opening in February 1984. By the end of the year 260 Starlight Ridge Homes had been sold. The Alcor Group had a similar success story. After purchasing 429 lots from Kaiser, Alcor opened its Rainbow Canyon Village Homes in September 1984 and had sold sixty homes by year's end. Certainly this growth is an indication that the Rancho California area will be one of the most significant housing areas in Southern California in the near future.

Part of Rancho California's attraction is the life-style the community affords. Single-family homes are available to those who were limited to less expensive forms of housing in Orange and Los Angeles counties. With Vail Lake, adjoining Butterfield Country RV Resort, and seventy miles of equestrian trails, there is much open space and a variety of recreational activities. Also, as a growing community, Rancho California provides numerous opportunities for community involvement. As one resident put it, "You can make a difference here. You're not swallowed up." One of those differences was the successful push for a local high school, which will open in September 1985.

The town of Temecula, across I-15 from Rancho California Plaza, offers a historical balance to the Plaza's

Rancho California encompasses many communities, recreational areas, and industrial parks spread over 87,500 acres.

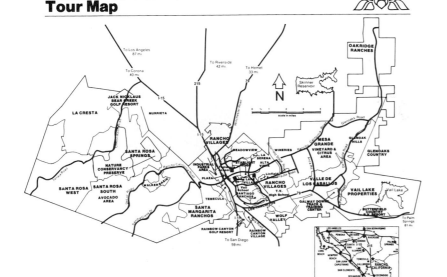

Rancho California Tour Map

Kaiser Development Company
A wholly owned subsidiary of Kaiser Aluminum & Chemical Corporation

modern setting, a balance most communities never dream of having. With the first post office in Riverside County, Temecula has existed as a commercial center since 1880.

Industrial and commercial construction began in 1968 and the first major industry opened in 1969. Since then over 250 industrial acres have been developed and sold out of the 1,200 planned. More than 600 businesses have located in the area, employing some 4,000 people. Attractions to industry have included clear skies without smog, industrial acreage 30 percent less than comparable developments in Orange, Los Angeles, or San Diego counties, and a work force of 400,000 within a forty-minute drive.

In 1983 Rancho California began a major advertising and promotional program aimed at increasing awareness among industrial site location decision makers on the major selling propositions of Rancho California. These were derived from market research and confirmed by two surveys of chief executives and their consultants. These propositions were the ample labor force, low-cost land, availability of affordable housing in all price ranges, freeway access to major metropolitan markets, and the clean air and attractive life-style available in southwest Riverside County.

This million-dollar program was designed by Cochrane Chase & Livingston in Newport Beach and was dubbed "The Major Employer Program." It was so successful in 1983 that the *Wall Street Journal* prepared a case study at its own expense. In 1984 the ads generated over 1,800 coupon responses.

The first major employer to move to Rancho California while this program was active was Advanced Cardiovascular Systems, which now employs 200 people and has been acquired by the Eli Lilly Corporation.

Rancho California Plaza

The second major employer to announce a move to Rancho was International Rectifier Corporation, whose Hexfet America Division is building a $90-million facility on twenty-nine acres in the newly completed business park near the airport. This plant will open in mid-1986 and ultimately employ 700 people in a 250,000-square-foot semiconductor production and assembly operation. The company joins the other major employers in Rancho California business parks, including Hudson Oxygen, Borg Warner Mechanical Seals, and Bianchi Leather.

The success to date of this market intervention program shows that Rancho California has a great deal to offer an industrial firm in the high-technology, bio-med, aerospace, and light manufacturing industries. In 1985 nearly two million square feet of industrial space was under construction and new firms were expressing interest in improved land and spec buildings almost daily. This industrial momentum has had a positive cross impact on the commercial and residential activity in the area.

Unlike other community developments of the 1960s, Rancho California has had only one developer—Kaiser. Its success has been due in part to its commitment to a balanced community. Its eighty employees have shown a high level of commu-

nity involvement, which has set the tone for later residents.

As Jeff Minkler, vice-president of Kaiser Development Company and general manager of Rancho California, has commented on Kaiser's commitment, "I believe we've more than kept the promise. Rancho California has taken a strong hold on its root system and now we see Rancho Californians themselves providing the impetus to further shape the community along the original guidelines. Our role has been that of the catalyst." The rest of the century will be the continuing proving ground for Kaiser Development's success.

Lake Village Homes

FIRST NATIONAL BANK IN COACHELLA

There was a time in the Coachella Valley when the rumor of a bank opening spread excitement like a growing fire, for no institution would lend money on valley real estate. December 4, 1912, was no exception. On that day the "Valley Bank for Valley People," capitalized at $25,000, received its first deposits of $2,010 in modest quarters near Seventh and Cantaloupe in Coachella.

The First National Bank in Coachella was the vision of John M. Westerfield, who had started a Banning bank in 1901. His brother, Harry A. Westerfield, had come to the valley to farm in July 1905 and had convinced his brother and their associates of the potential of the struggling pioneer community. At first the bank personnel consisted of John, his wife, Harry, and a bookkeeper.

Harry's two sons, John W. and Arthur M., later joined the institution. John attended the University of Omaha and Occidental College, and then farmed for a year before joining First National in 1915. From 1923 until 1938, however, he worked in Los Angeles, ending that period to farm

again near Coachella. Upon his father's death in 1942, John Westerfield reassumed his place in his family's bank.

Arthur Westerfield graduated from Occidental College in 1920 and returned to the valley to farm until 1923, when he joined First National.

The bank survived the Depression, and in 1932 it took over the assets of the First National Bank of Indio. That year the Coachella institution was placed in the hands of the conservator and allowed limited operations. Loyal, confident depositors formed a committee that presented the U.S. Comptroller of Currency with an unbelievable offer: to waive 50 percent of their profits if the bank was allowed full operation. So, on December 31, 1934, the reorganized bank reopened under the name of First National Bank in Coachella.

The institution had moved to another location in 1920, and again in 1948, this time to its present site, designed specifically for its needs. The new bank had state-of-the-art air conditioning and "up-to-date equipment, rare enough in any bank let

Arthur Westerfield was president of First National when this photograph was taken in 1948.

alone one in a community of this size," as one observer remarked.

First National has remained unchanged. The original Burroughs adding machine and gunmetal gray furniture are still there. Unlike most banks, it still does its own posting and has resisted the use of computers. It is proud of its old-fashioned reputation based on personalized service (employees know the names of all customers) and sound, conservative business: It is the fifth-safest bank in California.

When Arthur died in 1951, John became president and held that position until his death in 1984 at the age of ninety. The First National Bank in Coachella continues to be run by a Westerfield—Alice Lowery, John's widow, who has been with the bank since 1947 when she started as a file clerk.

In 1920 the First National Bank in Coachella moved to Sixth Street. Harry A. Westerfield is seated and John W. Westerfield is standing on the left.

DAVID FREEDMAN & COMPANY, INC.

To buy in 1951 over 800 acres on the Coachella slope and to somehow see beyond the sandy soil and seventy-mile-per-hour windstorms took an experienced eye and scientific validation. For Lionel Steinberg the decision also represented a passionate, steadfast desire to be a desert farmer.

Steinberg came from a well-established San Joaquin Valley farming family. His stepfather, David Freedman, began growing table and wine grapes in Fresno in 1922. He and his brothers had been in the produce business in New York City in the 1890s, working eighteen-hour days. With a vision of a better future, they moved to California to farm, something they knew nothing about. However, by the 1950s David Freedman & Company was growing twenty different crops in eight different counties from Imperial to Merced.

Lionel Steinberg was the first in his family to study agriculture. He graduated from California State University at Fresno with highest honors. Subsequently he received a fellowship to the American University in Washington, D.C., to study soil and agricultural economics. The U.S. Navy later sent him to the Harvard Graduate School of Business, U.S. Naval Supply Corps School. After World War II he returned to the family farming operations in 1946.

When his stepfather died in 1951, Steinberg was thirty-one and ready to focus gradually his energies in one place: the Coachella Valley. In 1950 Colorado River water became available to desert growers, making it feasible to farm the area productively and safely.

In order to stabilize the soil, he and a dozen people (some came with him from Fresno and stayed with him for thirty years) planted cotton between the young grapevines. Until the vineyards were profitable, he made a weekly commute by car to Fresno to supervise cotton, grain,

A typical harvest scene inspired by the vineyards of David Freedman & Company, Inc. This picture was painted in oil by Larry Neufeld.

melons, and vineyards. In 1958 Steinberg moved his family and business interests permanently to the Coachella Valley.

His son, Billy, although never intending to be a farmer, found himself in love with it after graduating from college and commenced in 1973 to work in the vineyards. He is presently in charge of most of the daily growing operations and the seasonal work force of 1,200. He finds time, however, between seasons for songwriting, which has brought him fame in the music industry. His own young son, Maxwell, seems interested in farming, taking pride in the Flame Seedless brand named after him.

David Freedman & Company, Inc., has been the largest grower and producer of table grapes in the valley. In 1983 the firm shipped 14 percent of five varieties of valley grapes from 9 percent of the acreage planted in table grapes. It farms 1,200 acres and has diversified into land development, recognizing that some farmland has a higher use potential as residential developments in the face of population encroachment.

Lionel Steinberg has for many years shared his company's expertise with others. For fourteen years he served as either a member or the president of the State Board of Food and Agriculture, advising three California governors. Subsequently, he served on U.S. commissions, traveling extensively on agricultural missions in Eastern Europe, the Middle East, and the People's Republic of China. In 1970 he negotiated the first labor contract with the United Farm Workers' Cesar Chavez, which brought an end to the crippling table grape boycott.

The Steinbergs are realists about farming. They know the risks involved but they also know the pleasure that beautiful grapes, carefully harvested, bring.

CURTIS-KIELEY, INC.

Curtis-Kieley, Inc., is the oldest insurance agency in Palm Springs, and probably the whole Coachella Valley. From its founding in 1927 to the present, Curtis-Kieley, Inc., has been a family-owned business with a strong personal and corporate inclination toward service to the community.

What is now Curtis-Kieley, Inc., was started as an insurance agency and real estate office by Dr. J.J. Kochner who was in 1927 Palm Springs' only resident physician. In addition to his business endeavors, Dr. Kochner was the first president of the Palm Springs Board of Trade, the forerunner of the present Chamber of Commerce, as well as advisor to many of the developing enterprises in the town. And when he was joined by Canadian emigré Herb Samson, he gained another public-spirited figure who was to become president of the Chamber of Commerce, chairman of Boy Scout activities, and a founding director of the Desert Water Agency.

Herb Samson eventually owned the agency by himself and after World War II was joined by Noble H. "Toby" Curtis. Toby Curtis continued the tradition of public service as president of the Palm Springs Chamber of Commerce and holding a series of posts in civic organizations and advisory boards over a period of twenty-six years. But after Samson left the agency, Curtis found it necessary to have additional help, and in 1955 he hired F.T. "Tom" Kieley, Jr., first as an agent and later as his partner.

Tom Kieley came to Palm Springs from North Dakota in 1936 as part of a personal plan to work, save money, and return to college. Instead he found himself the manager of Lykken's hardware store until 1942, when he entered the Army Air Corps for the duration of World War II. After the war he went to work for Earl Coffman at the old Desert Inn on a special "six-month" project that lasted for nine years, until Toby Curtis lured him away.

From its beginnings in Dr. Kochner's combination real estate office and insurance agency, Curtis-Kieley, Inc., has grown to include twenty persons, among them F.T. "Tom" Kieley III, a vice-president of the corporation.

Located in its new offices at 901 East Tahquitz-McCallum Way in Palm Springs, Curtis-Kieley, Inc., continues its earlier pattern of corporate and personal involvement in community affairs.

Tom Kieley, Jr., has been president of the Palm Springs Chamber of Commerce, Palm Springs Desert Museum, and the Palm Springs Lions' Club, as well as having been the first chairman of the Airport Commission and the youngest person ever elected to the Palm Springs City Council. He continues his interest in many of these activities, as well as the Boy Scouts of America.

Tom Kieley III has also been president of the Palm Springs Lions' Club and the Convention and Visitors Bureau, in addition to serving on the Riverside County Grand Jury and on

The Kieley father and son team—F.T. Jr. (seated) and son F.T. III.

the board of directors of the County Juvenile Facilities Commission.

In addition, members of the staff of Curtis-Kieley, Inc., give their time and energy to such organizations as the United Way of the Desert, the Rotary, Soroptomists, and the Lions' Club. The corporation, following the leadership of its owners, not only provides insurance to governmental entities and community and charitable organizations but cooperates with other local insurance agents to provide insurance services to cities, public service districts, and schools throughout the Coachella Valley. These combinations allow the agencies that serve the public to obtain competitive prices and local understanding and service for their insurance needs.

As a matter of good business Curtis-Kieley, Inc., has always sold all forms of insurance to all of the citizens of Palm Springs and surrounding desert communities. And as a matter of personal and corporate citizenship, Curtis-Kieley, Inc., through its owners and employees, continues to offer its collective knowledge and energy for the betterment of all of the residents of the desert.

Curtis-Kieley's new office, at 901 East Tahquitz-McCallum Way in Palm Springs, was completed in 1983.

RANCHO CONSULTANTS COMPANY, INC.

Prior to 1879 the Temecula Valley's only known residents were scattered among several Indian villages. A history of the first white men, carved into the town's historical monument, includes John C. Fremont and Kit Carson.

The town of Temecula, situated at the southern tip of Riverside County, is nestled at the core of the 97,500-acre master-planned community known as Rancho California.

In 1971 real estate broker Daniel Lee Stephenson, from Newport Beach, had a vision of potential growth for the area, which at the time had a population of only 700. "Pioneer" in Webster's dictionary is defined as "one of those who first enter or settle a region, thus opening it for occupation and development by others." Stephenson pursued his dream of pioneering with faith, courage, and a staff of three. Kaiser-Aetna, who had acquired Rancho California in 1964, welcomed Stephenson's enthusiasm and agreed to give his organization, Rancho Consultants Company, the exclusive right to sell residential lots in a prestigious area.

By 1972 the company opened La Cresta, 6,000 acres which were subdivided into twenty-acre exclusive custom homesites. Stephenson chose to build his 10,000-square-foot home here on a hilltop that offers a view of the Temecula Valley.

Residential developments were the grass-roots beginnings of a firm that today has five divisions, employing over 100 people. The brokerage division's real estate sales totaled over thirty-five million dollars in 1984.

Abundant land, suitable for avocado and citrus groves, became the company's early syndications, forming partnerships to acquire and develop the produce and to develop the real estate to higher and better uses for home and ranch development.

Daniel Lee Stephenson, chief executive officer.

Stephenson's further goals were now ready to be implemented. He began the formation of limited real estate partnerships for the purpose of developing commercial, industrial, and apartment complexes.

Meanwhile, Rancho Consultants Realty Fund partnerships had built

the 69,767-square-foot Winchester Square, complete with the area's first supermarket and movie theater, fourplex and apartment units, and the award-winning ninety-acre Winchester Commerce Center, whose major tenants include the Sizzler Restaurant, Overland Bank, a bowling alley, and an Auto Service Center.

Rancho Consultants Company, Inc., currently has a four-story, 41,200-square-foot building under construction, which will become its new corporate headquarters and offer professional office suites to other businesses. "Since making a commitment to encourage development in the Temecula Valley, I have thoroughly enjoyed taking a leadership role and am dedicated to giving my energies toward its continued growth," says Daniel Lee Stephenson.

Rancho Consultants' award-winning ninety-acre Winchester Commerce Center.

BEAUMONT CONCRETE COMPANY

L.R. Daniel certainly had no intention of putting Cross Roads, California (population forty), on the map with his ready-mixed concrete plant; he was just taking care of his own business. In the early 1950s he had leased 160 acres on the Colorado River to build a marina and trailer park for recreationists. With no ready-mix available he bought a Willard weigh-batcher loader and two three-cubic-yard truck mixers and produced his own. Immediately, he was in demand.

By the mid-1950s Daniel had a major contract to supply all of the concrete for the enlargement of the Colorado River aqueduct pumping stations. He purchased two new five-cubic-yard mixer trucks for the job. In January 1959 he lost his land lease and was given fifteen days to vacate. Earlier, by chance, Daniel had met Homer Vineyard who had started Beaumont Concrete Company in 1957 and now wanted to sell the business. At age sixty-six, with a wife and two sons, ages eleven and fifteen, L.R. Daniel decided to enter an industry new to him, and purchased Beaumont Concrete Company. "That same Saturday we finalized an agreement," recalls Daniel. He had purchased a business that had two mixer trucks, an obsolete batch plant, and a trailer for an office.

Daniel took over BCC with a staff of five. Bruce Hirter, who would later become general manager, started working for L.R. Daniel at the Colorado River project in 1957.

In 1960-1961 Daniel constructed a modern office/storage building and batch plant on the Beaumont property. He soon found it necessary to have his own aggregate source, and after investigating San Timoteo Canyon chose an 85-acre site in Cabazon. Daniel's oldest son, Bill, who had graduated from Beaumont High School in 1960, assisted the builder of the site's rock plant. Bill became

manager of the plant and has continued to run what is now one of the most efficient aggregate facilities in the West. The property has been expanded to 500 acres and includes a back-up batch plant.

Daniel's younger son, Tom, joined the company in June 1969 after receiving his bachelor of science degree in mechanical engineering. His father gave him free reign and, as production engineer, he immediately increased sales. In 1969 the firm was incorporated and leased three acres in Coachella Valley's Thousand Palms for a batch plant. By December sales for 1969 had increased 50 percent over the average of the previous ten years.

In 1971 Tom became president. In 1973 BCC started its first portable project at Lake Skinner. BCC continued its expansion program by purchasing Hemet's Mixed Concrete, Inc., in 1974. Since 1976 BCC has acquired three complete portable plants, which now ranks the firm as the largest supplier of site batched, transit-mixed concrete in Southern California. The new Thousand Palms plant was completed in 1982, expanding batch plant production from eighty yards per hour to 386 yards per hour.

Founder L.R. Daniel and his wife, Leila Mae.

What started as a small crew in 1959 has grown to eighty-two employees in 1985. The yearly average income during the first ten years is now created every week. Beaumont Concrete Company is the largest independently owned producer of ready-mixed concrete in the Inland Empire.

BCC's newest plant, in Thousand Palms, California.

NEWSPAPERS OF HEMET AND SAN JACINTO

Abundant water, an adobe general store, a dozen scattered homesteads, and endless tracts of arable land—that was the essence of the north side of the San Jacinto Valley in 1884. It wasn't much, but it was enough for two young pioneer publishers who thought they saw its promise.

With the publication of the first edition of the *San Jacinto Valley Register* on August 9, 1884, publishers Arthur G. Munn and Joseph P. Kerr began a crusade for prosperity and growth that was to continue for decades. They were, however, to part company before long and eventually become rival publishers.

THE HEMET NEWS

Joseph Kerr sold his interest in the *Valley Register* to Arthur Munn in 1889, but he was to turn up five years later as the fiery editor of *The Hemet News,* a weekly that began December 9, 1893, in the new town of Hemet, already stealing growth from San Jacinto just three miles away.

Kerr established a reputation as an independent thinker before he died in 1897. Succeeding owners, publishers, and editors tended to follow the tradition of Kerr and other early California publishers. Staunch supporters of freedom of the press, an informed public, and independence of viewpoint, they nevertheless were adamant in their belief that prosperity for all was linked to continued community growth.

Walter A. Potter purchased *The Hemet News* in 1913. It was operated and eventually acquired by John E. King, who ran it until his death in 1938. His son, Homer King, held the reins along with co-owner James W. Gill, Jr., until King's death in 1960.

Gill, who was business manager from 1938 to 1960, bought the other half-interest from the King estate and remained as editor and publisher until his death in 1983. Over time he

These frame buildings were the first offices of The Hemet News *and were on Florida Avenue and Carmalita Street, near where the Frank Regur Hardware Store is now located.*

converted the weekly newspaper to six days a week by 1967. In the meantime, he bought the *San Jacinto Valley Register.* The two newspapers now are published by the Hemet Valley Publishing Company, owned by the Gill family with James W. Gill III as editor and publisher.

SAN JACINTO VALLEY REGISTER

Arthur Munn, who owned the

The San Jacinto Register *office on Main Street also handled book and job printing when this photo was taken circa 1897.* Register *publisher A.G. Munn is second from right.*

weekly *Register* until he sold it to Chester Kline in 1912, was a San Jacinto booster without peer. Kline took up where Munn left off and ironically, it was Kline who first printed the idea for an outdoor pageant based on the 1884 novel *Ramona,* but it was eventually produced in Hemet, which got most of the credit for the nationally acclaimed Ramona Outdoor Play.

In 1983 publisher James W. Gill III made the commitment to revitalize what had become a declining publication. In August 1984 the newspaper celebrated its 100th birthday with a centennial edition and every expectation that it will live to celebrate its bicentennial.

T&S DEVELOPMENT, INC.

Jay Self, co-founder.

Mark Thompson, co-founder.

In November 1975 Mark Thompson, Jay Self, and Jerry Thompson founded T&S Development, Inc., with the objective of developing a limited number of neighborhood shopping centers over a period of four to five years. They started with a part-time secretary, a total overhead of less than $20,000 a year, and a combined forty years of expertise in their related fields.

Jerry, a resident of Riverside since 1947, was semiretired and wanted to remain that way. However, through his son, Mark Thompson, and Jay Self, Jerry had the opportunity to be a part of helping form a new company without the responsibilities of day-to-day management. His reputation in the community and his financial capability provided the new enterprise with the foundation needed for rapid growth.

Mark, born and raised in Riverside, graduated from California State University, Long Beach, with a degree in finance. Mark had chosen real estate as a career and had specialized in commercial sales and leasing of community and neighborhood

shopping centers. For several years he had gained valuable expertise and experience with Coldwell Banker in the dominant, fast-growing market of Orange County.

Jay, a native of Houston, Texas, had moved to Orange County in 1965. His career in banking with Bank of America and Union Bank exposed him to the dynamics of Southern California's premier real estate development firms that had located in Newport Beach. Ironically, Mark and Jay were, at the same time, providing different services to many of the same real estate firms but had never met.

The experience and expertise of the three partners—Jerry, with financial stability and a historical base in the community; Mark, with leasing and marketing contacts and knowledge; and Jay, with finance and legal background—formed a triangle of abilities that provided all of the skills required to build a successful development company.

Their future activities were foreshadowed by the selection of their first project: a 22-acre, 250,000-square-foot, mixed-use project that had been controversial for almost ten years.

In 1975 they purchased the property from a prominent major Southern California developer who had decided that the community opposition and controversy were too great and had abandoned the project. T&S Development chose a different approach and found it successful. Mark Thompson explains, "Because we were local, we could be a neighbor in the community; we weren't going to rape the community. This became our theme for all of our later projects, and we've taken on controversial sites where opposition has been strong. We feel nobody wins if anyone loses."

Today Canyon Crest Towne Centre is fully developed and is a monu-

ment to the success of that approach. It is representative of the company's commitment to quality-designed and -managed real estate developments.

As its knowledge of the fast-growing Riverside/San Bernardino marketplace grew, the company had decided to concentrate on the Inland Empire and to diversify by product rather than geographical location.

By 1983 the three partners had continued their program of aggressively building quality projects throughout the Inland Empire and had developed more than one million square feet of commercial, office, and industrial developments in Rancho Cucamonga, Chino, Hesperia, Woodcrest, Sunnymead, and the city of Riverside.

During the same period the company began to acquire several parcels of land that would become its most aggressive, creative, and profitable adventure—Canyon Springs. The project was so large and required such an enormous amount of financial resources and long-term commitment by the principals that the firm reached a new plateau. In 1982 Jerry decid-

Canyon Crest Towne Centre, a 22-acre, 250,000-square-foot, mixed-use development, was the firm's first project.

ed that the time had come for him to enjoy the fruits of his labor on a full-time rather than part-time basis.

By July 1983 the three partners had completed a reorganization that allowed Jerry to withdraw from the company and for Mark and Jay to assume total responsibility for its future financial and business plans.

From that point Mark and Jay embarked on a quest to establish T&S as a dominant organization in the Inland Empire, and Canyon Springs as a vision of the future business environment of Riverside County.

During the first two years after the reorganization, and apart from the Canyon Springs development, the company completed a small 40,000-square-foot center in Sunnymead; built a 100,000-square-foot center in Riverside, Lincoln Plaza; commenced construction on a 212-unit apartment project in Riverside; continued development on Park Sierra with a seventeen-acre mixed-use development west of Tyler Mall, to which El Torito and Seafood Broiler restaurants were added; acquired a forty-acre mixed-use project in Moreno Valley that will contain a 210-unit apartment project and a 300,000-square-foot community retail and entertainment center; and formed a joint venture to develop a 100-acre industrial park in the 1,100-acre Sycamore Canyon Business Park.

During the same period the Canyon Springs project has gone through a lengthy and highly controversial annexation to the City of Riverside. During 1985 the Canyon Springs project will begin construc-

tion of more than twenty million dollars in public infrastructure improvements.

Canyon Springs is a 400-acre, 6,000,000-square-foot mixed-use development at the intersection of Highway 60 and Interstate 215. It is master planned and designed to accommodate more than six million square feet of commercial, industrial, and office space.

The area's largest regional shopping center will be developed in a co-venture between T&S and the Edward J. DeBartolo Corporation. DeBartolo is one of the world's largest regional mall developers and brings a high degree of expertise and ability to the Canyon Springs Mall. The center will ultimately include six major stores and contain approximately 1,300,000 square feet.

Canyon Springs will include prime corporate and professional office parks, hotels, restaurants, research and business facilities, and many other compatible uses. With more

than two miles of freeway frontage, Canyon Springs will be the city of Riverside's showcase entrance from the east and south. At full build-out, estimated to be over ten to fifteen years, Canyon Springs will bring to the area more than one billion dollars in construction activity.

T&S had grown to become a major development company. It owns and operates a large 2,000-member health club (Roman Gabriel Sport Center), owns a major commercial construction company (Tascor), and has more than seventy-five total combined employees with a payroll that exceeds $1,200,000 annually.

Its future is based on a continued commitment of sensitivity to the communities its projects will serve. Although the firm plans to continue development of the type of projects that have made it successful, it will be Canyon Springs through which T&S will continue to be a vital part of Riverside's future, as well as its past.

This four-story, 80,000-square-foot office building is a part of the 22-acre office park in the Canyon Springs development.

HEMET CASTING COMPANY

Hemet was a sleepy town in the 1950s; only 13,000 lived in the Hemet/San Jacinto Valley. Police chief Walsh gave magic shows to the local schoolchildren to remove any fear of the police, and no one wore ties. The San Fernando Valley, on the other hand, was exploding; 3,000 to 15,000 houses were being built every month. After one look at the Ramona Pageant, Jack Tangeman and Don Malcomb knew there was no contest for the location of their new nonferrous investment castings business. That clients might ponder, "Where's Hemet?" mattered not. So, in 1957 they started Hemet Casting Company in 3,000 square feet of rental space on Acacia Avenue.

Tangeman had lived in the San Fernando Valley since age sixteen. He had been inspired by a mining engineer uncle to follow his example but instead found himself working for Douglas Aircraft in Santa Monica for sixty cents an hour. When World War II broke out Tangeman joined the Merchant Marines for three years. After the war he went to work for a heating and air conditioning company until 1954, when Duncan-Rohne, an investment casting company in the San Fernando Valley, offered him the presidency and his introduction to the business.

Don Malcomb was one of the two active partners in Duncan-Rohne. He had been trained after the war in dental technology, which employed the same process used in investment casting. He joined the firm and worked his way up to partner until the firm was sold in June 1957.

When the two men started Hemet Casting that year, Malcomb was the technician and Tangeman, the office staff and salesman. Since no one knew of this new company or of Hemet, he traveled a great deal.

The business grew and by 1964 the partners built an 18,000-square-foot facility at the present site. In 1969

Hemet Casting Company's facility in Hemet. The firm is the second-largest private industry in the area, employing 330.

they sold the company to Allied Equities, a small conglomerate, and retained a three-year management contract with them. However, by 1971 Allied wanted out of the business and the following January Tangeman and two new associates purchased the company. With the firm were still two people who had originally been trained by Malcomb.

Hemet Casting continued to grow and so did its facility, which reached 60,000 square feet. By 1976 Tangeman was again expanding his business interests. He helped create Hemet Steel Casting, which occupied a corner of the plant, and in 1977 started Hemet of Florida to service the East Coast market. In 1984 he moved Hemet Steel Casting to Rancho Cucamonga.

Now with 75,000 people in the Hemet/San Jacinto Valley, Hemet Casting is the second-largest private industry in the area, employing 330. It has grown nationally to become one of the three major nonferrous producers.

Since investment casting substan-

tially reduces the need for postmachining of parts, it has proven to be a better method than sand casting or forging. Thus, the industry has grown at a rapid rate for the past twenty years and Hemet Casting Company expects to continue to be a significant part of that growth.

Clusters of wax patterns on a conveyor begin the dipping cycle to put on a ceramic shell.

GAY HOOD PONTIAC

One of the seven original dealerships in Riverside's world-famous Auto Center, the Pontiac dealership, now Gay Hood Pontiac, began shortly after World War II. Don Gilmore opened his Pontiac franchise in February 1946. Located at Eighth and Lime streets in downtown Riverside, the dealership was then known as Don Gilmore, Riverside.

Among his employees was Jack Kennedy, Sr., who worked his way up to president and in April 1964 purchased the dealership from Gilmore. Kennedy brought his son, Jack Kennedy, Jr., into the business in the 1950s. When Kennedy Sr. died in 1965, just one year after purchasing the dealership, his son assumed control of the business. That year he changed the name to Kennedy Pontiac and moved the business to the newly constructed Auto Center.

In 1962 a friend of his, Gay Hood, joined the staff as a used-car salesman. Kennedy Jr. and Hood had grown up together in Riverside. Hood had joined the Coast Guard for three years and then attended Riverside City College, Fullerton Ju-

Gay Hood in front of his Pontiac showroom in Riverside's Auto Center.

nior College, and the University of Southern California before he settled on a career. The first place he chose was his father's business, Lee Hood Tire Company. Finding no future there, Gay Hood redirected his efforts toward the auto industry and joined Kennedy Pontiac.

In 1963 Hood advanced to new-car salesman and in 1966, to new-car sales manager. Three years later he left Kennedy Pontiac to become general sales manager for Whitney Tractor Company, the John Deere dealer for Riverside and San Bernardino counties. Don Whitney had been a good friend of Hood's and had presented to him the challenge of developing a sales staff at Whitney Tractor. He was in the mood for a change and the position was a natural for him.

In 1974, however, Gay Hood had another unbeatable offer for him: the opportunity to buy Kennedy Pontiac. He purchased the dealership in 1974 and changed the dealership's name to Gay Hood Pontiac and Iveco Trucks.

By the 1980s Hood's own sons were ready to join the business. His son Tobin started working full time in 1980 and became new-car manager in November 1982. Son Steve became manager of the Thrifty Rent-A-Car franchises for Riverside and San Bernardino counties when Hood purchased them in 1984.

Hood has made it a policy to be involved in the community that supported him as a youth. Gay Hood Pontiac continues to be a major sponsor of Riverside athletic programs. Riverside, in turn, continues to provide a productive base for his dealership, and as an active member of the National Dealer Council, Gay Hood is able to foresee a bright future for Pontiac everywhere.

Company policy as set forth by Gay Hood encompasses community involvement. Here he (left) and Tom Mazzetti emcee Riverside City College's Monte Carlo Night, which was sponsored by Gay Hood Pontiac and held on its showroom floor.

BOURNS, INC.

The groundbreaking ceremonies for the Columbia Avenue facility of Bourns, Inc. Marlan E. Bourns is pictured on the tractor.

In 1947, Marlan E. Bourns, a physics graduate from the University of Michigan, had an idea for new telemetry concepts. When no encouragement for his idea was forthcoming from his employers, he decided to start up a business of his own. In a cooperative effort on the Bourns' Altadena kitchen table, using their life savings to carry them through the first rounds of production, Marlan and his wife, Rosemary, worked on his potentiometer-transducer. This product would allow for the accurate electrical measurement of position, a capability greatly needed by the fledgling aerospace industry for the measurement of minute changes in position of flight-control surfaces on high-performance aircraft and missiles.

Marlan and Rosemary Bourns began building prototypes in their small garage and later, their converted chicken coop. Bourns was the technical-managerial head and Mrs. Bourns, the secretary. When the first prototype was ready, she covered a Whitman Sampler candy box to display the new product, which subsequently was patented.

From these inauspicious beginnings anchored in unshakable faith in their abilities, their company has grown to be a designer and manufacturer of quality high-technology products for military, scientific, and

Corporate offices and Bourns headquarters are located on Columbia Avenue in Riverside.

industrial applications. Today Bourns, Inc., employs over 6,500 people in twenty-six facilities worldwide. The firm owes much of this growth to a second invention created by Marlan Bourns and a design team in 1952: the TRIMPOT® trimming potentiometer.

In 1950 the company moved from a modest Pasadena storefront to a manufacturing facility on Riverside's Magnolia Avenue. Beginning with fifteen employees, Bourns Instruments, Inc., was expanding rapidly and two years later became a division of the newly formed Bourns, Inc. Expecting to sell but a handful of trimming potentiometers, the firm sold thousands because this cost-effective way of improving circuit performance allowed circuit designers to use inexpensive, wide-tolerance components. The TRIMPOT® potentiometer fit the needs of the time and Bourns, Inc., responded by expanding its work force to 1,000 over the next decade.

In 1962 the Bourns, Inc., corporate offices moved to the present location on Columbia Avenue. The facility is now also headquarters to Bourns Trimpot and Bourns IC Packages. Bourns Instruments, Inc., remained at the enlarged Magnolia plant. Bourns, Inc., further diversified in Riverside County by acquiring Pacific Magnetics, Inc., in 1967. Like the parent concern, the Magnetics Division started modestly in an old abandoned schoolhouse in the farmlands of Romoland.

From the mid-1950s through the early 1980s, Bourns, Inc., experienced great expansion with new facilities opening in two other states and six countries. Over the years the product line has grown to include precision controls, airborne reconnaissance cameras and related optical equipment, transformers, and high-performance linear integrated circuits.

The major activity for Bourns, Inc., has always been and will continue to be the design and manufacture of high-quality, innovative products based on customer needs. "Our philosophy," states Bert Snider, president and chief executive officer, "has been to invest in talented people, to encourage and support the development of new products and improved manufacturing techniques, and to provide the highest quality both in products and customer service."

DE ANZA CHEVROLET

George Reade, Sr., had worked for Chevrolet Motor Division for fifteen years when he had the urge to own his own dealership. After years in Great Falls, Montana, it was a pleasant surprise for him to find that the available dealership was in Riverside, California.

In 1943 he opened De Anza Chevrolet with twenty employees, selling twenty cars and trucks a month. He located the agency on Market Street in downtown Riverside. Three years later his son George "Cap" Reade, Jr., joined the business. Cap earned his bachelor of arts degree at the University of California at Berkeley and served as a captain in the Army in World War II before joining his father's agency.

George Reade, Sr., was known for his personable, gentlemanly demeanor and the time he took to enjoy people. He spent most of his time with his business. His son chose to spend some of his time in civic activities as well and became known for his work with the chamber of commerce, Riverside Community Hospital Foundation, and Republican politics.

By the late 1950s it had become apparent that the downtown area was becoming too crowded. George Reade, Sr., felt that the firm had outgrown its facilities, and along with Riverside auto dealers Red Moss and Woody Dutton, started looking for a large piece of property. They chose acreage off Adams that then was considered rural. It was the beginning of the first auto center.

De Anza Chevrolet opened in its new facility on eleven acres in 1965. It was an exciting time. Cap was continuing to build the business his father had started. In 1972 his son, George Reade III, started working full time and was made general manager. He had been working summers and vacations for years and had taken time out for his college training at

De Anza Chevrolet is located on eleven acres on Auto Drive in Riverside's Auto Center.

Cal Western University in San Diego and six years in the Air Force in Vietnam.

That same year George Reade, Sr., died while still working. Cap passed away in 1980. His son was then president of the dealership and he set out to expand upon what his grandfather and father had built.

In 1981 the family business began to branch out. The firm acquired a Chevrolet agency in San Diego that George's brother Jeff operates, a Chevrolet dealership in Hemet that brother Michael operates, and a Datsun dealership in Hemet. George,

who oversees all the agencies, comments, "This will continue to be a family business. We are expanding in response to the fast growth of the area and we will expand to six stores in the near future. The future is very bright and that is due in part to the Southern California life-style."

Having grown to 126 employees handling 5,000 sales of new and used trucks and cars in 1984, the present looks bright as well.

DESERT HOSPITAL

The roots of Palm Springs' modern-day image as a resort area can be traced back to the 1930s. It was at this time that many Hollywood stars, along with the rich and famous, discovered the natural beauty and near-perfect weather of the Coachella Valley.

A central point of this first influx of jet-setters was the famed El Mirador Hotel. The hotel's imposing pink Moorish tower gave the inn its name, which in Spanish means "the lookout." El Mirador, built in 1928, became a haven for such legendary actors as Eddie Cantor, George Raft, Jackie Cooper, Al Jolson, Jimmy Durante, Olivia De Havilland, Paulette Goddard, and Johnny Weismuller. Even Albert Einstein and the Duke of Windsor and other dignitaries enjoyed the hotel's ambience.

But an increase in Palm Springs' popularity meant an increase in the area's population. The number of people in the area swelled, due to the number of tourists and new year-round residents. This growth in population mandated a local hospital, as patients requiring hospitalization needed to be taken to one of a number of hospitals miles away. Up until this point, the only hospital in Palm Springs was the Tourney General Hospital, which was actually the renovated El Mirador Hotel. The federal government bought the hotel in 1942 to receive wounded soldiers from the South Pacific. After a conversion program, the military hospital had a 1,500-bed capacity and a staff of 1,300. But with the end of World War II the hospital ceased to exist, and Palm Springs was again without a hospital.

So, on Friday, March 10, 1944, a group of concerned citizens met at the Frances S. Stevens School in Palm Springs. Labeling themselves the Palm Springs Community Hospital Association, they discussed plans to establish a much-needed permanent hospital in the Palm Springs area.

This meeting at the Frances S. Stevens School was called to order by Culver Nichols. Nichols presented Philip L. Boyd, who addressed the crowd. The first order of business was to appoint directors of the association. Thirty-four persons were nominated and elected as directors, with C.J. Burket accepting the position of temporary chairman.

Other area residents who served as first-time directors of the association included Nichols, Lloyd Simon, Tom Holland, Nellie Coffman, Pearl McManus, Mrs. Tom Lipps, Alexander Baillie, Henry Weinberger, Mrs. John Hormel, Harry Williams, Robert Ransom, Raymond Wilson, F.G. Ingram, Harold West, Mrs. A. Turonnet, Francis Crocker, Mrs. Ruth Hardy, Earl Gray, Willard Hillary, H. Earl Hoover, Alice Guthrie, Clareta Kocher, William Dean, Mrs. Virginia Farrell, Alvin Weingarten, Mrs. Harold Hicks, Mrs. T.A. O'Donnell, E. Alshuler, Harry Klonick, Maxine Van Cleet, Farney Wurlitzer, Refugio Salazar, and Katherine Finchy.

With the directors selected, the association got under way to establish a hospital. During this time the directors had to grapple with such problems as raising funds, determining the location and design of the hospital, and establishing a medical staff. Several physicians in the area urged the association to include in its by-laws that only those doctors accredited by the American College of Physicians could be members of the hospital's medical staff. The directors heeded this recommendation.

Several parcels of land on which to build the hospital were reviewed by the Palm Springs Community Hospital Association. These included gifts from area residents, as well as property that was available for sale.

To make room for a much-needed expansion, the hospital purchased El Mirador Hotel. Its pink Moorish tower, which was a historic Palm Springs landmark, has become a symbol for the Desert Hospital.

After much consideration, the association voted to secure the title of the Tourney General Hospital as the temporary location of the Palm Springs Community Hospital. The directors also applied for immediate use of the building, which they received in early 1947, and the Palm Springs Community Hospital, once an idea, now became a reality.

One of the first orders of business was to staff the new hospital with employees and to establish a medical staff. The first physicians appointed to the medical staff's active section were H.M.F. Behneman, James B. Oliver, J.W. Potter, Frank A. Purcell, and P.A. Staley, who became the hospital's first chief of staff. In addition, a courtesy medical staff was established, with the first members being Clyde E. Harner, George Kaplan, C.H. Peppers, Hugh E. Stephens, and C.H. Woodmansee.

The Palm Springs Community Hospital continued to grow, but the directors realized that the facility could only be useful for a limited time. So, on December 18, 1947, at a meeting of the board of directors led by president Frank Bennett, discussion took place concerning a district hospital plan. The idea was met favorably by the board, and petitions were sent to Riverside to conduct an election in 1948 to establish a district. The residents voted in favor of the plan, and in 1948 the Desert Hospital District was formed.

The board of directors felt it was important to keep the Palm Springs Community Hospital open until Desert Hospital was ready. On August 1, 1951, the doors of the Palm Springs hospital were finally closed, and Desert Hospital opened on September 26 of the same year.

On that autumn day in 1951, the hospital was a single building on 7.85 acres of land. It cost a modest $500,000: $450,000 for the building and another $50,000 for equipment. By noon the next day, Desert Hospital had six inpatients.

The hospital district was created to serve a 457-square-mile area that includes Palm Springs, Desert Hot Springs, Cathedral City, Rancho Mirage, Thousand Palms, Palm Desert, and outlying communities. With the rapid rise in the local population and the growth in popularity of Palm Springs as a resort area, expansion was inevitable.

In 1962 ground was broken for Desert Hospital's first expansion of

twenty-two beds. By November 1968 the East Tower was completed, bringing the bed total to 217. The hospital continued its expansion between 1969 and 1973 by adding the Frederick Loewe Pediatrics Wing, the Joseph M. Shapiro Eye Center, a diagnostic treatment center, and the Martin Anthony Sinatra Educational Center.

In the meantime El Mirador Hotel, which was located adjacent to Desert Hospital, again flourished until its doors were closed for the final time

in 1973. The hospital purchased the hotel, making room for a much-needed expansion program. Original architectural drawings called for the destruction of the old hotel, but the board voted to preserve the building's pink Moorish tower as a historic site. The tower was then adopted as the hospital's logo.

Phase one of the expansion project was completed in January 1980, with

Desert Hospital, 1985.

Comparing notes with Larry N. Minden (left), chief executive officer since April 1969, on the progress of Desert Hospital are three former presidents of the board (left to right): George Beebe (1978-1981), Howard Wietels (1978-1981), and S. Duke Kosslyn (1982, 1984-1985).

the dedication of the $33-million Sinatra Patient Tower, named in honor of hospital benefactor Frank Sinatra. The five-story structure houses 159 single-care rooms, the fifteen-bed Frederick Loewe Intensive Care Unit, and the sixteen-bed Herbert E. Toor Cardiac Center. The addition, which more than doubled the size of the hospital, includes the ten-suite Ever J. Hammes Surgical Pavilion, outpatient surgery center, the Daniel and Natalie Schwartz Patient Lobby, and many support services.

The second phase of the construction project was completed in January 1982 and includes a psychiatric pavilion and the David and Dorothy Greene Rehabilitation Center for stroke patients and those with head or spinal injuries. In addition, a new maternity pavilion, the expanded Regional Trauma Center, an oncology unit, several specialized laboratories, respiratory and pulmonary departments, the Augusta Morse Fried Cardiac Rehabilitation Center, and the Grace Petrie Chapel were opened. These were added to the basic services at Desert Hospital, including 194 general medical-surgical beds, eighteen pediatric beds in the Frederick Loewe Children's Pavilion, and twelve beds for specialized eye care in the Joseph M. Shapiro Eye Center.

From an initial handful of employees, the staff has grown to more than 1,400 today. Currently the medical staff, with membership of 250 physicians, encompasses virtually all of the specialties. The Desert Hospital Foundation, comprised of the area's civic-minded philanthropists and leading citizens, has raised millions of dollars in funds since its inception in 1967. The 1,200-member auxiliary, with some 450 active in-house volunteers, has contributed more than two million dollars through fund-raising projects and has donated an average of 65,000 hours of service each year to Desert Hospital. It was also instrumental in the construction of Desert Hospital's Regional Trauma Center. Tiempo de los Niños, a support group whose Spanish name translates to "time of the children," is credited with raising funds to help establish the Tiempo de los Niños Maternity Pavilion and is a major source of funds for the pediatrics unit.

Combined, these efforts have gained the 350-bed acute care facility a wide-spread recognition for providing excellence and professionalism in health care for the Coachella Valley's residents and visitors.

Desert Hospital is accredited by the Joint Commission of Hospitals and is a member of the American Hospital Association, the California Hospital Association, the Association of Western Hospitals, the Hospital Council of Southern California, and the Association of California Hospital Districts.

Throughout its colorful history, which began with the concern of a few citizens, Desert Hospital has evolved into one of the most comprehensive health care facilities in Southern California. Its mission, however, has remained stable with an unwavering dedication reflected in the hospital's motto: "Care, Compassion, Commitment."

LAS CASUELAS RESTAURANTS

From the early Colton days of Armida's Drive-In, Mexican food with twelve-seat service, to Las Casuelas Terraza, Palm Spring's Veracruz-style dinner house, the Delgado family has worked to establish the nationwide standard for judging Mexican dinner houses.

The history of this remarkable family really begins with Maria Delgado, for she proved to be the inspiration for five of her six children to undertake the restaurant business. Florencio Delgado was two years old when his father, an Arizona miner, died in 1926 and his widowed mother decided to enter the restaurant business. When Florencio was in the Navy during World War II, Maria decided to move to San Bernardino and start a tortilla factory so that her only son would not become a miner. There in 1946 he married Mary Tagle.

In the late 1940s and early 1950s Florencio worked in construction and Mary for H.S. Kress & Company. By 1954 Maria Delgado thought it time they went into business and helped them start Armida's. Soon after, they also took over a 150-seat res-

taurant, the Spanish Kitchen, on Colton's main street. Four years later the new freeway claimed both the restaurant and drive-in.

Customers suggested they try Palm Springs next. With their four children, Florence, Patty, Joaquin, and Armida, they explored Palm Canyon Drive. That the location they liked had failed twice before as a restaurant mattered not. What was important was its placement across the street from city hall, and the Delgados believed that if they took care of the locals, the tourists would follow. So, in early 1958, Las Casuelas opened in an area half its present size with all the family working there, in addition to one waitress from Colton who commuted for two years because she did not think it would last.

By the early 1970s Las Casuelas had more business than the family could handle. In 1972 the Delgados began construction of Las Casuelas Nuevas, the first free-standing, hacienda-style restaurant in the United States. They were criticized for their extravagance in construction in an area where even the post office did

not know what the address would be. However, from the time of the restaurant's opening in 1973, this concept of a Mexican dinner house has been widely copied. Joaquin and his wife, Sharon, now operate it.

In 1977 the Delgados, facing the loss of the lease on their original restaurant, began an extensive search for a new location and ended by choosing a site five blocks from the old restaurant. Patty and her husband, Rick Service, had been in training for four years and were ready to undertake the task of establishing their own restaurant. Encouraged by Florencio and Mary, they opened Las Casuelas Terraza with its climate-controlled outdoor seating, tropical decor, and live music, and received the restaurant industry's highest design award in 1979.

For a family that has been honored by Cornell University's renowned restaurant school, the future can only be a worthy challenge. "Mexican food will continue to grow as an art form," states Rick Service, "and Las Casuelas will continue to be at the cutting edge of the Mexican food industry."

HARRIS' DEPARTMENT STORES

When the Harris brothers opened their dry-goods store in San Bernardino on April 18, 1905, they offered the community a new policy—no bargaining. "Anybody from the youngest child to the oldest person can shop in our store and they will only pay one price. We will not barter."

Today there are stores in five locations with three in Riverside County. Each was opened in response to customer desires and each emphasizes Harris' commitment to customer service: to provide each with merchandise to serve the community it is in.

Herman and Philip Harris, who were joined by brother Arthur in 1906, were not new to the business. Their father, Morris, had been a merchant in West Prussia, Germany, where they were born and raised. The brothers had come to the United States in the late 1800s. Each worked for relatives in the dry-goods business in Southern California.

The first store, a 25- by 100-foot storeroom in the old armory at 462 Third Street in San Bernardino, had three employees. After little more than a year at this location, business had so improved that Harris' moved to larger quarters across the street. In their first advertisement in 1905, Herman and Philip had offered "courteous treatment, low prices,

good goods, and honest methods." Their policies and earnest efforts were obviously appreciated; by 1919 the store had expanded to 23,500 square feet.

Not only did the San Bernardino store grow, but Harris' opened a series of branch stores beginning in 1907. The first, in Colton, was sold after a year. The second, in Redlands, opened in 1908 with the purchase of the Randall Merriman store.

In 1926 a branch store was opened on Miles Avenue in Indio to serve the Coachella Valley. Indio had been a booming railroad town and was a natural choice for a branch. Ralph Crom managed it with his wife in

concept, it seemed ideal. On September 30, 1957, Harris' opened with two floors and half the basement. A third floor for home furnishings, toys, and a budget store was ready for operation in 1963 and offered an auditorium for community use. "Community service for community advancement" has always been part of the Harris' tradition. The additional floor had expanded the floor space to 208,000 square feet.

By 1967 a 20,000-square-foot basement store was created to meet increasing business. In 1985 a complete remodeling was undertaken to continue to improve service to the community.

In October 1980 the fifth Harris' opened at the Hemet Valley Mall, the first enclosed mall in the area of 140,000 population. Construction of the 50,400-square-foot Harris' began in May of that year and was in keeping with the Spanish and American Indian architectural themes of the mall. Located on the west end of the $10-million complex, the store opened with a series of special events.

By the late 1970s few Harris family members were left in the business and they were ready to find an appropriate buyer. In 1981 El Corte Inglés purchased Harris'. The largest retailer in Spain, with fifteen stores, 22,000 employees, and $1.7 billion in annual sales, El Corte Inglés was ideal because it was a service-oriented company like Harris' and their business philosophies were harmonious.

"Harris' has only one commitment: to fulfill the needs of our customers," remarks Jorge Pont, president and chief executive officer of the Harris Company. "We are very involved in the growth of the Inland Empire. We do our best to make Harris' unique and special every day of the year in every city we serve. We don't have branch stores; we have community stores."

charge of the office. By 1955, when the head office decided to close the store, employees numbered eleven.

After studying the area's potential for growth for several years, the Harris Company returned to Indio in 1975 to anchor the Indio Fashion Mall. Two hundred people were hired to operate the 60,000-square-foot store. The store was completely renovated in 1982 to make shopping easier; emphasis was placed on goods within easy reach, proper lighting for better viewing, and good placement for merchandise selection.

Another area that was growing rapidly and was frequently suggested by customers as a prime location for

Harris', which opened in the Riverside Plaza in 1957, was completely remodeled in 1985 to improve service to the community.

a new store was Riverside. Certainly Riverside County's impressive population growth, which reached 36 percent by the early 1960s, far above the rest of Southern California, warranted another Harris'.

The company had long considered a downtown location, but when it was approached with the concept of the Riverside Plaza, the first mall in California to use the anchor-store

ALUMAX MILL PRODUCTS, INC.

The Alumax Mill Products facility is on Columbia Avenue in Riverside.

the casting and forming of aluminum. The continuous aluminum strip caster invented by Hunter in 1948 was used by Hunter-Douglas, Inc., in the production of venetian blinds.

Both Hunter brothers were involved in the new enterprise. However, by 1954, Joe, yearning to be immersed again in research and development, formed a new alliance with Olin Industries under the cor-

Employees work with aluminum plate, one of the firm's products.

In a small metal facility, simply labeled Building 6 and now covered with the aluminum siding made famous by the company it housed, Joseph L. Hunter started one of his unique ventures, Eureka Scrap Iron and Metal. By the late 1950s the firm began producing aluminum irrigation pipe by the cold extrusion process and the name was changed to Eureka Aluminum Pipe Company. It was the precursor of the mill products division that would later become Alumax Mill Products, Inc.

Hunter and his brother, Eddie, were fascinated with machinery. Products of Riverside schools, they initially went into business in Riverside. Joe was a genius at invention, determining what an industry needed to improve production. Eddie, the more mechanically minded, designed the machinery that Joe dreamed up. From the 1930s through the 1950s they were an unbeatable team. Working in a small machine shop on Joe's 100-acre ranch off Columbia Avenue in Riverside, they created processing equipment that greatly changed the aluminum industry.

Joe Hunter established Hunter Engineering Company to market a hydraulically powered hacksaw in

1932. This development company and machine shop had, by 1935, revolutionized metal venetian blind production with new processing equipment.

During World War II Hunter Engineering retooled for the war effort, producing different types of narrow strip aluminum products. Until the postwar years the company had been involved solely with machine-tool invention and building.

Hunter Engineering became inactive in 1946, when Hunter-Douglas, Inc., was established to utilize the processes developed by Hunter for

A coil of aluminum, 15,000 to 20,000 pounds in weight, being prepped for the cold mill.

porate name Hunter Engineering Company. In July 1954 construction began on a building to be devoted to research and development. Now housing Alumax Mill Products, Inc., the facility was ready for Hunter Engineering in 1955.

When Hunter-Douglas was acquired by the Bridgeport Brass Company in 1956, Joe Hunter withdrew from the company to further devote himself to research. Both he and brother Eddie were again working full time for Hunter Engineering. It didn't bother them if their prototypes did not work; they were motivated by the creativity and satisfaction of the process. One associate remembered Joe Hunter spending $50,000 for an unsuccessful invention and, unperturbed, moving on to another idea.

He incorporated Eureka Aluminum Pipe Company in 1956. It continued to operate out of the corrugated metal building adjacent to the new facility and functioned as Hunter's link with the aluminum products industry.

By 1958 Olin Industries had purchased Joe Hunter's interest in the joint venture, Hunter Engineering Company. Concurrently, Eureka Aluminum Pipe Company purchased all the assets of Hunter Engineering Company. This effort cost Hunter ten million dollars, for which he willingly incurred debt in order to secure this outlet for his creative ideas.

One year after the firm went public in 1962, American Metal Climax, Inc., acquired the business and divided it into four divisions, one of which, mill products, became the forerunner of Alumax Mill Products, Inc.

Eddie Hunter eventually left Hunter Engineering to join Toro, Inc. In 1965 Joe Hunter died at the age of fifty-four, having established a national reputation as an industrial developer. Yet this man who had made revolutionary advances in the aluminum industry had not forgotten his hometown. He had given thirty-five acres of his Columbia Avenue ranch for a city park and had established a foundation to aid local students in the fields of science, engineering, and agriculture. He had treated his employees as part of his family and they responded with loyalty and dedica-

tion. One longtime employee with Eureka Aluminum Pipe Company remembered the times when their duties included cutting and baling the hay on the ranch's nearby fields.

In 1967 Amax Aluminum Mill Products, Inc., incorporated with Hunter Engineering as a division of this new entity. Three years later Amax sold the division, which was reorganized as an independent company and headquartered in a new building next door to the present Alumax Mill Products, Inc., facility.

The Aluminum Group, including Amax Aluminum Mill Products, Inc., of American Metal Climax, Inc., was incorporated in late 1973 and renamed Amax Aluminum Company, Inc. Through name changes over the next two years, Amax Aluminum Company became Alumax and the mill products division, Alumax Mill Products, Inc. AMAX, Inc., sold 50 percent of Alumax, Inc., to Mitsui & Co. in 1974.

Through the years the Riverside plant has housed many departments: rod and bar facility and pipe, foil, and panel facilities. Some of the original casters built by the Hunters as prototypes have remained in operation in this plant. In 1978 and 1980 new Hunter Engineering equipment was added when mill and paint lines were installed.

With a short history in the aluminum industry, Alumax Mill Products, Inc., has grown from a small producer of irrigation pipe to a major producer of aluminum plate and painted and mill finish aluminum sheet, based on the brilliance and dedication of men like Joseph L. Hunter.

This aerial of Joseph L. Hunter's property shows the location of the present Alumax and Hunter Engineering facilities and the metal building above the site which housed Eureka Scrap Iron and Metal, predecessor of Alumax, Inc.

SANBORN/WEBB, INC.

In 1922 G.K. Sanborn brought his wife to Riverside at the invitation of his uncle, Kingsbury Sanborn, who offered him work as a surveyor at Riverside Water Company. G.K. Sanborn later went to work for Davidson and Fulmore, land surveyors and civil engineers. The firm sent him to Palm Springs in 1935 to establish an office, and Sanborn became city engineer from 1938 until World War II when the city had grown enough to have its own staff.

In 1945 Sanborn opened his own office, the first and only local surveying firm in the Coachella Valley until 1953. With a staff of four he operated out of his house until 1958.

The previous year his son, John, joined the firm, having studied civil engineering at Riverside Junior College and the University of New Mexico. Although G.K. Sanborn had done 60 percent of the subdivisions in Palm Springs, he was content with a small firm. By the time he passed away in 1968, the business had eight employees.

John, however, was young and energetic. Palm Springs was growing and he wanted Sanborn Engineering to grow along with it. So, in 1968 he incorporated with Albert Webb Associates in Riverside. Albert Webb had initially worked with G.K.'s uncle and had employed John when he was going to college. John worked very closely with Albert's son, Hubert, his close friend. It seemed a natural association since it provided a variety of expertise and services that Sanborn alone could not supply. Webb expertise combined with Sanborn's intimate knowledge of the Coachella Valley ensured the best service.

Over the years the firm acted as city engineers or consultants for all of the valley's cities and the Coachella Valley Water District. It has also worked on such projects as the Springs, Morningside, and Mission Hills country clubs; Desert Hospital; Eisenhower Medical Center; Rancho Mirage storm drainage system; Sheraton Plaza Hotel; and Desert Fashion Plaza.

By 1983 the association with Webb had become nominal and a reformation of the business created Sanborn/Webb, Inc. The company now has thirty-five employees with John Sanborn's daughter, Lisa, the full-time receptionist, and his architect son, Allen, looking forward to joining the firm in a few years.

G.K. Sanborn had the philosophy that you must give back to the community what you take out of it. In return for his success he spent several years on the Palm Springs City Council and served two years as mayor. John has shared this commitment to community involvement, serving on numerous boards including the Palm Springs Board of Education, Riverside County Parks Commission, and the Youth Center Board.

As John Sanborn has said: "The Coachella Valley will continue to be one of the strongest and most productive areas for development in the nation." Five decades of experience give Sanborn/Webb, Inc., the capability of continuing to be on the leading edge of the valley's growth.

John L. Sanborn, president.

Rancho Mirage storm drain—a Sanborn/Webb, Inc., project.

Patrons

The following individuals, companies, and organizations have made a valuable commitment to the quality of this publication. Windsor Publications, the Riverside County Historical Commission, and the Riverside County Board of Supervisors gratefully acknowledge their participation in *Harvest of the Sun: An Illustrated History of Riverside County.*

Lorne L. Allmon
Alumax Mill Products, Inc.*
The Ames Group*
Beaumont Concrete Company*
Beverly Manor Convalescent Hospital
Blue Banner Company, Inc.*
Bourns, Inc.*
LVW Brown Estate*
Centre Brands, Inc.*
Coachella Valley Historical Society's Museum and
    Cultural Center
Corona Community Hospital*
Corona Historic Preservation Society
Curtis-Kieley, Inc.*
De Anza Chevrolet*
The Depot Center
Desert Center Historical Society
Desert Hospital*
Deutsch Electronic Components Division*
Ernst & Whinney*
First National Bank in Coachella*
Mr. and Mrs. Robert J. Fitch
David Freedman & Company, Inc.*
Harris' Department Stores*
Hemet Area Museum Association
Hemet Casting Company*
Gay Hood Pontiac*
Hunter Engineering Company, Inc.*
Johnson Tractor Co.*
Kaiser Development Company/Rancho
    California*
R.G. Kercheval
Krieger & Stewart, Incorporated
La Quinta Hotel*

Las Casuelas Restaurants*
Lemonava Land & Cattle Company, Ltd.
Alfred M. Lewis, Inc.*
Loma Linda Foods*
Loma Linda University/La Sierra Campus*
Modtech, Inc.
Mr. and Mrs. Bill Mohn
Newspapers of Hemet and San Jacinto*
Parkview Community Hospital*
Press-Enterprise*
Paul and Nancy Racicot
Rancho Consultants Company, Inc.*
Rancho Temecula Escrow
Riverside Community Hospital-Medical Center*
Riverside Dental Group
Riverside International Raceway*
Rohr Industries, Inc.*
Rubidoux Motor Company*
Sanborn/Webb, Inc.*
San Gorgonio Pass Memorial Hospital*
San Jacinto Valley Museum Association
Shadow Mountain Resort and Racquet Club*
SYNATEK/Dave Tucker & Assoc., Inc.
T&S Development, Inc.*
Angie L. Thill
University of California, Riverside*
Washburn & Sons*
Duane and Evelyn Welk

*Partners in Progress of *Harvest of the Sun: An Illustrated History of Riverside County.* The histories of these companies and organizations appear in Chapter IX, beginning on page 185.

Bibliography

Bean, Lowell John. *Mukat's People: The Cahuilla Indians of Southern California.* Berkeley: University of California Press, 1972.

Bean, Lowell John and Katherine Siva Saubel. *Temalpakh: Cahuilla Indian Knowledge and Usage of Plants.* Morongo Indian Reservation: Malki Museum Press, 1972.

Beck, Warren A. and Inez D. Haase. *Historical Atlas of California.* Norman, Oklahoma: University of Oklahoma Press, 1974.

Becker, Stephen and Jeffrey Birmingham, eds. *The San Jacintos: A History and Natural History.* Riverside: Historical Commission Press, 1981.

Bell, Major Horace. *Reminiscences of a Ranger or Early Times in Southern California.* Santa Barbara: Wallace Hebberd, 1927.

Bolton, Herbert Eugene. *Outposts of Empire.* New York: A. Knopf, 1939.

Bourne, A. Ross. *Some Major Aspects of the Historical Development of Palm Springs between 1880 and 1938.* PhD Diss. Occidental College, 1953.

Brewer, William H. *Up and Down California in 1860-1864: The Journal of William H. Brewer.* Berkeley: University of California Press, 1974. (First published by Yale University Press, 1930.)

Bright, Marjorie Belle. *Nellie's Boarding House.* Palm Springs: ETC Publications, 1981.

Brown, John, Jr. and James Boyd. *History of San Bernardino and Riverside Counties.* Chicago: Lewis Publishing Co., 1922.

Brumgardt, John R., ed. *Historical Portraits of Riverside County.* Riverside: Historical Commission Press, 1977.

Dekens, Camiel. *Riverman-Desertman.* Riverside: Press Enterprise Co., 1962.

Elliot, Wallace. *History of San Bernardino and San Diego Counties.* San Francisco: Elliot Publishing Co., 1883.

Forbes, Jack. *Warriors of the Colorado.* Norman, Oklahoma: University of Oklahoma Press, 1965.

Harley, Dr. R. Bruce. *The March Field Story: 1918-1978.* March Air Force Base, California: Office of the Historian, Headquarters, Fifteenth Air Force, 1978.

Heizer, Robert F. and C.W. Clewlow, Jr. *Prehistoric Rock Art of California.* Ramona California: Ballena Press, 1973.

Hornbeck, Robert. *Rubidoux's Ranch in the Seventies.* Riverside: Press Publishing Co., 1913.

Jaeger, Edmund C. *The California Deserts.* Fourth ed., Stanford: Stanford University Press, 1965.

Kahrl, William L. *The California Water Atlas.* Sacramento: Governor's Office of Planning and Research, 1978.

Klotz, Esther. *Riverside and the Day the Bank Broke.* Riverside: Rubidoux Press, 1972.

Klotz, Esther, Harry Lawton, and Joan Hall. *A History of Citrus in the Riverside Area.* Riverside: Riverside Museum Press, 1969.

Lingenfelter, Richard E. *Steamboats on the Colorado River, 1852-1916.* Tucson, Arizona: University of Arizona Press, 1978.

McWilliams, Carey. *Southern California: An Island on the Land.* Santa Barbara: Peregrine Smith, Inc., 1973. (c. 1946).

Patencio, Chief Francisco, as told to Margaret Boynton. *Stories and Legends of the Palm Springs Indians.* Los Angeles: Times-Mirror, 1943.

Patterson, Tom. *A Colony for California: Riverside's First Hundred Years.* Riverside: Press-Enterprise Co., 1971.

Paul, Arthur G. *Riverside Community Book.* Riverside: Arthur H. Cawston, 1954.

Phillips, George Harwood. *Chiefs and Challengers: Indian Resistance and Cooperation in Southern California.* Berkeley: University of California Press, 1975.

Pourade, Richard F. *Anza Conquers the Desert.* San Diego: Copley Press, Inc., 1971.

Robinson, W.W. *The Story of Riverside County.* Riverside: Riverside Title Co., 1957.

Seiler, Hansjakob. *Cahuilla Texts with an Introduction.* Bloomington, Indiana: Indiana University Press, 1970.

Setzler, Grady. *Another Wilderness Conquered.* Blythe: N.P., 1967.

Sharp, Robert P. *Geology Field Guide to Southern California.* Dubuque, Iowa: Wm. C. Brown Co., 1972.

Smith, Gerald A. and Wilson Turner. *Indian Rock Art of Southern California.* San Bernardino, California: San Bernardino County Museum Association, 1975.

Spier, Leslie. *Yuman Tribes of the Gila River.* Chicago: University of Chicago Press, 1933.

Stonehouse, Merlin. *John W. North and the Reform Frontier.* Minneapolis: University of Minnesota Press, 1965.

Strong, William Duncan. *Aboriginal Society in Southern California.* Berkeley: University of California Publications in American Archaeology and Ethnology, Vol. 26, 1929.

Tapper, Violet and Nellie Lolmaugh, eds. *The Friendliest Valley: Memories of the San Jacinto-Hemet Area.* Hemet: private printing, 1971.

Wilke, Philip J. *Late Prehistoric Human Ecology at Lake Cahuilla, Coachella Valley, California.* Berkeley: Contributions of the University of California Archaeological Research Facility, No. 38, May, 1978.

Weymouth, F.E. *History and First Annual Report.* Los Angeles: The Metropolitan Water District of Southern California, 1939.

Index